Cataloging Library Resources

LIBRARY SUPPORT STAFF HANDBOOKS

The Library Support Staff Handbook series is designed for to meet the learning needs of both students in library support staff programs and library support staff working in libraries who want to increase their knowledge and skills.

The series was designed and is edited by Hali Keeler and Marie Shaw, both of whom teach in support staff programs and have managed libraries.

The content of each volume aligns to the competencies of the required and elective courses of the American Library Association–Allied Professional Association (ALA-APA) Library Support Staff Certification (LSSC) program. These books are both textbooks for library instructional programs and current resources for working library staff. Each book is available in both print and e-book versions.

Published books in the series include:

1. *Foundations of Library Services: An Introduction for Support Staff*
2. *Library Technology and Digital Resources: An Introduction for Support Staff*
3. *Cataloging Library Resources: An Introduction for Support Staff*
4. *Working with Library Collections: An Introduction for Support Staff*

Cataloging Library Resources

An Introduction

Marie Keen Shaw

ROWMAN & LITTLEFIELD
Lanham • Boulder • New York • London

Published by Rowman & Littlefield
A wholly owned subsidiary of The Rowman & Littlefield Publishing Group, Inc.
4501 Forbes Boulevard, Suite 200, Lanham, Maryland 20706
www.rowman.com

Unit A, Whitacre Mews, 26-34 Stannary Street, London SE11 4AB

British Library Cataloguing in Publication Information Available

Library of Congress Cataloging-in-Publication Data Available

ISBN 978-1-4422-7485-3 (cloth : alk. paper)
ISBN 978-1-4422-7486-0 (pbk : alk. paper)
ISBN 978-1-4422-7487-7 (electronic)

∞™ The paper used in this publication meets the minimum requirements of American National Standard for Information Sciences—Permanence of Paper for Printed Library Materials, ANSI/NISO Z39.48-1992.

Printed in the United States of America

To my parents, Mildred E. Keen and Harry J. Keen,
who taught their children how to make order
of their world—with love and admiration

Contents

Illustrations

PHOTOGRAPHS

Tables

Preface

Aligned with the revised national American Library Association Library Support Staff Certification (ALA-LSSC) competency standards for cataloging and classification, *Cataloging Library Resources: An Introduction* provides clear explanations, suggestions, and examples on how to successfully create catalog records using current RDA rules and practices. This book is essential for those who need to know how to interpret revised cataloging rules and standards in order to apply them in practice to all types of library materials. Embedded throughout the book are textboxes that simplify cataloging processes. At the end of each chapter is an extensive list of online references and suggested readings for further exploration of the topics. This important handbook is geared to improve the reader's knowledge and skills of cataloging. Each chapter is broken down into short subheadings to make complex topics easy to find, read, and understand. Tables and illustrations are abundantly used throughout the text to present key ideas simply and clearly.

The text is written for three intended audiences: working library staff, college instructors, and students in college library certificate or degree programs. No matter the type of library, there is even greater need today for skilled catalogers whose work conforms to the latest standards. Throughout the country accurate cataloging records from the smallest school to the largest academic and public libraries are being shared publicly in regional and statewide catalogs.

There is a shortage of practical texts written for library staff on the new standards of cataloging. Beginning or intermediate catalogers who work in technical services will want this book because it provides understandable explanations about today's cataloging standards. At the end of each chapter there are discussion questions and guided practice exercises aimed at creating bibliographic records that meet the current RDA rules and MARC21 specifications appropriate for classroom or individual use.

Instructors in library technology certificate or associate degree programs will want this book as a primary instructional resource. With extensive chapter bibliographies, this book supports curriculum on fundamentals of RDA cataloging, authority control, classification, copy cataloging, metadata, and future developments of BIBFRAME.

Students will find this a useful text for the way the information is presented in clear, non-technical language. An abundance of tables and figures make concepts easier to understand. Suggested websites and readings at the end of each chapter can further students' knowledge of topics that are introduced in the book. Many references are from academic journals that are cited for further reading.

The scope of the book addresses many different aspects of the cataloging process staff should know about and the skills they should be able to perform to create full bibliographic MARC and item records that meet the highest requirements. Sequenced in three parts, the book contains the following:

Fundamentals of the Cataloging Process. The basics of cataloging, including how to use Library of Congress tools and other resources available to us

Classification of Library Materials. The application of call numbers and subject headings to any type of library material

Cataloging Library Materials. RDA cataloging rules as well as the future impact on cataloging with the development of BIBFRAME

Cataloging Practice. Practice cataloging activities for many types of library resources, included at the end of chapter 12

Part 1 begins with the introduction, where we learn the background purpose of cataloging, what a bibliographic record is, and how catalogers apply specific steps in the cataloging process. This section includes thorough explanations on the topics of online catalogs, collaborations, tools, and resources for the cataloger. RDA rules and BIBFRAME, topics that are later covered in depth in Part III, are also introduced here. Chapter 3 addresses the importance of name and title authority control to ensure uniformity to searching. In chapter 4 the reader gains practice with the revised MARC21 format that includes RDA descriptive and access fields. Chapter 5 provides options to the cataloger when they can copy catalog records or draw upon bibliographic records created from other sources. Part 1 concludes with a chapter on metadata and how it enhances searching.

Part 2 focuses on classification of library resources, which is the assignment of call numbers and subject headings. Call number assignments follow specific rules and guidelines depending upon the system the library selects. Most K–12 and public libraries use the Dewey Decimal system, while larger public and academic libraries often use the Library of Congress classification system. For those who classify with the Dewey Decimal system, chapter 7 describes the logic of the tables and how to assign call numbers. Chapter 8 delves into the Library of Congress classification system with its classes, enumeration system, and expansions. How collections and individual materials are classified with Library of Congress subject authority control is the topic of chapter 9.

Part 3 provides the reader many practical and hands-on examples of cataloging types of library resources. Chapter 10 covers the new cataloging rules of Resource Description and Access (RDA) that replace AACR2. This chapter would be helpful to any cataloger who is grappling with the ongoing changes in cataloging and classification rapidly being developed and adopted by the Library of Congress and the American Library Association. Chapter 11 prepares us for the near future of BIBFRAME cataloging that will radically alter cataloging practices so that libraries will be able to fully utilize the upcoming semantic web or Web 3.0. Chapter 12 provides cataloging examples and exercises for many of the common types of library resources such as books, serials, e-books, music, film, software and databases. Answers to and examples of how to do the work of these exercises are given at the end.

The structure of each chapter begins with the specific ALA-LSSC cataloging competency standard it will address. Following subchapter headings are definitions of key terms that explain how the term applies in cataloging. The key terms are defined in the context of both their importance to cataloging but also how that cataloging relates to library services such as the online catalog and circulation. Each chapter has an introduction where the upcoming topics and content are foreshadowed. Background knowledge, practical examples, and many step-by-step instructions abound in every chapter. The aim of this book is to describe cataloging in clear and direct ways so that the reader has both a basic understanding and the immediate knowledge of how to apply rules and processes to their work. This book has broad appeal because of its topic coverage and practical suggestions. The reader can immediately put into practice many of the ideas and skills gleaned from each chapter.

Cataloging Library Resources: An Introduction covers new ground with its content aligned with the cataloging competencies established by the American Library Association Library Support Staff Certification Program (ALA-LSSC). Each chapter addresses one or more of the cataloging competencies in ways that the reader can understand each requirement in real and practical applications and examples. In this book the cataloging competencies are turned into examples of library practice that catalogers deal with on the job each day.

This text provides a different perspective than most books or materials written for library professionals. Simply put, the majority of library literature is aimed at professional or graduate-level librarians. Works are often highly theoretical and not practical. Other books on this topic of cataloging are written at a level that is aimed for professional librarians and not support staff. However, 85 percent of library support staff members do not hold professional degrees. This book is written in clear language so its readers can become effective catalogers.

There are many examples of how this book can help the reader to become more proficient and confident performing cataloging functions. At the end of each chapter are discussion questions that are written to refocus the reader on the more important or salient parts of the chapter. There are either one or two learning activities at the end of each chapter that an instructor can use with a class or the reader can work through independently or with other staff to gain experience or additional practice with ideas or processes described in the text.

Just a few examples of how the information in this book helps people are in chapter 4 on the MARC21 record. By using template examples, the reader will learn how to maximize his or her potential to populate exact fields and subfields with data so that library items will have a better chance to be found by patrons. Another example of how this book can help people is chapter 10 on RDA, FRBR, and FRAD. There are tables in this chapter to help the reader understand the terminology and how it relates to the thinking, research, and work of the cataloger. The goal of this book is to provide hands-on, real experiences of learning for library staff and students who can either refer to the book for specific topics or read it in its entirety for a thorough and practical understanding of library cataloging and classification of resources.

This book is needed because there is a shortage of comprehensive books written on the topics of cataloging and classification at this level. Library support staff is often required in their work to have practical knowledge of cataloging as it permeates many of the other library services such as circulation, interlibrary loan, online catalog, or reserves. This book was developed around both the ALA-LSSC competencies for cataloging and the course curriculum of cataloging and classification taught at Three Rivers Community College that has been approved by the American Library Association as an accredited course that meets the LSSC standards. Because of the lack of textbooks for LTA programs on cataloging, the author developed the content from her own research and teaching cataloging. The author also has extensive practical experiences with cataloging as a member library cataloger for more than twenty-five years in the Libraries Online consortium.

I wrote this book to instill confidence in new or intermediate support staff catalogers who are often required to learn on the job how to perform aspects of this complicated and demanding skill. Approaching the vast and ever-changing world of cataloging takes a level head and extensive knowledge of and being able to apply in each situation the rules, policies, and standards specific for each item. In a world of shared records that are public to everyone via the Internet, a cataloger's work must be accurate. When library staff have the skills to catalog, they become invaluable employees in this shortage area to any library. This book is intended as a handbook for all staff and students so that they, in turn, will be able to confidently and smartly catalog library resources that will enhance patrons' library experiences. Following are chapter descriptions:

Chapter 1: The Basics. Users of libraries expect to be able to search, select, locate, and check out materials, yet few people understand the knowledge and skills required by library staff to make these processes work. Libraries describe, organize, and manage materials in a process called cataloging and classification that is unique to libraries rather than any other type of institution that collects and inventories items.

Chapter 2: Catalogs, Collaborations, and Tools. Cataloging is steeped in practices and history that go back to ancient civilization. An appreciation of the historical roots of cataloging gives us appreciation for the dynamic online catalogs we have available to us today via the Internet. Online catalogs are the result of cooperation and collaborative practices led by institutions such as the Library of Congress and the American Library Association that have been embraced by catalogers in all types of libraries. There are many tools catalogers must know how to use so that they may create bibliographic records of high quality that are accepted in union or shared online catalogs.

Chapter 3: Authority Control. The value of authority control is that it provides catalogers with the means to create and maintain a quality library catalog that uses names, titles, and subjects in a standard way and with consistency. The LC authorities, AACR2 rules, and MARC21 work together to ensure the cataloger can use authority control no matter the type or size of the library. Because with technology the records of the local catalog will potentially be shared in a union catalog, authority control is more important today than ever before.

Chapter 4: MARC21 Records. MARC21 is the standard computer language and code used in libraries in the United States and around the world for inputting the bibliographic information required by AACR2 rules so it can be processed and retrieved from any online library system.

Chapter 5: Copy Cataloging. Catalogers copy, edit, and import outside bibliographic records as part of their work, and in the United States, bibliographic sources with millions of MARC records are available for our use. The value of cooperative or collaborative cataloging practices cannot be minimized as they save enormous amounts of time and funds for libraries. Catalogers must be knowledgeable about the content and purpose of bibliographic, holding, and item records so that they can appropriately integrate them into their ILS.

Chapter 6: Metadata. This chapter compares cataloging books to cataloging digital collections and objects in order to explain what metadata is and how it can be used. Because libraries are rapidly becoming centers for creating, storing, and promoting digital objects that are cataloged with metadata, it is important for library staff to be able to use metadata to help patrons find and locate digital objects.

Chapter 7: Dewey Decimal Classification System. In this chapter library staff is introduced to the art and science of classifying materials using the Dewey Decimal Classification, the oldest system most used by libraries in the United States. Using Dewey, catalogers can apply the basics of classification and organization schemes for any type of library resource collection or format. Catalogers who know DDC can explain the value and purpose of cataloging and classification to help users find the resources that they seek.

Chapter 8: Library of Congress Classification System. Library items are grouped together on similar subjects by their call numbers. As the LCC was developed with just one collection—its own—in mind, the classes are created for the Library of Congress resources. Its collection was primarily developed to be a depository of the items that are vetted through U.S. copyright law. The LC was originally established to provide library service to both the House and the Senate, and it continues to do so. Because of this mission, much of its collections are in the areas of law, politics, military, and administration and less strong in the arts, science, and technology. Thus the twenty-one main classes reflect these collection biases.

Chapter 9: Classification—Collections and Subject Headings. Through the application of the rules and authorities of Library of Congress subject headings, catalogers help users find the resources they seek through a well-maintained and fully functional online library catalog. When subject headings are applied or created following the standards set by the Library of Congress, subject headings are a powerful access point to the resources of libraries found in both their individual and shared catalogs.

Chapter 10: RDA, FRBR, and FRAD. As with anything new there can be bumps along the road. RDA is in its infancy, and there will undoubtedly be refinements to make the rules more understandable. Library support staff who learn the rules and authorities of RDA, FRBR, and FRAD will be able to apply and manage the appropriate current processes for cataloging and classification. Participating in RDA workshops, webinars, and other trainings is even more important today for catalogers as they become conceptual thinkers who can apply new rules and entities relationships in the process of creating quality records.

Chapter 11: BIBFRAME: Preparing Catalogers for the Future. RDA rules and the current MARC21 and emerging BIBFRAME standards challenge LSS catalogers to apply and manage appropriate processes, computer technology, and equipment for cataloging and classification. More than ever before catalogers are challenged to continually learn new ways to extract and input bibliographic data of library resources so that it can be searched and located on the semantic web.

Chapter 12: Practice Cataloging Library Resources in RDA and MARC21. The exercises are developed to give the reader guided practice cataloging nonfiction and fiction books, e-books, serials, audio sound, film, and computer files based on current MARC21 template and RDA rules.

Acknowledgments

I would like to thank all the catalogers who have guided me through the years, in particular Lydia Main, who was always so gracious in sharing with me her new learning about RDA and other aspects of cataloging. I would also like to thank Karan Conover, who for years reviewed my work and offered helpful suggestions to improve my bibliographic records for the Libraries Online consortium. I am especially grateful to Kris Jacobi, head cataloger at Eastern Connecticut State University, who volunteered to review this text for technical accuracy.

With special appreciation, I acknowledge members of the editorial advisory board, who provided important feedback during many stages of this book. Each board member made thoughtful suggestions from the proposal phase thorough the final copy. Their hard work and book endorsements mean much to me.

I am once again grateful for my collaboration of Hali Keeler as we add new books to the Library Support Staff Handbooks series. I thank our editor, Charles Harmon, for his confidence in me as a writer and for his constructive advice.

To my children, their spouses, and their grandchildren: Joe, Jiayi, AJ, Alyssa, Ken, Sarah, and Nora. I thank them for their ongoing interest that sustains my writing.

I would not have begun—or completed—this book without the love and support of my husband, A.J. I remain grateful for his encouragement throughout my writing process.

Editorial Advisory Board

PART 1

Fundamentals of the Cataloging Process

CHAPTER 1

Introduction to Cataloging and Classification

LSS apply and manage the appropriate processes, computer technology, and equipment for cataloging and classification. (ALA-LSSC Cataloging and Classification Competency 1)

Key Terms

AACR2. Anglo-American Cataloguing Rules, second edition. These rules govern the work of those who catalog in English-speaking countries including the United States, Canada, the United Kingdom, and Australia.

Bibliographic record. Information such as the title, author, publisher, ISBN, size, or edition that describes a unique book or other library item.

Cataloging. The process of analyzing and selecting key identifying information about an object and organizing this information in ways that can be easily retrieved by those who wish to locate and use the object.

Classification. The process of assigning subjects and location codes to library materials. Library of Congress (LC) and Dewey Decimal are the common codes used in the United States. LC subjects are assigned so that materials can be searched by topic.

Cloud computing. A library leases storage space for their catalog data on computer servers located off-site and managed by a company that guarantees technical support, backup, and security.

Consortium. Libraries that form a partnership to share an ILS.

FRBR. Functional Requirements for Bibliographic Records, a conceptual model that explains the relationships between an author's work, how it is expressed, the way it is manifested or produced, and the final item to be cataloged.

Holding library. The library in a consortium that owns or "holds" a particular item.

Integrated library system (ILS). The hardware and software used by a library or libraries to provide for a common online catalog and circulation, cataloging, acquisitions, interlibrary loans, reserves, and other library services.

Item record. Attached to the bibliographic record, this second record contains local information, unique to a specific library, about the resource being cataloged such as its
circulation rules, call number, barcode, replacement cost, and collection type.

Library of Congress. An agency of the legislative branch of the federal government. Among
its many services is its leadership in establishing cataloging standards and the rules and
practices for librarians to follow in the United States.

Library support staff (LSS). The term used by the American Library Association for people
who work in libraries who do not have professional (graduate) library degrees. These
staff constitute approximately 85 percent of library workers today and perform a wide
variety of duties and services.

MARC record. An acronym for machine readable cataloging, the computer coding system
developed by the Library of Congress in the 1970s that established a standard way to
enter and format bibliographic data about library material.

RDA. The initialism for Resource Description and Access, the new cataloging standard that
replaces the *Anglo-American Cataloguing Rules* (AACR2). It was created in 2010, and
most libraries have adopted it as their standard for cataloging.

INTRODUCTION

Library users expect to be able to search, select, locate, and check out materials, yet
few people understand the knowledge and skills required by library staff to make
these processes work. Library staff describe, organize, and manage materials in a
process called **cataloging** and **classification** that is different from that used by any
other institution that collects and inventories items. The national standards for cataloging and classification are developed by the **Library of Congress** (LC) and are
used in all school, public, special, and academic libraries in the United States. In
most libraries cataloging is considered a technical service, and the work often takes
place behind the scenes on networks and computers out of public view.

This book, which is divided into three parts, provides an introduction to the
knowledge and skills **library support staff (LSS)** need to catalog and classify materials. Part 1 provides readers an introduction to the fundamentals of the cataloging
process. Beginning with the development of cataloging in libraries, the reader learns
about common procedures and rules, cataloging tools and technology, authority
control, Machine Readable Cataloging (MARC) records, copy cataloging, and metadata. Skilled catalogers are always in high demand. Having fundamental knowledge
of cataloging skills increases work opportunities for library staff as they become
more versatile employees.

Part 2, Classification of Library Materials, explains how catalogers analyze and
organize materials around common topics or themes. Classification is the basis for
the Library of Congress and Dewey Decimal schemes that are used by libraries to
arrange resources so patrons can find specific items on a shelf. In part 2 readers will
also learn about assigning multiple subject headings to materials so that patrons can
find an item about a topic of interest when its title or author is not known.

In the final section of this book, the process of cataloging is explained and opportunities for practice are offered. This is an exciting time for cataloging as many new changes have been adopted so that library materials can better be located and used via the Internet. The reader will learn about Resource Description and Access (**RDA**), which has replaced **AACR2** as the standard for cataloging, and Functional Requirements for Bibliographic Records (**FRBR**), which explains the relationships that occur from authorship to cataloging an item. RDA and FRBR will enhance future cataloging changes through BIBRRAME, which will support full use of library resources in Web 3.0. The goal of part 3 is to give library staff information about RDA and BIBFRAME and also to provide practical experiences using these new procedures to catalog books, media, e-books, and other library materials. The book concludes with a chapter on future trends in cataloging services.

CATALOGING AND CLASSIFICATION: A SCIENCE AND AN ART

We humans use information constantly to make sense of our world. We identify, sort, and compare information about items to help us make decisions. For example, in the grocery store we seek information about the quality, quantity, color, shape, price, weight, and date of food before we select an item to put in our cart. An analogy can be made between shopping and cataloging library resources. In cataloging we also identify numerous facts or pieces of information about an item in order to help patrons decide if it will be of interest or helpful to them. The work of the cataloger is very important to the decisions made by patrons.

The phrase "a science and an art" describes a task that requires both discipline and flexible thinking. The phrase applies here because, as a science, cataloging requires adherence to exact rules and procedures. Yet, as an art, librarians have some flexibility to create records that meet the local needs of their collections and patrons. For example, the descriptive data of an item is set in the rigid code of the **MARC record** so that information such as its author and title are displayed consistently in all libraries. But the cataloger may add a unique classification label that applies only to her library so that the item is shelved in its local history collection.

The RDA and *Anglo-American Cataloguing Rules* (AACR2) must be strictly followed in order to have consistent descriptive data. There are hundreds of rules a cataloger must follow, each numbered and explained. For example, always use the form of the author's name that appears chiefly in their main works, such as "D. H. Lawrence" and not "David Herbert Lawrence" (Rule 31B1). By following this rule, all books by D. H. Lawrence are found in a search under this one form of his name. AACR2 will be described in greater detail in the following chapters. The science of cataloging makes searching both easier and also more consistent, complete, and comprehensive.

But cataloging is also an art because the cataloger has leeway for interpretation. Some librarians may wish to classify a nonfiction work on the life and inventions of Thomas Edison in their biography collection, while others librarians may wish to classify the book as "technology" and locate it with other books about electricity. Throughout this book we will toggle back and forth between the science and the art, the rules and the flexibility, that govern the work of catalogers.

Library Resources

Catalogers create records for all types of library resources, and in this text we show how to do this for many different material formats such as e-books, magazines, digital files, media, and music as well as traditional print materials. While electronic and digital items have very different formats than books, they have much in common. For example, all books, regardless of whether they are e-books or print books, have a title, most likely an author, call number, publisher, copyright date, subjects, and so forth. What differs is the material format, and catalogers account for this in the descriptions. E-books also have a unique tag for the URL or hyperlink so that patrons will be able to acquire access to the digital file. More and more common are catalog records accompanying subscription databases of e-books, journals, and other digital resources that are available through the local library online catalog. These records provide patrons links to digital resources to which the library has access through means other than book purchase.

Background

Prior to the late nineteenth century, most libraries in the United States were either small or private collections, and there was no need for a common cataloging system. Colleges typically required students to read only the Greek and Roman classics, so there was no need for many other texts. If there was an academic library, it held books mostly on theology or sociology. It was not until the inventions that spurred the growth of the Industrial Revolution in the mid- to late nineteenth century that the number of public and academic libraries expanded in the United States. Nouveau riche benefactors established libraries in their towns and cities. As our country began to emerge as a technological and world leader, people began to perceive a need to collect and share information on all kinds of topics. Libraries did not begin to organize their books in a standard way until Melvil Dewey established a classification code scheme in 1872 for how books should be located on shelves. Prior to that, books were arranged by size, donor, subject, author, or any scheme that made sense to the librarian.[1]

Classification codes tell us where to locate a book. Simultaneous with the growth of libraries, there was a need to establish common rules about how to describe a book so that patrons would know the exact items a library had in its collection. This descriptive list of items became the first library catalog, and the process of describing items became known as "cataloging." In England in 1876, Charles Ammi Cutter published *Rules for the Dictionary Catalog* with principles for library cataloging. In 1883 the American Library Association published *Condensed Rules for an Author and Title Catalog.* These rules were revised in 1902 in partnership with the Library of Congress. A few years later the first Anglo-American rules were unified through a revision of cataloging code and procedures that included the previous works of the British Museum, Cutter, Melvil Dewey, the American Library Association, and the Library of Congress.[2]

Since the early twentieth century, there have been many revisions to AACR. Today the American Library Association and the Library of Congress continue to set the rules and practices of cataloging. These two organizations, working in consultation with the British Library and other national libraries, respond to the modern needs

Table 1.1.　Key Dates in the Early History of Cataloging

Date	Event
1839	British Museum creates its own code for cataloging its items.
1872	Melvil Dewey invents the Dewey Decimal System at age twenty-one.
1876	Charles Cutter publishes *Rules for the Dictionary Catalog* in England.
1895	ALA establishes the first list of common subject headings for libraries to use.
1898	The LC adopts the ALA list of subject headings, beginning its own authority file.
1901	The LC begins distributing catalog cards to other libraries.
1908	The ALA publishes an accepted cataloging code based on Library of Congress (LC) standards that describes items but does not classify (provide subject headings).
1909	The LC publishes the first edition of *Subject Headings Used in the Dictionary Catalogs of the Library of Congress*. Now the *Library of Congress Subject Headings* has had thirty-three print editions and is now available on the Internet as a database.
1935	Over five thousand libraries in the United States use LC catalog cards and adopt its standards for cataloging.
Late 1960s	MARC record is established and begins to be accepted by libraries in the early 1970s.
1971	Online Computer Library Center (OCLC) is established.

Source: Steven A. Knowlton, "Power and Change in the U.S. Cataloging Community," *Library Resources and Technical Services* 58, no. 2 (April 2014).

in the cataloging and classification of materials and practices of libraries in the English-speaking world. Revisions continue to occur because of the Internet and advancing technology.

Bibliographic Records

A resource displayed in an online library catalog has many lines of description about the item; among them are its author, title, place of publication, publisher, copyright date, size, and ISBN. This descriptive information is written in a standard format called a **bibliographic record**. The word "bibliographic" is the adjective form of the noun "bibliography," meaning a list of books. The term "bibliography" is derived from the Greek word *biblio* for "book" and *graphy* for something "drawn or written." Today bibliographic records are used for all types of library materials including DVDs, serials, audiobooks, and e-books. The MARC bibliographic record contains all fields for information established by the Library of Congress to describe an item.

There are three main ways a library acquires bibliographic records for the items in its collections:

1. accepting another library's record when it is an exact match and needs no changes
2. customizing another library's record
3. creating a new record from scratch

Catalogers use all three methods in their practice, and all three require training. Many staff members are involved with the first two levels, but in small libraries or where staff have advanced knowledge of cataloging, they may be responsible for creating original MARC records.

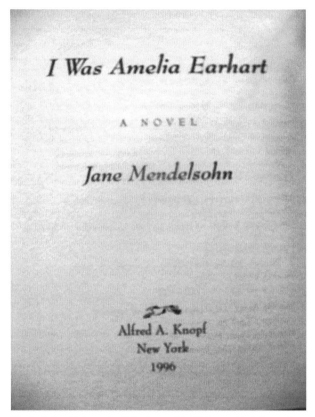

Photo 1.1.   Picture of a Title Page with Bibliographic Information.

In this book we will focus on the skills to modify and create original records. However, any staff person who works with cataloging should be trained, as even to accept a record without modification requires comparing and contrasting it to the local collection and patrons' needs.

Item Records

Once a bibliographic record has been secured or created, the cataloger adds local information into a second record called an **item record**. The item record contains information for the book or other resource in hand, such as the local library call number, circulation rules, barcode, replacement price, the collection it will be shelved in, and so forth.

In a shared catalog, all of the libraries will use the same bibliographic record for a unique resource, but the item records will vary according to the needs of the local or **holding library**.

LIBRARY STAFF APPLY AND MANAGE APPROPRIATE PROCESSES

There are many steps to cataloging a library resource, and this book focuses on the many ways staff can apply and manage these steps. When staff can perform and

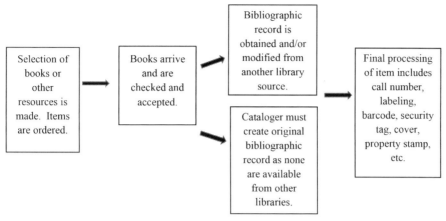

Figure 1.1. Flowchart Showing the Process of Cataloging and Management.

apply accepted rules and requirements of cataloging to their work, they become essential members of the technical services department of the library.

These accepted rules and requirements are numerous and ever changing. We are presently at an exciting time for cataloging as new standards in RDA and BIBFRAME prepare libraries to use the Internet not only to share their own resources with patrons but also to establish links between their library catalog and valuable informational websites. One way to think about cataloging is as a sequential framework. Library staff apply their skills in each of these steps of the cataloging process:

Table 1.2. Steps in the Cataloging Process

Step	Process
1	**Acquisitions.** At this initial step of buying new materials, libraries often also select catalog records for what they are ordering so that the pending items can be displayed as "on order" in the catalog. Matching the right record to the ordered item allows patrons to anticipate and place holds on new items that have not yet arrived.
2	**Receiving.** Here is where the books and other materials that have been selected by the collections development staff arrive in boxes at the library receiving area. Items must be checked and inspected before they are accepted.
3	**Cataloging.** The acquisitions record is accepted as is or modified (more about this in chapter 5 on copy cataloging). If a bibliographic record is not available, the cataloger creates an original one.
4	**Classifying.** Once the bibliographic record is made, classification information for the library is added such as the Dewey or LC code, a collection designation, circulation rules, fines, replacement cost, and so forth.
5	**Final Processing.** After cataloging and classification, the item still needs final processing such as adhering special collection labels, covering, securing barcode and security tags on the item, and other steps such as property stamping for ownership.

Library staff reliably apply many of the steps in the process. However, for cataloging and classification (steps 3 and 4) the cataloger must professionally apply the LC and AACR2 standards so that library catalogs will be accurate not only for their patrons but for anyone in the world to view. This book provides this knowledge so staff can competently and confidently apply the standards of the cataloging process to library materials.

Library staff may have a role in managing the cataloging process. Each library has a technical services department where resources are handled. In a very small library, this could be one dedicated desk and computer. Around the desk could be tools such as a local bibliographic guide established by a school district or public library consortium, *Anglo-American Cataloguing Rules,* and other handbooks. In large academic or public libraries, cataloging may take place in its own department of several members, each of whom completes specific tasks in the process. No matter what size a library may be, all need a managed work sequence so that new resources are correctly cataloged and are on the shelf as soon as possible for patrons to check out. In order for staff to aid in their library's cataloging process, they must demonstrate the following:

- extensive knowledge of the collection and classification scheme used by the library
- accuracy in editing and matching content
- productivity, as the average number of books to copy catalog is approximately fifteen per hour and the average number of original records created may be only three or four per hour[3]
- competent computer skills, as today's cataloger works almost exclusively with database technology

COMPUTER TECHNOLOGY

More than fifty years ago librarians recognized that computers could make the work of cataloging more efficient and available. Because the U.S. government was using mainframe computers in the military and other strategic areas in the 1960s, the Library of Congress and other federal government departments benefited from what was being learned about how computers could be used to store and retrieve data and to make work more efficient. Cataloging the vast collections of the Library of Congress could be expedited with computers.

The MARC record was created for use with LC mainframe computers. By the mid-1970s catalogers in U.S. libraries were encouraged to adapt the MARC format for typing catalog cards as a step in standardization among libraries. With the advances and affordability of the personal computer in the late 1980s, most libraries switched from typing MARC catalog cards to creating MARC records on the computer. Computer hardware and software have replaced the typewriter and catalog cards of the past. Where once catalogers typed cards with basic information about a book that were filed in wooden cases, today they create databases for immediate retrieval of information about each library item or resource.

Equipment for Cataloging and Classification

All libraries need computer equipment to support cataloging and a network infrastructure to efficiently move data. Devices are used for creating records, storing records, and displaying records. Networks support the transmission of data between these devices. Catalogers have workstations that are part of the **integrated library system (ILS)** with access to software where they review, modify, and create bibliographic

Photo 1.2. Traditional shelf list with catalog cards. Bill Memorial Library. Groton, CT.

records. These workstations are typically personal computers, but they may, in a large library, be dedicated terminals. The mainframe computer has long been replaced in the workplace by the personal computer, or PC. Data that was once input through cards or analog tapes is today input digitally through keyboards, voice, or touchscreen.

Libraries also need secure storage for their catalog of bibliographic and item records. A small school or public library may keep records locally on a dedicated PC. Catalogers whose library has a stand-alone PC may be responsible for backing up or making copies of the cataloging data at the end of each day. Most medium and large libraries transmit their data to one or more servers with some degree of dedicated technical support. If the server is off-site, it may be in a central location that supports the ILS of multiple libraries at an institutional, district, regional, or state level.

Patrons are able to view catalog records on a variety of devices. Even in the library, they may use the online catalog computer found at a library station or access the catalog through any number of wireless devices, such as tablets, laptops, or smartphones that provide interactive web access.[4] Near field communication (NFC) used for banking and other consumer interactions could also be used, in some libraries, to pay fines, place holds, and access catalog and patron records.

High-speed network infrastructure is very important to catalogers. While this was once a problem, fiber optic and other broadband communications technology provide libraries today with have options for high-speed transmission of data.[5] Depending upon a library's location, it may use fiber, cable, DSL, satellite, or BPL (broadband over power lines) for Internet connectivity. If there is a performance lag, boosters can be used to increase capacity.

Consortiums

Many libraries have moved from having separate catalogs to sharing a common database of records with other libraries in a **consortium** arrangement using a shared integrated library system.

The ILS combines hardware and software for the many services and functions of the library, including circulation and cataloging. An ILS has servers, library PCs, network infrastructure, and the proprietary applications used for each of the services, including the online library catalog. Staff should know about their library ILS, the vendor or provider, and the staff who run the ILS. Bibliographic and item records are created through the cataloging function of the ILS so that they can be displayed for the public via the online library catalog. In a consortium the database of bibliographic records, and often patron records, are shared. As a result, the information of one library can be used for the benefit of another. We will learn more about this in chapter 5 on copy cataloging.

A library may opt for **cloud computing** whereby an outside company guarantees the security and management of the library catalog records. Depending on the size of a library and its resources, storage devices and processes will vary, but all need to have secure space for the catalog with backup and redundancy for both the cataloger and the patron.

LIBRARY OF CONGRESS

The Library of Congress (LC) has been mentioned several times in this chapter as a major influence on cataloging history and practices. The Library of Congress plays a critical role in the cataloger's day-to-day work and provides resources to support that work. Each chapter of this book refers to LC resources and applies them to cataloging and classification. Because the LC is a federal government agency dependent on taxpayers, librarians benefit from the free availability of its resources. Because the LC has taken the leadership role in the United States for establishing standards for cataloging and classification, we not only have excellent management of our libraries' materials but also are primed to use our data with the latest technologies to enhance world knowledge through resource sharing.

SUMMARY

This first chapter introduces some of the fundamental terminology, practices, and agencies you will encounter as you learn how to catalog and classify library materials. Library staff who know about cataloging and classification can apply their skills to get materials more quickly to patrons. They also use their skills to modify or create records for online library catalogs. Computer technology and equipment are important tools for cataloging, and staff who catalog must become adept in using them. Finally, the Library of Congress, along with the American Library Association, creates the procedures and rules for library cataloging in the United States. We will begin to look at some of the cataloging resources of the Library of Congress in chapter 2.

DISCUSSION QUESTIONS AND ACTIVITIES

Discussion Questions

1. Why can the process of cataloging and classification be called both a science and an art? Explain.
2. Who were two key people who influenced early cataloging and classification? What did they do?
3. Explain a major difference between a bibliographic record and an item record.
4. Name some of the information found in a bibliographic record.
5. What are some ways patrons can view their online library catalog? Which method do you prefer and why?

Activity

This activity helps library staff become familiar with the work of the cataloger at the library he or she frequents. Arrange for a visit to your public or college library and ask for an appointment with the cataloging librarian to learn about the processes and equipment the staff use to catalog new library materials. Explain that you are new to the cataloging process but are eager to learn how the library handles this work. During the interview, ask these questions:

1. How many members are there in the technical services department, and what are their job descriptions? (You may ask to talk later with other staff about their work.)
2. Describe the steps of processing this library uses from the time a book is ordered to when it is ready for the shelf. In these steps, when is a catalog record accepted, modified, or created?
3. Ask about the integrated library system this library uses for the cataloging function. Do they share the ILS with other libraries? If so, with whom?
4. What roles and responsibilities do staff have in the cataloging process in this library? What work do they do? What work do they not do? Why?
5. Does the cataloging librarian have suggestions for how staff can improve their cataloging skills?

In a two-page, double-spaced paper, summarize the interview data you obtained. In a final paragraph, provide your opinion about what you saw. Does the library have adequate staff and resources to do the cataloging work in a timely way? What were the most interesting parts of the process you observed?

NOTES

1. Most books in libraries were theological works, though there were also some classics and standard treatises in philosophy, logic, and history. There was no standard way to categorize books, so they were arranged by size, donor, subject, or author until the adoption of the Dewey Decimal classification scheme in 1876.

2. "Anglo-America" refers to the English-speaking countries of the United Kingdom, the United States, and Canada. "A Brief History of AACR," Joint Steering Committee for the Development of RDA, last modified July 1, 2009, at www.rda-jsc.org/archivedsite/history.html (accessed November 1, 2015).

3. Richard Walser and Melissa VanTine, "Cataloging a Small Library Using LibraryThing," Cataloging with LibraryThing, last modified 2008, at home.southernct.edu/~walserr1/courses/585LibraryThing.htm#workflow (accessed November 11, 2015).

4. Marshall Breeding, "Library Technology Forecast for 2015 and Beyond," *Computers in Libraries* 34, no. 10 (December 2014), 22–24, available at www.infotoday.com/cilmag/dec14/Breeding--Library-Technology-Forecast-for-2015-and-Beyond.shtml.

5. "Types of Broadband Connections," Broadband.gov, Federal Communications Commission, at www.broadband.gov/broadband_types.html (accessed November 21, 2015).

REFERENCES, SUGGESTED READINGS, AND WEBSITES

Breeding, Marshall. "Library Technology Forecast for 2015 and Beyond." *Computers in Libraries* 34, no. 10 (December 2014): 22–24. Available at www.infotoday.com/cilmag/dec14/Breeding--Library-Technology-Forecast-for-2015-and-Beyond.shtml.

Federal Communications Commission. "Types of Broadband Connections." Broadband.gov. Accessed November 21, 2015, at www.broadband.gov/broadband_types.html.

JSC-RDA. "A Brief History of AACR." Joint Steering Committee for the Development of RDA. Last modified July 1, 2009. Accessed November 1, 2015, at www.rda-jsc.org/archivedsite/history.html.

Knowlton, Steven A. "Power and Change in the U.S. Cataloging Community." *Library Resources and Technical Services* 58, no. 2 (April 2014): 111–26.

Library of Congress. "About the Library." Accessed October 25, 2015, at www.loc.gov/about/.

Rider, Mary M. "Developing New Roles for Paraprofessionals in Cataloging." *Journal of Academic Librarianship* 22, no. 1 (January 1996): 26.

Walser, Richard, and Melissa VanTine. "Cataloging a Small Library Using LibraryThing." Cataloging with LibraryThing. Accessed November 11, 2015, at home.southernct.edu/~walserr1/courses/585LibraryThing.htm#workflow.

Weiner, Sharon Gray. "The History of Academic Libraries in the United States: A Review of the Literature." *Library Philosophy and Practice* 7, no. 2 (Spring 2005). Available at www.webpages.uidaho.edu/~mbolin/weiner.htm.

Zhu, Lihong. "The Role of Paraprofessionals in Technical Services in Academic Libraries." *Library Resources and Technical Services* 56, no. 3 (July 2012): 127–54.

CHAPTER 2

Catalogs, Collaborations, and Tools

LSS know and can use the basic cataloging and classification tools, both print and online, including bibliographic utilities and format standards. (ALA-LSSC Cataloging and Classification Competency 2)

LSS are able to explain the value and advantages of cooperative or collaborative cataloging practices to enhance services. (ALA-LSSC Cataloging and Classification Competency 6)

Key Terms

AACR2. The abbreviation for the *Anglo-American Cataloguing Rules*, second edition. These rules govern the work of those who catalog in English-speaking countries including the United States, Canada, the United Kingdom, and Australia.

Accession book. A ledger used by librarians to record bibliographic and item information about each item acquired by the library in the order that it was received.

Copy cataloging. The process of making a local record based on an acquired bibliographic record created from another source.

Integrated library system (ILS). The hardware and software used by a library or libraries to provide a common online catalog and circulation, cataloging, acquisitions, interlibrary loans, reserves, and other library services.

MARC21 record. The standard for creating a bibliographic catalog record based on the rules of AACR2.

Modules. The different functions or services of the ILS such as circulation, cataloging, online catalog, and so on.

Online Public Access Catalog. Also known as OPAC, this is how patrons view, place holds, and manage their accounts both within and outside the library using the Internet.

Open source. Software available to the public at either minimal or no cost.

Union catalog. A library catalog that contains the bibliographic records of more than one library interfiled in the dictionary format.

INTRODUCTION

We will begin to explore the different basic cataloging and classification tools in this chapter and will continue to look at important bibliographic tools, utilities, and formats throughout part 1. The library catalog is the repository of bibliographic records, and a library catalog's appearance and use by staff and patrons has rapidly changed with technology. Where once the catalog was a list of a library's holdings, today the catalog is a dynamic database with active links to websites and information about the library's resources.

Because of technology, today the cataloger does much more than create a repository. Cataloging supports all other modules or services such as circulation, interlibrary loan, acquisitions, readers' advisory, and reference. Shared catalogs between and among libraries also provide important benefits.

The Library of Congress (LC), the American Library Association, and other large libraries and agencies guide and support the work of catalogers. Some of the most important cataloging tools and resources for library staff are available from the LC. The LC develops the national standards for library cataloging in the United States and provides many tools and resources for accurate and current cataloging practices. We look at the LC catalog and learn how its bibliographic data can be used as a resource for other libraries.

LIBRARY CATALOGS

Over the past century library catalogs in the United States have evolved from bound lists of titles to online databases with search tags and fields. Likewise, technology has changed the role of the cataloger from clerical typist to database manager. Library staff perform many of the professional cataloger's database management tasks today. They search, edit, and export catalog records from national sources. They also retrieve and import records into their local **integrated library system (ILS)**, create holding records, and complete the processing of materials.[1]

Library catalogs are categorized based on two major considerations. First, what is the order or arrangement of the bibliographic data? Second, what is the physical construction of the catalog?

Searchable Catalogs

Access to bibliographic data has evolved over time through four types of searchable library catalogs beginning with the classified catalog, moving next to the dictionary catalog, and ending today with the online catalog. Some libraries also maintain a shelf list catalog. The actual catalogs are constructed from available materials and systems to provide the greatest ease of access. Library catalogs first began with the book, then the card catalog, followed by microfilm or microfiche and CD-ROM. Today, with almost universal Internet access, library catalogs are online databases. We will look at the four types of searchable library catalogs.

Classified Catalog. Historians found evidence that the ancient libraries of Babylonia, Alexandra, Rome, and Athens created topic or subject inventories of their scripts, books, and reading and visual materials. Library items were classified, or grouped, by topic. People interested in a subject could find all of the similar materials on that topic through the classified catalog, no matter where they were kept in the library. The Carnegie Library of Pittsburgh long used the classified catalog system for organizing its scientific collections.[2]

Dictionary Catalog. In this type of catalog, author, title, and subject cards are interfiled alphabetically. When the Library of Congress moved into its new building in 1898, staff there decided that the classified catalog of subjects was inadequate for its rapidly expanding collections. Rewritten onto alphabetical subject lists, the first edition of *Subject Headings Used in the Dictionary Catalogue of the Library of Congress* was printed in 1909.[3] The classified catalog became less useful with the adoption of the Dewey Decimal Classification System by libraries in the late nineteenth century. The dictionary catalog had been used by libraries for over a century until its recent replacement by **online public access catalogs**.

Online Public Access Catalog (OPAC). The OPAC is a database of the library holdings searchable by multiple points of data such as keyword, author, title, subject, ISBN, call number, barcode, and collection type. The OPAC may offer search limiters such as "NOT"; in the search "boy NOT scouts," books on Boy Scouts will not be shown. Libraries today have already or soon will be abandoning card catalogs in favor of OPACs because they provide more thorough searching via the Internet. In a study by the Pew Research Center of the 25 percent of adults sixteen years and older who said they went to a library website in the past twelve months, 84 percent of them searched the library OPAC for books, e-books, CDs, or DVDs.

Shelf List Catalog. Neither a classified catalog nor a dictionary catalog, the shelf list is an aging anomaly that some libraries still maintain for inventory purposes. The shelf list is a list or a set of drawers of cards arranged in the classification order of the library. For catalogers who work in libraries where shelves are periodically inventoried, the shelf list can speed the process of confirming the presence of items not in circulation.

Photo 2.1.   Picture of Shelf List Cards. Bill Memorial Library. Groton, CT.

Construction

The construction of the actual catalog has significantly changed over time. Early libraries used the book catalog, but today libraries present their holdings to the public through the Internet.

Book catalog. Books or volumes are the oldest form of catalogs, beginning with people in ancient civilizations who made classified lists or subject list inventories of scripts, manuscripts, and books. A major problem with book classified catalogs was that they were fixed with little to no flexibility for recording new items. Some catalogers may work in libraries today that still have an **accession book**. The library staff entered concise bibliographic information into the accession book about every new book in the order that it was received.

Card Catalog. Introduced by Melvil Dewey in the late eighteenth century, this piece of cabinetry held multiple drawers for filing catalog slips or cards. Librarians took to the card catalog very quickly, dooming the book catalog to obviation. The card catalog was not replaced until the **MARC21** record could be searched and retrieved through computer database software in the late twentieth century.

Microfiche. Photographed bibliographic records were reduced in size on plastic cards or film. Creating microfiche was time consuming and costly as the majority of libraries needed to outsource the work. Special readers for microfiche are very expensive and not affordable for busy public access.

CD-ROM. These storage devices of the 1980s, concurrent with the advent of the personal computer (PC), could hold great amounts of data. Using CD-ROMs, libraries could render backup copies of their catalogs and offer patrons access to statewide or other catalogs. CD-ROMs and DVDs were quickly and widely accepted as media for accessing bibliographic data because they were easy to use and affordable for libraries.

Databases. Online Public Access Catalogs (OPACS) are databases of bibliographic information about library holdings searchable by multiple terms. The databases reside on library servers or may be outsourced to commercial enterprises that offer cloud computing. The public can access the OPAC any time of the day or night with the Internet. Most libraries offer abridged versions of their OPAC that are more practical for mobile devices.

INTEGRATED LIBRARY SYSTEMS

Libraries of all types and sizes use integrated library systems (ILSs) to input data and manage such services as circulation, cataloging, online catalog, acquisitions, serials, reserves, e-resource management, and inventory. Software as a Service (SaaS) has become a common feature of ILSs for managing much of the other software used by staff and patrons, such as word processing and the like. ILSs vary depending on the the type of library, its budget, technical expertise of staff, and other needs. It is common for libraries to purchase or lease an ILS as a consortium.

An ILS is a bundle of software applications that work with each other to provide effective library services. These software applications are often called **modules**. Each module focuses on a particular library service. For instance, the cataloging module

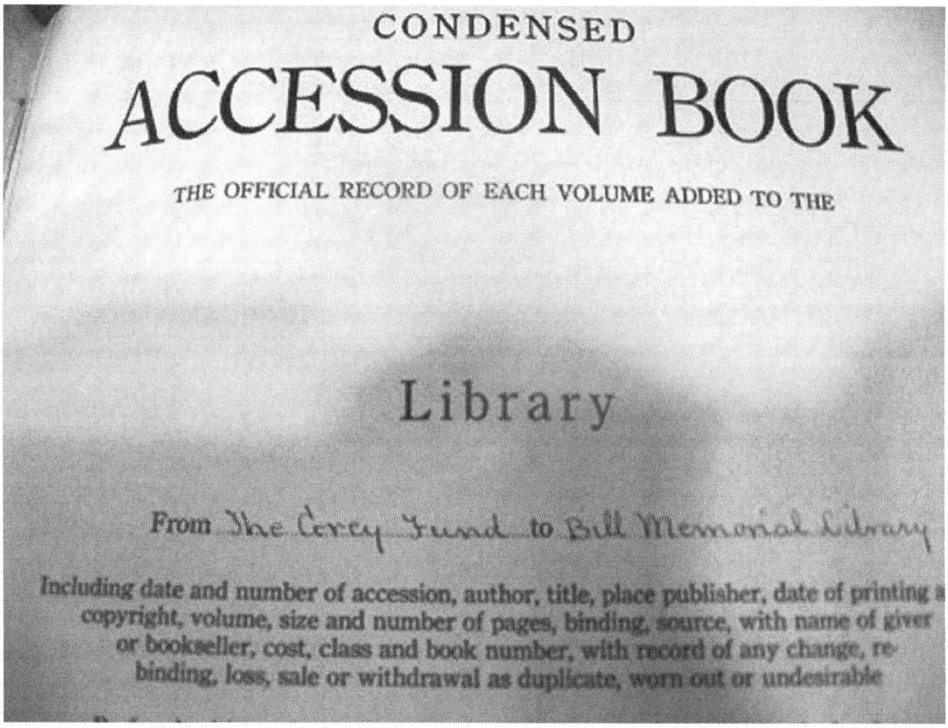

Photo 2.2. Accession Book . Bill Memorial Library, Groton, CT.

Photo 2.3. Entry page of the accession book. Bill Memorial Library, Groton, CT.

Table 2.1. Evolution of Library Catalogs

Time Period	Type of Access to Bibliographic Data	Type of Physical Construction
300 BC to the mid-nineteenth century	Classified catalog	Lists bound in books
1840	Dictionary catalog	Harvard College Librarian Thaddeus Harris creates a "slip catalogue" consisting of the title of every work in the library on pieces of card 6½ inches long by 1½ inches wide.
Late nineteenth century	Dictionary catalog	Melvil Dewey sells the first card catalog cabinets through his supply store.
1970s–1980s	Dictionary catalog	Microfilm, microfiche
1990s–2000s	Digital discs	CD-ROMs or DVDs that contain the bibliographic information of the library collections
1990s–2000	Online Public Access Catalog (OPAC)	Databases of bibliographic text information searchable via the Internet
Twenty-first century	Online Public Access Catalog (WebOPAC)	Online public access catalog that provides availability of library services using the Internet.

supports the work of the cataloger while the circulation module supports the management of lending materials. An ILS is efficient because the data inputted in one module is used in other modules. For example, the bibliographic record created for a particular book in the cataloging module will be linked to and used in the circulation module when the patron checks out this book. The same thing takes place between acquisitions (purchasing) and cataloging. Information or data created for the order record for a new item in acquisitions is carried over into the catalog record once the item arrives. This sharing of data among modules avoids duplicating staff time and effort.

Vendors

Integrated library systems today must manage both print and electronic resources.[4] There is competition among commercial vendors for market share. At the same time, there is also a successful movement for libraries to cut costs and use open-source ILSs that are inexpensive and reliable. Depending on the ILS a library adopts, staff need training to become proficient users of its functions and features. While the end result in each case is to create bibliographic records using the MARC standard, there is variation among ILSs in ease of use, support, and so forth. Librarians often help and train each other, forming user groups for each module. Some of the major commercial vendors of ILSs for public libraries are Innovative, SIRSI-Dynix, BiblioCommons, and Auto-graphics.[5] Academic libraries seek ILS platforms that can manage print and electronic resources. OCLC WorldShare Management Services, ExLibris, and ProQuest Intota are competing with Voyager, Aleph, Symphony, and Horizon. SirsiDynix offers BLUEcloud Campus aimed at the academic market. Follett Destiny has dominated K–12 library automation with 70 percent of market share reported. Book Systems and Library Solutions are also ILS vendors. Special libraries have differing requirements for their ILSs. Many business, medical, law, and other special libraries use products from Lucidea.

While contracting with commercial vendors is not without significant expense to libraries, there are many benefits. First, software development is ongoing, tested, and competitive. Second, vendors offer excellent software support for migrating to their system, installing new releases, and offering updates to existing modules. Third, commercial vendors provide libraries with system reliability, training, cloud computing and storage, backup and disaster recovery, and discounts on hardware and software.

But many small to mid-sized libraries are choosing open-source software because of the low cost. Evergreen and Koha are currently the two largest open-source ILSs. Performance and reliability are proving to be good, and the modules can be customized. Regardless of whether an ILS is from a commercial vendor or available as open-source code, cataloging modules are a key function.

Cataloging Modules

The cataloging module is the key module in an ILS. Without the bibliographic record, there is no circulation. A patron searches and then checks out a book, and that book information—its title, author, location, and so forth—comes from the catalog record. In other words, the work of the cataloger is needed for the ILS to be used for any other services.

The cataloging module of any ILS supports the work of the cataloger and provides many of the online tools required to create the MARC record and ensure it is robust and accurate. Other chapters in this book explain and demonstrate how the cataloger uses the functions and features of the cataloging module. Table 2.2 outlines typical supports provided by the ILS.

Table 2.2. Common Functions and Features of an ILS Cataloging Module

Function	Features
Creating new MARC records	MARC templates are provided for each type of library resource or material. Help-screen prompts are easy to understand.
Importing and editing MARC records	Depending on the vendor contract, outside resources such as OCLC, the LC, and other statewide, regional, and local catalogs are available to search and import records. Editing tools are easy to use for copying and changing lines of information. Simple and clear instructions are available for importing records into the local system.
Importing authority records	Author and subject authority files from the LC as well as consortium or other members of a shared catalog are easy to access and import or overlay into records.
Replacing or overlaying records	Upgrading a bibliographic record in the system with either a more robust record or one that is more accurate is a simple process without losing local information.
Adding holding information	After the bibliographic record is created, local information such as the call number, collection code, barcode, circulation parameters, and so on is easy to add.
Administration	Customized reports, statistics, and bibliographic and local records as well as other information and alerts about the use and management of cataloging is easy to obtain. Data created in the cataloging module is used in other ILS modules.
Resources	Links are available to codes, lists, authority files, catalogs, and other tools.

It is important that the ILS offers training to catalogers, clearly written manuals, and opportunities for practice with robust help screens. Most cataloging courses do not provide enough hands-on practice with real ILS cataloging modules, making the supports of the cataloging module even more important for both the novice and the experienced cataloger.[6]

Online Public Access Catalog

The ILS module patrons are most familiar with is the online catalog, or OPAC. The OPAC displays all of the library holdings. Bibliographic records are created in the cataloging module in MARC and displayed to the public in a readable format in OPAC, providing the patron with author, title, publisher, ISBN, and other descriptive data about each library resource. Not only does the OPAC display bibliographic records from the cataloging module, it also provides active shelf status from the circulation module.

Because the ILS modules are relational databases—that is, they are designed to use and share information—the OPAC is a combination of cataloging, circulation, reserves, and electronic management features. The data the cataloger creates or imports into the cataloging module will immediately be visible from the OPAC module. Likewise, the moment an item is checked out, its status will show as not on the shelf in OPAC.

It is important for all catalogers to maintain the highest standards when they are entering data as their work is immediately public on the OPAC. Misspellings or any other grammatical or editing inaccuracies will be visible on the OPAC.

OPACS are evolving, and, for most libraries, provide access to many different library services through the Internet in addition to the collection. For example, OPACs offer patrons remote access to electronic books, music, magazines, databases, and newspapers.

Figure 2.1.   Screen shot of a OPAC Display. Libraires Online, Middletown, CT.

As online access changes and improves, so will the work of the cataloger change. Another evolution in cataloging is Library Resource Discovery, which is positioning itself to replace OPACS and ILS modules.[7] Library Resource Discovery will allow patrons to submit queries, receive results, and make content selections more easily and fully. Users will be able to create advanced searches whose results provide hyperlinks to the full text of relevant related web and library resources. There will be improved searching capability for local searches, and patrons will be better able to place holds and manage their accounts. No doubt Library Resource Discovery will impact catalogers' work as it will create an ongoing need for robust information that can be used and retrieved for multiple purposes for each library resource.

COOPERATIVE OR COLLABORATIVE CATALOGING

The good news is that not all catalog records need to be created from scratch. A proficient cataloger may take upwards of fifteen minutes to create an original MARC record, so approximately four to five books could be cataloged in an hour. For a library that acquires five thousand books per year, it would take an unacceptable thousand hours to originally create these MARC records.

Cooperative cataloging has led to shared catalogs. A catalog with cards from more than one library interfiled in an alphabetical, dictionary format is known as a **union catalog**. While interfiling more than one library's cards is not an easy task with a physical card catalog, integrated library systems have made union catalogs both feasible and practical. Patrons respond enthusiastically to being able to search not only their own library's collections but the collections of other towns, universities, or schools. Libraries establish logical cooperatives, collaborations, or consortiums with each other based on one or more of these practical considerations:

TEXTBOX 2.1. SOME REASONS LIBRARIES PARTICIPATE IN COOPERATIVE CATALOGING

- Leverage budget for cost savings
- Gain efficiency and save staff time
- Share technical support and expertise
- Share items between libraries with geographic proximity
- Share common objectives and policies because of similar library type
- Increase depth and breadth of collection because of access to dissimilar library resources

---

National Catalogs

The majority of countries in the world have online library catalogs for the institution designated to develop collections supported by the national government. Browsing through the catalogs using a site such as LibWeb lets us compare not only the types of materials countries collect but also their cataloging standards.[8] The MARC record in the Anglo-American standard is used not only by libraries in the United States but also by libraries in other English-speaking countries, such as the British Library in London and the National Library of Australia. The International Federation of Library Associations (IFLA) in 1961 established the first cataloging principles based on the fields of the MARC record.[9] Cataloging standards across the world are adopted so that library catalogs have a similar format and utility. In other words, people using the Biblioteca Nacional do Brazil can rely on the fact that its library display adheres to the standards of description and access found in the United States. Because the international standards for cataloging are continually updated under the direction of IFLA, the technology of library catalogs should be current around the world, which is important because research is not confined to one country. Today, people comfortably use world Internet resources, and IFLA cataloging standards are in place for better access to searching and finding information in libraries.

The Library of Congress initiated cooperative cataloging in the United States by sharing the information on its catalog cards with other libraries who were purchasing the same items that the LC had in its collections. The LC continues to be a leader in collaboration by sharing its catalog records with libraries in their online catalog, which is found at catalog.loc.gov. Why should a cataloger create another bibliographic record of the same item when the LC has already made one?

The LC catalog originated in 1898 and today contains over eighteen million bibliographic records that describe its collections; the catalog is searchable by keyword, author, title, or call number.[10] Other LC collections, such as its E-Resources Online Catalog of e-books, e-journals, and quality websites, are linked to the LC catalog. Dedicated to keeping up with current browsers and cataloging software, the LC is developing easier and more practical ways for catalogers to import or adapt its records. The sharing of records is referred to as **copy cataloging**, and chapter 5 is dedicated in detail to this topic, including how to copy records from the LC catalog.

State Catalogs

State libraries are an excellent model for cooperation and collaboration among library catalogers. Each state in the United States has a state library, and the majority have dedicated staff and resources to creating a statewide online catalog of the bibliographic records of their public, school, and academic libraries. One of the main features of these online catalogs is the ability to share library resources so that residents have statewide interlibrary loan privileges. Catalogers also benefit from statewide catalogs when they can copy, import, and share bibliographic records.

The statewide catalogs are created by libraries that export their records to a central database. A comprehensive list with links to the fifty state libraries and their online catalogs can be easily found by searching the Internet.[11] Catalogers can learn how to access the cataloging module of their state library catalog and explore its resources through instructions often posted on the state library website. Authorized library users may import records into the catalog, following specific steps. Most state online catalogs are developed by commercial vendors, but a few are moving to open source code. Each contracted vendor has specific protocols for moving records, and state libraries hire their own staff to interface with the contractors and supervise the quality of the online catalog.

Many states offer online libraries; some, like the state of Texas, provide access primarily to state archives and state library collections. Other online state library catalogs, like Connecticut's researchIT, Virtual Illinois Catalog, and Ohio Libraries Share MORE (OLS:MORE), are fully comprehensive.[12] Residents have access to the catalogs and digital libraries of state, public, school, academic, and special libraries as well as electronic databases. Over a hundred libraries with seventeen million volumes and 2.5 million patrons participate in Ohio Libraries Share MORE.[13] A great feature of Ohio's system is that catalogers can share MARC records. With just a click, the display record can be shown in the MARC format. If another library in the state has an item in its collection, particularly if it is fairly unusual and would require original cataloging, searching the statewide catalog to see if another library already owns it is very efficient.

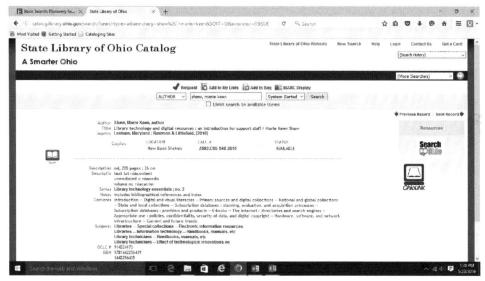

Figure 2.2. Screen Shot of an OLS:MORE Regular Display Record and its MARC Record. Ohio State Library Catalog.

Figure 2.3. Screen Short of an OLS:MORE MARC Display Record. Ohio State Library Catalog.

Region Catalogs

It has become more common than not for libraries to join with others to create online shared catalogs in order to share resources and expenses. Cataloging begins at the local level, and consistency is required so that there is only one bibliographic record per unique item. We will look more closely at examples of regional systems and how they share resources in chapter 5 on copy cataloging.

CATALOGERS' TOOLS

This section is a mere introduction to the many resources and tools catalogers use to support their work. We will use many of these tools in the subsequent chapters. Catalogers learn both formally and informally. College courses accredited by the American Library Association provide an excellent foundation for a beginning cataloger. While much about cataloging can be learned informally on the job, cataloging is a complicated and exacting process that requires solid knowledge of its fundamentals. Ongoing professional development from workshops, webinars, websites, books, and other sources is necessary to maintain and update cataloging skills. In other words, a proficient and accurate cataloger is a lifelong learner!

We will end this chapter by introducing some of the more common and important tools for cataloging and classification. Throughout the remainder of this book we will refer to and use many of these tools as we perform and practice cataloging. Some of the tools are in print format, but today many are only available online so that they stay current. Libraries must purchase and invest in resources that are published by nongovernmental agencies.

AACR2

We begin with the *Anglo-American Cataloguing Rules* (AACR2), which is the comprehensive and definitive "gold standard" of the rules for cataloging library materials for the United States, Canada, the United Kingdom, Australia, and other English-speaking countries. Each action performed by the cataloger in the process of creating a bibliographic record is done only under the guidance of a clearly defined and specific rule found in AACR2. The rules are published jointly by the American Library Association and other international library agencies and are updated regularly. Rules are numbered and hierarchically organized. All catalogers must be familiar with and be able to reference AACR2 in order to do their work.

American Library Association (ALA) Publications

The ALA offers many important tools for catalogers, both print and online. Two critical ones are the *RDA Toolkit* and the *ALA Filing Rules*.

The *RDA Toolkit* is an online database of the updated resource description and access instructions for catalogers. The toolkit also contains the cataloging rules from AACR2 that were carried over into RDA. A subscription to the toolkit provides workflows, maps, and other templates that teach catalogers how to create searchable Internet bibliographic records. RDA supports technology that today can provide a new exposure to the items in library collections.

The *ALA Filing Rules* provide the official governance for how bibliographic records of library materials of any format, including those online, are arranged. For example, one ALA rule is that the articles *a, an,* and *the* are ignored when they begin the title of a bibliographic record. All library staff should be familiar and know the rules as they govern title, author, subject, and other entries of library catalogs.

Library of Congress (LC) Cataloging Tools

Libraries both in the United States and elsewhere benefit from the work of the LC Cataloging and Acquisitions Division.[14] In addition to maintaining the LC online catalog, this division provides web access to the LC bibliographic records, provides unprecedented leadership in collaborative practices, sets cataloging standards for access, and develops and shares those standards through online instructions and training.

There is a plethora of print and online cataloging tools provided by the LC. Print materials generally have a cost, but today much that was once in print has been uploaded to free online databases. By having tools online, updates and new releases can be readily shared with catalogers. Just a few of the many essential tools provided by LC are the following:

Library of Congress MARC21 Standards describe and explain how to convert information from any library resource into a bibliographic record based on the AACR2. We will rely on the templates, guides, training, and other materials provided by the LC as we practice creating MARC records.

With the expansion of the MARC record to Resource Description and Access (RDA), the LC has begun to provide excellent documentation and training in RDA. The *LC RDA Core Elements,* for example, is a practical guide for the cataloger that we will use in later chapters.

BIBFRAME is the Library of Congress initiative that will one day replace MARC21 as the standard for cataloging on the web and in the broader networked world.[15] The LC provides general information about the project, including presentations, FAQs, and links to working documents. A major focus of the initiative will be to determine a transition path for the MARC21 formats.

Library of Congress Subject Headings (LCSH) are available and free online. Since 1898 LCSH has been the subject authority to catalog materials held at the Library of Congress. As the national and international authority for subject headings, LCSH is used by other libraries around the United States to provide subject access to their collections. We will use LCSH often in subsequent chapters.

Used by K–12 schools and small- to medium-sized public libraries, the *Sears List of Subject Headings* is a one-volume abridged version, available from H. W. Wilson, of more commonly used headings in the LCSH. Now in its twenty-first edition, many catalogers prefer *Sears* because of its ease of use.

The *Library of Congress Classification* (LCC) was first developed in the late nineteenth and early twentieth centuries to organize and arrange the book collections of the Library of Congress. LLC is used in most academic, special, and large public libraries.

The *Cutter Table* is also available online from the LC. Academic libraries use Cutter to formulate the author's surname into a number to create a unique call number for ease of filing.

OCLC Resources

The OCLC is an international member services cooperative of thousands of libraries across the globe who come together to share cataloging and other resources and services.[16] We will often refer to OCLC products, including the Dewey Decimal Classification System (DDC) that is now in its twenty-third edition. DDC is the more common classification system for school and public libraries in the United States.

Table 2.3.   Essential Tools for the Cataloger

Category	Title	Source
Rules	RDA Toolkit	ALA (purchase)
	Anglo-American Cataloguing Rules (AACR2)	ALA (purchase)
	ALA Filing Rules	ALA (purchase)
MARC21	MARC21 Standards	www.loc.gov/marc/marc.html
Cataloger's Desktop	Electronic access to AACR2 and the LC's most heavily used cataloging publications	www.loc.gov/cds/desktop/help/en/contents.html
Classifications	Library of Congress Classification (LCC)	www.loc.gov/catdir/cpso/lcco/
	Dewey Decimal Classification	www.org/dewey/features/summaries.en.html (Purchase)
	Cutter Table	www.loc.gov/aba/pcc/053/table.html
Subjects	Library of Congress Subject Headings (LCSH)	id.loc.gov/authorities/subjects.html
	Sears List of Subject Headings, twenty-first edition	www.hwwilsoninprint.com/sears.php
RDA	RDA Core Elements	www.loc.gov/aba/rda/
BIBFRAME	Bibliographic Framework Initiative	www.loc.gov/bibframe/

Other Print and Web Resources

There are numerous books and websites to help catalogers with their work available from the Library of Congress, ALA, publishers such as Rowman & Littlefield, professional national and state library organizations, universities, library consortiums, online catalogs, and other sources. We will use many of these resources and references to demonstrate cataloging in sequential and logical steps.

Beginning with the next chapter on authority control, we will put into practice the theories and rules of cataloging.

SUMMARY

Cataloging is steeped in practices and history that go back to ancient civilization. Understanding the historical roots of cataloging lets us appreciate the dynamic online catalogs available to us today via the Internet. Online catalogs are the result of cooperation and collaborative practices led by institutions such as the Library of

Congress and the American Library Association that have been embraced by catalogers in all types of libraries. There are many tools catalogers must know how to use so that they can create bibliographic records of high quality that are accepted in union or shared online catalogs.

DISCUSSION QUESTIONS AND ACTIVITIES

Discussion Questions

1. Describe the evolution of libraries from using classified book catalogs in ancient times to using online public access catalogs (OPAC) today.
2. Define the term "integrated library system (ILS)" and explain how are they used by libraries.
3. How does the work of the cataloger affect the other modules of the ILS?
4. Why is cooperation and collaboration important among catalogers at both the local and national levels?
5. What cataloging benefits do libraries derive from belonging to a consortium or collaborative?
6. Who are the main providers of cataloging tools, and what are the purposes of these important resources?

Activity: Tools of the Cataloger

Many cataloging tools were introduced in this chapter. We will soon be using these tools, and it is important that you be able to find them quickly and are familiar with their overall purpose. This assignment will help you gain familiarity with several of the Internet-based tools presented here. Using table 2.4, go to each of these resources, read the introductory paragraphs that describe the tool, and try each one out!

Table 2.4. Internet-Based Cataloging Tools

Tool	URL	Purpose	How Did You Use It?
MARC21	www.loc.gov/marc/marc.html		
Library of Congress Classification (LCC)	www.loc.gov/catdir/cpso/lcco/		
Dewey Decimal Classification	www.oclc.org/dewey/features/ summaries.en.html		
Cutter Table	www.loc.gov/aba/pcc/053/ table. html		
Library of Congress Subject Headings (LCSH)	id.loc.gov/authorities/subjects .html		

NOTES

1. "Catalog," Alcorn State University, at www.alcorn.edu/academics/library/library-de
partments/catalog/index.aspx (accessed December 3, 2015).

2. Richard Cox, Jane Greenberg, and Cynthia Porter, "Access Denied: The Discarding of
Library History," *American Libraries* 29, no. 4 (April 1998): 57–62.

3. Introduction to *Library of Congress Subject Headings*, 37th edition, Library of Congress
Publications, at www.loc.gov/aba/publications/FreeLCSH/lcshintro.pdf (accessed December
6, 2015).

4. Marshall Breeding, "Library Systems Report 2015," *American Libraries*, May 1, 2015
at americanlibrariesmagazine. org/2015/05/01/library-systems-report/ (accessed December
7, 2015).

5. Ibid.

6. Karen Snow and Gretchen Hoffman, "What Makes an Effective Cataloging Course?,"
Library Resources and Technical Services 59, no. 4 (October 2015): 187–99.

7. Marshall Breeding, "The Future of Library Resource Discovery," NISO White Paper,
February 2015, availabe at www.niso.org/apps/group_public/download.php/14487/future
_library_resource_discovery.pdf.

8. "Browse Online Libraries Worldwide," LibWeb, Library Servers via WWW, at www.lib
-web.org/ (accessed December 9, 2015).

9. "Statement of International Cataloguing Principles," International Federation of Library Associations and Institutions (IFLA), 2009, at www.ifla.org/files/assets/cataloguing/icp/
icp_2009-en.pdf (accessed December 9, 2015).

10. "About the LC Online Catalog," Library of Congress Online Catalog, at catalog.loc.gov/
vwebv/ui/en_US/htdocs/help/index.html (accessed December 9, 2015).

11. "State Libraries," Public Libraries, at www.publiclibraries.com/state_library.htm (accessed December 9, 2015).

12. See "researchIT CT," Connecticut State Library, at iconn.org/ (accessed December 12,
2015); "Statewide Cataloging Standards," Illinois State Library, at www.cyberdriveillinois
.com/departments/library/libraries/cataloging_standards.html; and "Find Books, Articles,
and More," State Library of Ohio, at library.ohio.gov/ (accessed December 12, 2015).

13. "Statewide Resource Sharing," Ohio Libraries Share MORE, State Library of Ohio,
at library.ohio.gov/services-for-libraries/library-programs-development/ohio-libraries-share
-more/ (accessed December 12, 2015).

14. "About the Organization," Cataloging and Acquisitions, Library of Congress, at www
.loc.gov/aba/about/ (accessed December 12, 2015).

15. "Bibliographic Framework Initiative," BIBFRAME, Library of Congress, at www.loc
.gov/bibframe/ (accessed December 13, 2015).

16. "Membership," OCLC, at www.oclc.org/membership.en.html (accessed December 13,
2015).

REFERENCES, SUGGESTED READINGS, AND WEBSITES

Alcorn State University. "Catalog." Alcorn State University Library Catalog. Accessed December 3, 2015, at www.alcorn.edu/academics/library/library-departments/catalog/index.aspx.
Baga, John, Linda Hoover, and Robert Wolverton Jr. "Online, Practical, and Free Cataloging
Resources." *Library Resources and Technical Services* 57, no. 2 (April 2013):100–17.
Breeding, Marshall. "The Future of Library Resource Discovery." NISO White Paper. Last modified February 2015. Available at www.niso.org/apps/group_public/download.php/14487/
future_library_resource_discovery.pdf.

————. "Library Systems Report 2015." *American Libraries*, May 1, 2015. Accessed December 7, 2015, at americanlibrariesmagazine.org/2015/05/01/library-systems-report/.

Connecticut State Library. "researchIT CT." Accessed September 15, 2016, at researchitct.org/.

Cox, Richard, Jane Greenberg, and Cynthia Porter. "Access Denied: The Discarding of Library History." *American Libraries* 29, no. 4 (April 1998): 57–62.

Enis, Matt. "Putting the Pieces Together." *Library Journal* 139, no. 6 (April 1, 2014): 32.

Fu, Ping, and Moira Fitzgerald. "A Comparative Analysis of the Effect of the Integrated Library System on Staffing Models in Academic Libraries." *Information Technology and Libraries* 32, no. 3 (September 2013): 47–58.

Illinois State Library. "Statewide Cataloging Standards." Statewide Cataloging Standards. Accessed December 12, 2015, at www.cyberdriveillinois.com/departments/library/libraries/cataloging_standards.html.

International Federation of Library Associations. "Statement of Internatioanl Cataloguing Principles." 2009. Accessed December 9, 2015, at www.ifla.org/files/assets/cataloguing/icp/icp_2009-en.pdf.

Kao, Mary L. *Cataloging and Classification for Library Technicians*. 2nd ed. New York: Haworth, 2001.

Library of Congress. "About the LC Online Catalog." Library of Congress Online Catalog. Accessed December 9, 2015, at catalog.loc.gov/vwebv/ui/en_US/htdocs/help/index.html.

————. "About the Organization." Cataloging and Acquisitions. Accessed December 12, 2015, at www.loc.gov/aba/about/.

————. "Bibliographic Framework Initiative." BIBFRAME. Accessed December 13, 2015, at www.loc.gov/bibframe/.

————. Introduction to *Library of Congress Subject Headings*. 37th edition Library of Congress Publications. Accessed December 6, 2015, at www.loc.gov/aba/publications/FreeLCSH/lcshintro.pdf.

LibWeb. "Browse Online Libraries Worldwide." Library Servers via WWW. Accessed December 9, 2015, at www.lib-web.org/.

OCLC. "Membership." Accessed December 13, 2015, at www.oclc.org/membership.en.html.

PublicLibraries.com. "State Libraries." Accessed December 9, 2015, at www.publiclibraries.com/state_library.htm.

Rainie, Lee, Kathryn Zickuhr, and Maeve Duggan. "Mobile Connections to Libraries." Pew Internet and American Life Project. December 31, 2012. Accessed December 6, 2015, at libraries.pewinternet.org/2012/12/31/mobile-connections-to-libraries/.

Snow, Karen, and Gretchen Hoffman. "What Makes an Effective Cataloging Course?" *Library Resources and Technical Services* 59, no. 4 (October 2015): 187–99.

State Library of Ohio. "Find Books, Articles, and More." Accessed December 12, 2015, at library.ohio.gov/.

————. "Statewide Resource Sharing." Ohio Libraries Share MORE. Accessed December 12, 2015, at library.ohio.gov/services-for-libraries/library-programs-development/ohio-libraries-share-more/.

CHAPTER 3

Authority Control

LSS understand the value of authority control and its basic principles, and can identify and apply appropriate access points for personal names, corporate bodies, series, and subjects. (ALA-LSSC Cataloging and Classification Competency #5)

Key Terms

Access points. Words or terms, such as author, title, series, subject, or keyword, that can be used to locate a bibliographic record in a library catalog.

Authority control. The establishment of one standard form of a name, word, or term for an access point that occurs in multiple MARC records.

Cataloging in Publication. Also known as CIP, this is both the print display form found on the reverse side of the title page and the MARC record that is created by the Library of Congress during the prepublication stage of a new book or manuscript.

Field. The place where specific information related to the topic of the tag is inputted on a line of a MARC record.

FRBR. The initialism for Functional Requirements for Bibliographic Records, a conceptual model of the relationships between works, expressions of the work, the manifestation or production of the work, and the final item to be cataloged. FRBR supports RDA, which expands access points in bibliographic MARC records.

Keyword searching. A search using natural language that does not weigh or control the context of the word, as would be the case for a LC subject heading.

Library of Congress Authorities. Free and online searchable MARC authority records of the preferred forms of names, titles, places, subject phrases, and topical terms to be used for author, title, subject, tracings, and added entry access points.

MARC authority records. Records available in the Library of Congress Authorities of standardized headings for names, titles, places, subject phrases, or topical terms to be used by catalogers in the United States.

RDA. Resource Description and Access, the new cataloging standard that replaces the *Anglo-American Cataloguing Rules* (AACR2). Created in 2010, RDA is a content standard that works with AACR2 to expand description access points in bibliographic MARC records. Most libraries have adopted it as their standard for cataloging.

Tag. The three-character code that begins a line of bibliographic information in a MARC record.

Tracings. The 400-level tags of a MARC record where alternate forms of an author's name are entered so that any searches using these forms will retrieve the records with LC name authority headings.

Uniform access. The ability to search and obtain access to all items by the same author or with the same title or subject in one search.

Uniform title. The preferred title chosen by the Library of Congress for a work that is published or known by multiple titles.

INTRODUCTION

A MARC bibliographic record contains such data as the author's name, title of the work, publisher, copyright date, size, subjects, and many other pieces of descriptive information. Patrons use the information of a MARC bibliographic record to search and locate specific library resources. The cataloger does his or her best job to fully identify all of the **access points** required by a MARC record. Some decisions, such as the ISBN, size, or number of pages, are straightforward, following from close examination of the object. Others are not as clear.

In the creation of every MARC record there is ambiguity. This uncertainty may occur around the bibliographic data access points of some names, titles, places, and subjects when more than one form or option is available. For example, should the cataloger use an author's full name, "Thomas," when he goes by "Tom," as in the case of Tom Clancy? How does the cataloger answer this question?

TEXTBOX 3.1. DETERMINING THE PERSONAL NAME OF AN AUTHOR

1. Go to the AACR2. The answer is found in AACR2 rule 22.1, which states, "In general, choose, as the basis of the heading for a person, the name by which he or she is commonly known."
2. Look up "Clancy, Tom" in LC Authorities, available at authorities.loc.gov. The standard way to enter Tom Clancy is with his birth and death dates: *Clancy, Tom, 1947–2013.*

In this simple example we learn that the answer was determined by both AACR2 rule 22.1 and the Library of Congress (LC) authority file. We will learn about how these two essential tools work together to help the cataloger with the important job of standardization.

PRINCIPLES OF AUTHORITY CONTROL

What if some of the popular author's books were filed under "Thomas Clancy" and others under "Tom Clancy"? If that were the case, Clancy's titles would not all be listed under one of these forms of his name or the other.

The above is an example of **uniform access**. Uniform access is the ability to search and obtain access to all items by the same author or with the same title or subject heading in one search. In other words, all items written or created by the same author, or all items with similar titles, or all items on the same topic should be able to be retrieved from the catalog with one search. Libraries provide uniform access to materials that often have or could have multiple variable terms so that patrons avoid confused and incomplete searches. Uniform access provides clear identification for authors and subjects.[1]

Why not just rely on **keyword searching** instead of authority control? Isn't the patron going to find the items anyway using keywords? Yes and no. Keyword searching is very expansive, but the enormity of the results could be a real deterrent to making immediate use of the results. Authority control narrows the scope of the results and provides patrons with reliable records on topic. The larger the collection, the more important authority control becomes. With large union catalogs at the state and regional level, authority control is even more important to support reliable searches.

Library of Congress Authority

The LC recognized early on that where there is the possibility for multiple forms for the same access point, a decision that carried final authority had to be made so that all items under the term would be filed together. In the United States, the Library of Congress has the authority to make decisions about the format of authors, titles, and subjects. These decisions are made following AACR2 rules. LC authority decisions about which words or terms to use in these areas are definitive for all catalogers in the United States, no matter the size or type of library. Union catalogs would be haphazard, inefficient, and unworkable if access points for the same piece of information were not the same. The LC has the vested **authority control** to select the one word or words catalogers will use to avoid splitting a search among two or more terms. Because the LC leads the country in sharing library records, it is appropriate that it determine authority control for library catalogs in the United States that will build on its work. Authority control for names, uniform titles, series, and subjects is ultimately determined by the Library of Congress because all catalogers use the records from the LC's vast collections. Those records are available from a variety of places, including Cataloging in Publication.

Cataloging in Publication (CIP)

Catalogers have looked to the Library of Congress as an authoritative source of cataloging since the late nineteenth century. Wouldn't it save time and staff resources if each new book came with LC authority cataloging? Not until 1958 was prepublication cataloging tested when 157 publishers sent 1,203 unpublished texts to the LC for cataloging.[2] This trial, which became Cataloging in Source, was very successful and became the basis in 1971 for Cataloging in Publication (CIP), a service that continues today.

CIP fulfills several important objectives. First, it is a great aid to catalogers who use LC cataloging in their own work and import it to their ILS. Second, LC cataloging establishes authority for the form of the author's name, a uniform title if required, and the subject headings for the book. No matter what library a book is in, its cataloging will be the same. Third, collaborative catalogs shared among multiple libraries will use the one authoritative LC bibliographic record for each unique book title that goes through CIP. This avoids the problem of having multiple locally made bibliographic records for the same book that have variations or errors. Last, the speed at which a new book can be shelf ready is accelerated because CIP has done most of the work of the local cataloger.

Not every book or library resource is eligible for CIP. There is still much work for a cataloger to do!

TEXTBOX 3.2. CRITERIA FOR CIP PROGRAM[3]

1. Limited to titles likely to be acquired by U.S. libraries
2. Must be forthcoming monographs with a U.S. place of publication on the title page
3. U.S. publisher must maintain editorial and production offices in the United States and be available for questions

---

Most other types of library resources are ineligible for CIP. For example, books that are already published, works available only as e-books, translations other than Spanish, serials, music scores, audio and media files, computer software, and prints are ineligible. In other words, books with anticipated general interest and government-published monographs are the primary items that receive CIP.

The CIP process begins with the approved publisher sending no more than twenty CIP applications at a time.[4] A Library of Congress Control Number (LCCN) is assigned prior to the cataloger completing descriptive cataloging that includes authority forms of the author's name, subject headings, and classification numbers. The publisher receives the CIP record and inserts it on the back of the title page prior to the book going to press. At the same time, a MARC record is entered into the LC catalog and distributed to large libraries, bibliographic utilities such as OCLC, and book vendors. On the return side, the publisher is obligated to send the LC a copy of the published book that will be considered for its collection. An LC cataloger verifies the CIP with the book in hand and makes any updates to the MARC record.

CIP and the resulting MARC record save a tremendous amount of labor and time to libraries in the United States, and they also establish the LC authority of the book's record. In chapter 5 on copy cataloging, we will look more closely at how catalogers use the CIP program.

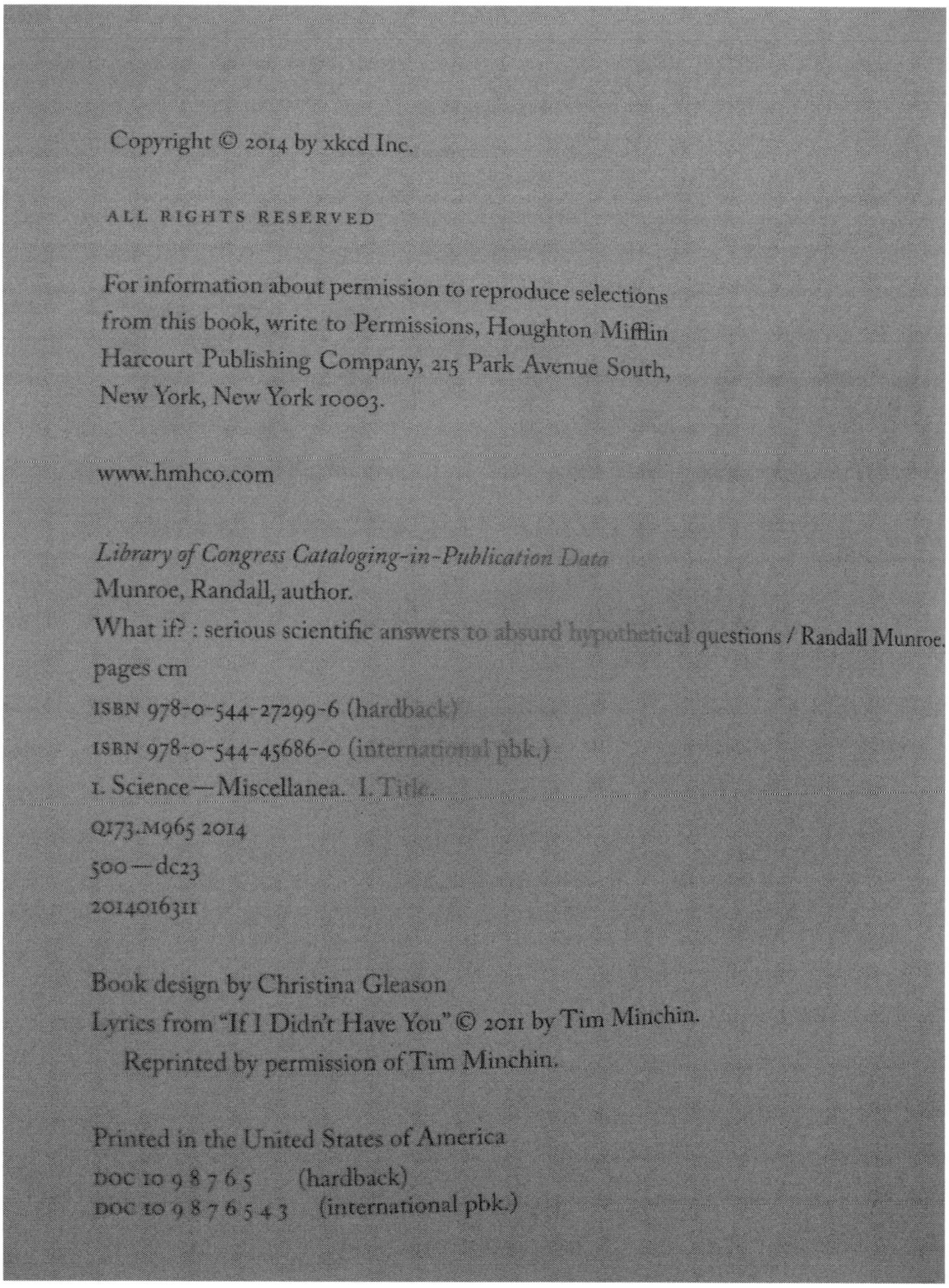

Copyright © 2014 by xkcd Inc.

ALL RIGHTS RESERVED

For information about permission to reproduce selections from this book, write to Permissions, Houghton Mifflin Harcourt Publishing Company, 215 Park Avenue South, New York, New York 10003.

www.hmhco.com

Library of Congress Cataloging-in-Publication Data
Munroe, Randall, author.
What if? : serious scientific answers to absurd hypothetical questions / Randall Munroe.
pages cm
ISBN 978-0-544-27299-6 (hardback)
ISBN 978-0-544-45686-0 (international pbk.)
1. Science—Miscellanea. I. Title.
Q173.M965 2014
500—dc23
2014016311

Book design by Christina Gleason
Lyrics from "If I Didn't Have You" © 2011 by Tim Minchin.
Reprinted by permission of Tim Minchin.

Printed in the United States of America
DOC 10 9 8 7 6 5 (hardback)
DOC 10 9 8 7 6 5 4 3 (international pbk.)

Figure 3.1. CIP Record from the Back of a Title Page.

MARC AUTHORITY RECORDS

MARC stands for machine readable cataloging, the format for catalog records. MARC is the computer coding system developed by the Library of Congress in the 1970s that established a standard way to create and format bibliographic data for library materials. MARC is now in its twenty-first edition and is officially referred to as MARC21.

MARC is made up of lines of computer code that begin with **tags**. Chapter 4 describes in detail how to create MARC bibliographic records. Each piece of data such as the author's name or the book title in a catalog record is assigned a three-digit label called a **tag**. For example, the 100 tag is the line where a cataloger always enters a personal author's name. The 245 tag is set aside only for the title of the book. The 600 and 700 tags are always for subjects.

Two Types of MARC Records

There are two types of MARC records: bibliographic records and authority records. The MARC bibliographic record is the complete descriptive cataloging of a library resource. It contains all of the descriptive information of a unique book or other library resource. MARC bibliographic records are the records in the online catalog, searchable by patrons to learn about and locate items in the library. Included in the MARC bibliographic record are the author, title, publisher, copyright date, size, illustrations, volumes, and many other access points of descriptive data for an item.

A **MARC authority record** is different. For one, the MARC authority record is *not* in the library online catalog. This is a big distinction. The records in the MARC authority files are tools for the cataloger to help standardize the information in the bibliographic records. The LC has the authority to determine which words and terms are to be used for consistency of names, places, and topics.

The remainder of this chapter shows how MARC authority records are used by the cataloger.

Tags and Fields

Tags are the three-character codes that begin each line of distinct code of a MARC bibliographic record. A MARC record is made up of many tags in a prescribed order going from 000 to 999. The first tag, 001, identifies the institution creating the record. Depending on the item being cataloged, the record usually ends in the 700 tags with heading entries or 800 tags if the item is an electronic format. The 900 tags are rarely used for local information.

Since the LC is responsible for setting the rules about how catalogers create bibliographic MARC records that become online library catalogs, it is logical that the LC would also be responsible for determining when to standardize information within the tags. The type of information that goes into a tag is called a **field**. Certain fields of information, such as the author's name, must be standardized so that there is consistency among library catalogs in the United States. The fields that could be ambiguous without standard headings are those with names, subjects, and variant titles. These fields are found in the 100, 130, 600, and 700 tags of the MARC records.

MARC authority headings solve the problem of inconsistency when catalogers use only the one format the LC has selected in conjunction with AACR2.

Table 3.1.   Common Tags and Fields that Require MARC Authority

Tag	Field	Reason
100	Author	People have more than one form of their name.
110	Corporate	Institutions have more than one form of their name.
130	Uniform Title	Some items have more than one title.
600	Subject	Topics, places, and things are known by multiple words or terms.
700	Subject	People as subjects have more than one form of their name.

LC Authorities Files

The LC creates a MARC authority record for each authorized form of an author, subject, or uniform title heading.[5] These standardized headings are searchable in the **Library of Congress Authorities** files.[6] These files are available online and are free to the public. MARC authority records are created by the Library of Congress (LC) when there is a need to standardize information for the sake of consistency.

Figure 3.2.   Search the Library of Congress Authorities by Author, Subject, or Title. Library of Congress.

RDA and FRBR

Authority records are updated by LC catalogers, and new terms are added to keep up with current trends and the contributions of people, new places, and things. Changes created by the inclusion of RDA (Resource Description and Access) and FRBR (Functional Requirements for Bibliographic Records) rules also influence authorities and how catalogers use them. Chapter 10 provides an in-depth explanation about these two sets of rules. Both RDA and FRBR require MARC records to contain much more information about the relationships between the item and other resources.

RDA requires a more thorough description of the item as well as ways to access the item. The cataloger provides detailed description in multiple tags. RDA requires more access points so that patrons could, for instance, locate a book by knowing the author's famous brother's name even though the brother had nothing to do with writing the book. These descriptions and access points correspond to elements describing people, families, and corporate bodies. RDA also requires catalogers to include relationships to concepts, objects, events, and places. As catalogers enhance MARC records with more description and data access points, they must be mindful to use LC authorities for standardized terms, phrases, and names.

FRBR identifies relationships that occurred in the process between the creation of the work and its final format. For example, the FRBR of a film could be the fields of data shown in table 3.2. Prior to FRBR, many of these access points would not be considered for the MARC record. Today, catalogers identify and include relationships in the process of a work becoming an item.

Table 3.2. Relationships of a Film Identified by FRBR

Work	Cataloger identifies the key people, places, or things involved in the script of the film.
Expression	Cataloger identifies the key people, places, or things involved in the filming of the script into a film.
Manifestation	Cataloger identifies the key people, places, or things involved in the production process of the film.
Item	Cataloger identifies the key people, places, or things involved in the showing of the film, sale of the DVD, and so on.

RDA works closely with FRBR; it created some significant rule changes from AACR2 and expanded the MARC template. As catalogers create FRBR and RDA tags and fields, they must be sure to filter the terms and names they use through the LC authorities to ensure catalog quality.

Compliance

Do catalogers have the option not to use MARC authority records? What difference does it make to patrons in a very small library? The cataloger must think beyond his or her own library when a record is created.

The local benefit of using MARC authority records is that the library catalog produces high-quality searches in the most efficient manner. All items searched under a name, title, or subject will be displayed in one results list. This efficiency will translate into patrons and staff successfully locating related items, thus giving them maximum choice among library resources. The more success a user has, the more likely the user will rely on the library catalog for future searches.

A second reason the cataloger uses MARC authority records is that most libraries—no matter the size—are members of district, regional, or statewide union catalogs. Even if the library has a cooperative catalog with just one other library, the need for standardized forms for authors, titles, and subjects is very important so that all resources can be jointly displayed. Most consortiums with shared catalogs set policy that requires the use of MARC authority records to ensure the quality of the catalog. Catalogers in consortiums who do not use MARC authority records will be quickly identified for their inferior work and be required to upgrade their records because catalogs without MARC authority will be confusing and yield incomplete searches. The remainder of this chapter will examine MARC authority headings for names, uniform titles, and subjects.

LC NAME AUTHORITY

The LC Name Authority is the tool catalogers use to find the standard heading for an author's name. They will enter this form of the author's name in the appropriate 100-level tag as a field of information. Names can be personal or can be assigned to corporations, institutions, professional organizations, and other entities responsible for writing and publishing.

Author Personal Names—100 Tag

Names are one of the most widely used LC authority files. The AACR2 general rule of personal authorship states: "A personal author is the person who is chiefly responsible for the content of a work (Rule 23A1)."[7] Personal authors can be writers of texts, composers of music, photographers, artists, or any person chiefly responsible for the content of a work. Once the cataloger has established there is a person or persons responsible for the content of a work, the next step is to determine how the person's name is to be expressed. Generally the format is as follows:

TEXTBOX 3.3. LC FORMAT FOR ENTERING AN AUTHOR'S NAME

Surname, First name, Initial. year of birth–year of death (if no longer living)

If the item is being originally cataloged, the cataloger checks the LC Authorities for confirmation. While most authors will follow this format, there are surprises. For example, many entertainers and even some authors are not known by their given names. The musician Cher has had several legal name changes. The LC Name Authority has standardized any work by Cher to be under her most-recognized name. In textbox 3.4 we see the relationship between the LC Name Authority and MARC:

TEXTBOX 3.4. USING LC NAME AUTHORITY IN A MARC 100 TAG

1. Find standardized person heading in LC Name Authority: `Cher, 1946—`
2. Use authority in MARC 100 tag entry: `100 0_|a Cher, |d 1946—`

Corporate Body Names—110 Tag

A corporate body is an organization or group of persons that has a name. Enter a work issued by a corporate body under the heading of that body if it is an administrative work, a law, a report, a collection of papers, media performed by a group, or a map (AACR2 Rule 23B2).[8] The MARC tag for a corporate name heading is 110. When cataloging a special report by GE, would the cataloger use GE, General Electric, or something else?

TEXTBOX 3.5. USING LC NAME AUTHORITY IN A MARC 110 TAG

1. Find standardized corporate heading in LC Name Authority: `General Electric Company`
2. Use authority in MARC 110 tag entry: `110 2_|a General Electric Company`

Similar to corporate bodies, conferences and meetings can also author works. The meeting or conference name is entered in the 111 MARC tag.

Tracings—400 Tag

However, what happened to those other forms of Cher's name? Only one form was standardized by the LC Name Authority. What does the cataloger do with the other forms? Perhaps a patron does not search with "Cher" but rather searches the last names of "Allman" or "Bono."

There is a nifty reference called **tracings** that the cataloger uses to be sure all of the other forms of the author's name are traced back to the LC Name Authority heading. The cataloger creates tracings of the other forms of the name in the 400 tag. The other forms of the name are "traced" to the LC Authority name in the 100, 600, or 700 tags. Tracings for Cher's multiple names would look like this in a MARC record:

TEXTBOX 3.6. 400 TAG TRACINGS FOR "CHER" IN A MARC RECORD[9]

```
400 _|a Allman, Cher, |d 1946—
400 _|aBono, Cher, |d 1946—
400 _|aCleo, |d 1946—
400 _|aLa Piere, Cherilyn,|d 1946—
400 _|aLaPierre, Cherilyn, |d 1946—
400 _|aSakesian, Cherilyn,|d 1946—
400 _|aSakisian, Cherilyn, |d 1946—
400 _|aSarkisian, Cherilyn, |d 1946—
400 _|aSarkisian, Cheryl, |d 1946—
```

Anyone who searched under any of these legal or commonly misspelled forms of Cher's name will have that search traced back to the LC Name Authority of

"Cher, 1946–." The search is not lost. All items under Cher will be retrieved under any of these other forms of her name provided there are 400-tag tracings in the MARC record.

From this example you may be able to appreciate the importance of the LC Name Authority. Not only has the LC standardized the format of one name per author, it also gives the cataloger the alternate names to be added as 400-tag tracings. The tracings are also called "See References," which means that if you are looking up this term, you really need to "see" this other term. In the old days of card catalogs, a patron would read the clue on the "see card" and then find the card to which it pointed in another drawer.

Uniform Titles—130 Tag

On occasion a cataloger will use the LC Name Authority to find the standard title of a book. This would occur if the book could have been republished with a slight variation to its title. In such cases, the LC has found all of these slight variations and will not let them cause havoc in a library catalog. Without a standard title, patrons could use one of the variations to search and not be able to find all of the copies or slightly modified copies of the item. With the LC deciding on the name of the title and making the heading "uniform," all searches of the variant titles will lead back to one format. **Uniform titles** are most often created for classic works whose titles may become slightly altered over time, an abridged or revised edition, a translation, an arrangement of music, a reproduced artwork, or other adaptations that do not change the essence of the original work. Because many uniform titles begin with a name, they are found in the LC Name Authority.

The anonymous classic *Beowulf* provides an example of how a uniform title is used.[10] There are many versions of *Beowulf*, and without a uniform title each would stand alone in the catalog and might be missed by the patron. The uniform title is entered into the 130 tag. Because that tag was used, all title searches with the word "Beowulf" would be collected and displayed together no matter the version or edition.

Series

The authority control of titles can also be used for series. Over time the series name can become abridged or changed. Is the series name for the film "Star Wars" or "Star Wars Adventures"? By using the LC Title Authority the cataloger learns the first name is for the films and the second is for the Dark Horse Comics series. If there is any doubt or question about the correct form of the series, the cataloger should check the LC Authorities.

SUBJECT HEADINGS AUTHORITY

The MARC tags in the 600 and 700 series are dedicated to providing subjects that describe the item. Most of the time patrons do not know the exact title of an item or even its author. However, they do know the topic they wish information on, and therefore they search the catalog under subject or keyword.

There are many different ways to describe a library item, and a catalog that is indiscriminate will be confusing and yield incomplete searches. Catalogers use an authority file for LC preferred subject headings in order to yield the largest quantity of quality results.[11] Chapter 9 provides an in-depth explanation of how catalogers create and use subject headings. Here our focus is on controlled LC authority for subjects.

Topical Subject Headings—650 Tag

Subject headings may be a noun, a phrase, an inverted phrase, a name, or a place that reflects the topic of an item. A subject heading may be subdivided by geography or by chronology. Most items have multiple subject headings and provide expanded access. The LC is undergoing changes to its subject authority files to accommodate RDA, making terms more descriptive, removing abbreviations, and using phrases that are more clear and up-to-date.[12] In other words, a goal of RDA is to make the LC Subject Authorities more patron-friendly and searchable.

A search of the word "computers" in the LC Subject Authorities provides a list of more specific or narrow terms that are accepted, such as "art and computers" and "used computers." Continuing with the heading "computers," the authority record suggests a number of terms in the 450 tags that, while seemingly reasonable (such as "electronic computers"), should not be used in any other tag because they do not have LC authority. The LC Subject Authorities suggest these tips for searching:

1. Begin with word roots.
2. Truncation is automatic.
3. Retain punctuation found in the middle of words and numbers.[13]

Geographical Subject Headings—651 Tag

Many library resources have a relationship to a place, whether that be where the item was made or where the author lived, the setting of the story, or the influence of a country or culture. LC authorities standardize the name and format of cities, states, parks, landmarks, countries, oceans, mountains, and other geographic places and features. Sometimes the time period is important:

**TEXTBOX 3.7. GEOGRAPHICAL
SUBJECT HEADINGS BY TIME PERIOD**

```
Arizona—1890—1910
Arizona—1890—1920
Arizona—1900—1910
```

Added Entries—700 Tags

The 700 tags provide for additional name entries. Similar to that found in the 100 tags of the LC Name Authority, these same names can also be used in records as subjects. When used in this way, these (people) subjects are called "added entries." Added entries are used when persons, corporate bodies, or meetings have some form of responsibility, but not primary responsibility, for the creation of the work and when they have an important relationship to the work.[14] Use the LC Name Authority to find the proper way to express the name when you are going to use it as an added entry.

Added entries are also needed when a book is known by multiple titles. The example below has discrepancies between the title page ("Evidence in Oregon civil trials"), the cover ("The Oregon lawyer's trial book"), and the spine ("Trial book"). Added entries are important because they bring patrons to the bibliographic record regardless of which of the three titles they use to search for this book. While multiple titles are not the norm, they do occur with enough regularity to warrant 700-tag added entries.

TEXTBOX 3.8. AN EXAMPLE OF AN ADDED ENTRY[15]

```
110   1_   |a Oregon State Bar. |b Committee on Continuing
              Legal Education.
245   10   |a Evidence in Oregon civil trials.
500   __   |a Cover title: The Oregon lawyer's trial book.
500   __   |a On spine: Trial book.
740   0_   |a Oregon lawyer's trial book.
740   0_   |a Trial book.
```

SUMMARY

The value of authority control is that it provides catalogers with the means to create and maintain a quality library catalog that uses names, titles, and subjects in a standard way and with consistency. The LC Authorities, AACR2, and the MARC21 work together to ensure the cataloger can use authority control no matter the type or size of library. Because the records of the local catalog will potentially be shared in a union catalog, authority control is more important today than ever before.

DISCUSSION QUESTIONS AND ACTIVITIES

Discussion Questions

1. What is uniform access and how does it enhance library catalog searching?
2. Explain the process of the Cataloging in Publication (CIP) program. What are its benefits to catalogers?

3. How does the Library of Congress share its authority files with catalogers? What is the format of the files?
4. Explain the differences between a MARC authority record and a bibliographic MARC record.
5. How do tracings work and why should a cataloger create them? What benefit do they give patrons?
6. Why should a cataloger use and be compliant with LC Authorities?

Activity

The activity in table 3.3 will give you practice using the LC Authorities.

Table 3.3. Steps to Search LC Authorities

Step	Action
1	Go to authorities.loc.gov/cgi-bin/Pwebrecon.cgi?DB=local&PAGE=First.
2	Select Name Authority Headings.
3	Search textbox for the author *Stephen King*. Select the line with the most bib records.
4	Click Authority Record.
5	What is the LC name authority for this author? Does he have an alternate name? If so, where did you find it? Are there tracings associated with his authority record? What is the relationship between King and the tracings?
6	Repeat steps two through five and repeat the search for the names *Isaac Asimov*, *Charlotte Brontë*, and *Lady Gaga*. Explain your findings.
7	Now do a new search and select "Subject Authority Headings." Search for *Vietnam* and select the option with the most bib records.
8	Select the authority record and select *Vietnam* again.
9	Review the large number of 451 tracings. Why are there so many tracings for Vietnam? Do many of them make sense to you as alternate forms of the country or the war? Explain.

NOTES

1. "Frequently Asked Questions," Library of Congress Authorities, at authorities.loc.gov/help/auth-faq.htm (accessed December 14, 2015).

2. Robert R. Newlen, "The Power of CIP," *Library Journal* 116, no. 12 (July 1, 1991): 38–42.

3. "About CIP," Cataloging in Publication Program, Library of Congress, at www.loc.gov/publish/cip/about/eligible.html (accessed December 17, 2015).

4. Ibid.

5. "What Is a MARC Record and Why Is It Important?," Understanding MARC Authority Records, Library of Congress, at www.loc.gov/marc/uma/pt1-7.html (accessed December 13, 2015).

6. "Library of Congress Authorities," Library of Congress, at authorities.loc.gov/ (accessed December 20, 2015).

7. Michael Gorman, *The Concise AACR2*, 4th ed. (Chicago: American Library Association, 2004), 64.

8. Ibid., 66–67.

9. "MARC Display," Library of Congress Authorities, at authorities.loc.gov/cgi-bin/Pweb recon.cgi?AuthRecID=3265170&v1=1&HC=3&SEQ=20151220160141&PID=T6n8hiw1ajvkc UE9hPxE9UxtQO70I (accessed December 20, 2015).

10. "Tag of the Month," Follett School Solutions, at www.follettsoftware.com/tagofthe month.cfm?tagID=52 (accessed December 20, 2015).

11. "Library of Congress Authorities."

12. "Changes to Headings in the LC Catalog to Accommodate RDA," Library of Congress, at loc.gov/aba/rda/pdf/rdaheadingchanges.pdf (accessed December 20, 2015).

13. "Library of Congress Authorities."

14. "70X–75X—Added Entry Fields—General Information," MARC21 Bibliographic Format, Library of Congress, at www.loc.gov/marc/bibliographic/bd70x75x.html (accessed December 20, 2015).

15. "Evidence in Oregon Civil Trials," LC Online Catalog, at catalog.loc.gov/vwebv/ staffView?searchId=2250&recPointer=0&recCount=25&bibId=2650443 (accessed December 21, 2015).

REFERENCES, SUGGESTED READINGS, AND WEBSITES

El-Shirbini, Magda. "Bibliotheca Alexandrina's Model for Arabic Name Authority Control." *Library Resources and Technical Services* 57, no. 1 (January 2013): 4–17.

Ferguson, Bobby. *MARC/AACR2 Authority Control Tagging*. 2nd ed. Westport, CT: Libraries Unlimited, 2005.

Follett School Solutions. "Tag of the Month." Follett Customer Portal. Accessed December 20, 2015, at www.follettsoftware.com/tagofthemonth.cfm?tagID=52.

Gorman, Michael. *The Concise AACR2*. 4th ed. Chicago: American Library Association, 2004.

Hart, Amy. *The RDA Primer: A Guide for the Occasional Cataloger*. Santa Barbara, CA: Linworth, 2010.

Library of Congress. "70X–75X—Added Entry Fields—General Information." MARC21 Bibliographic Format. Accessed December 20, 2015, at www.loc.gov/marc/bibliographic/bd70x75x .html.

———. "About CIP." Cataloging in Publication Program. Accessed December 17, 2015, at www.loc.gov/publish/cip/about/eligible.html.

———. "Changes to Headings in the LC Catalog to Accommodate RDA." Accessed December 20, 2015, at loc.gov/aba/rda/pdf/rdaheadingchanges.pdf.

———. "Evidence in Oregon Civil Trials." LC Online Catalog. Accessed December 21, 2015, at catalog.loc.gov/vwebv/staffView?searchId=2250&recPointer=0&recCount=25&bib Id=2650443.

———. "Frequently Asked Questions." Library of Congress Authorities. Accessed December 14, 2015, at authorities.loc.gov/help/auth-faq.htm.

———. "Library of Congress Authorities." Library of Congress Authorities. Last modified 2015. Accessed December 20, 2015. authorities.loc.gov/.

———. "MARC Display." Library of Congress Authorities. Accessed December 20, 2015, at authorities.loc.gov/cgi-bin/Pwebrecon.cgi?AuthRecID=3265170&v1=1&HC=3&SEQ =20151220160141&PID=T6n8hiw1ajvkcUE9hPxE9UxtQO70I.

———. "What Is a MARC Authority Record?" Subsection of "What Is a MARC Record and Why Is It Important?" October 28, 2005. Accessed December 20, 2015, at www.loc.gov/marc/ uma/pt1-7.html#pt4.

———. "What Is a MARC Record and Why Is It Important?" October 28, 2005. Accessed December 13, 2015, at www.loc.gov/marc/uma/pt1-7.html.

Maxwell, Robert L. *Maxwell's Guide to Authority Work*. Chicago: American Library Association, 2002.

Newlen, Robert R. "The Power of CIP." *Library Journal* 116, no. 12 (July 1, 1991): 38–42.

Penn State University Libraries. "Intro to MARC Tagging." Cataloging and Metadata Services. Accessed December 20, 2015, at www.libraries.psu.edu/psul/cataloging/training/marctagg ingintro.html.

Sandstrom, John, and Liz Miller. *Fundamentals of Technical Services*. ALA Fundamentals Series. Chicago: Neal-Schuman, 2015.

CHAPTER 4

MARC21 Records

LSS apply and manage the appropriate processes, computer technology, and equipment for cataloging and classification. (ALA-LSSC Competency 1)

LSS know and can use the basic cataloging and classification tools, both print and online, including bibliographic utilities and format standards. (ALA-LSSC Competency 2)

Key Terms

Area. Called a "field" in MARC21, it is the term for a line of bibliographic information in AACR2.

Bibliographic. In cataloging the term refers to the descriptive information and data of a library resource that is entered into the fields of a MARC record.

Bibliographic record. Information such as the title, author, publisher, ISBN, size, or edition that describes a unique book or other library item.

Catalog display. This is the patron view of a MARC record that does not include the computer coding language.

Delimiters. The letters or numbers used as part of the computer code that separates subfields of information in a line of a MARC record.

Element. A word, phrase, or groups of characters forming a field or subfield.

Field. A unique piece of bibliographic information about an item such as its author, title, ISBN, or media type that corresponds to an area in AACR2.

Fixed field. Data in a MARC record that is limited to an exact number of characters.

Indicator. Used in variable fields, these two numeric characters are part of the programming of a MARC field that helps to set up the patron display screen properly. Each indicator's meaning varies according to the tag.

Initial articles. The articles "a," "an," and "the" when used as the first word of a book title.

Nonfiling. A word, such as an initial article, that is ignored or not used for filing purposes.

Subfield. A part or subdivision of a variable field that relates to the main theme of the tag. Subfields are separated in the tag line by alphabetical or numerical delimiters.

Tags. The three-character code that begins a line of bibliographic information in a MARC record.

Template. The format for coding bibliographic information and data of an item in MARC so that it can be read and interpreted by software applications.

Variable field. This field in a MARC record allows a flexible number of characters.

INTRODUCTION

AACR2 and RDA provide the rules for cataloging. The Library of Congress (LC) provides the means by which those rules apply to an item and are expressed in computer code that results in library catalog records. This chapter introduces the fundamental concepts behind the construction of MARC21 records. The third part of this book expands our knowledge of MARC21 with opportunities to practice making records for all types of library resources. Readers will also practice transforming and converting MARC records to the emerging initiative called BIBFRAME. However, before we can confidently create MARC records, we need to understand many of the underlying principles behind the coded form of each tag and field of bibliographic information.

DEVELOPMENT OF MARC

In the mid- to late 1950s mainframe computers were being developed by the U.S. government for military use. The size of an entire room, mainframes could do far less than a child's digital toy today. The Library of Congress, as part of the government, benefited from the research taking place with these new machines. Believing that mainframe computers might in some way be able to support the sharing of the Library of Congress's national catalog, Librarian of Congress L. Quincy Mumford embarked on a project in the late 1960s to investigate the feasibility of using computers.[1] To do so, a common computer language was needed for librarians to use to display "catalog card" information in a consistent and standard way. Specifications for the standard **bibliographic** information for a union **catalog display** were also needed. If expectations for cataloging items were consistent and standardized, catalog records could be shared among libraries. Mumford hired Henriette Avram to lead a project to find a way this could be done.

Henriette Avram

In the mid-1950s Avram began work for the National Security Agency, where she learned to program computers. Although she did not have a library degree, Avram joined the LC in 1965 as a highly qualified programmer and in just three years developed the Machine Readable Cataloging (MARC) standard that fostered electronic

Photo 4.1. Photo of Henriette Avram from LC. Library of Congress.

catalog access.[2] By 1970 the LC was sharing copies of catalog records on magnetic tape using the MARC standard with many libraries. Avram continued to work for the LC until her retirement in 1992, overseeing refinements to the MARC record and exploring its uses. Interviewed in 1989 about her early work on MARC, she said the automation of library operations is very complex and librarians have done wonders because, as a profession, they understood the need for and adopted standards.[3] Because they had the foresight to do this, librarians have had a leadership role in resource sharing that no other profession can claim.

The MARC record has proven to be an excellent tool for building online catalogs. By designing a template to be used for all digital **bibliographic records**, librarians in the United States established a common language that could be incorporated into online catalogs. Occurring as it did early in the development of digital technology, the MARC record serves as a model for establishing standards.[4]

MARC21

As one would expect, the template we use today has changed in many ways from the original 1968 MARC. MARC is how computers exchange, use, and interpret bibliographic information, and its data elements are fundamental to library cataloging. MARC became USMARC in the 1980s. USMARC, however, had limited utility because of the new technologies libraries were rapidly adopting in the 1990s. USMARC and the Canadian form of MARC (CAN/MARC) merged in 1997 to become MARC21, the current edition.[5]

As we have seen in chapter 3, cataloging rules and standards from the American Library Association (AACR2) and the Library of Congress (MARC21 template) continue to change with the times. FRBR and RDA standards have added new tags and fields to the MARC template to include more access points that describe items. Functional relationships between and among people and the creation of the work and its expression are now also cataloged data. Today, cataloging in MARC21 goes far beyond the title page, physical dimensions, and packaging of the item. Catalogers are researchers who discover relationships about authorship, production, and other descriptive attributes of an item to enhance patrons' ability to search and locate it using multiple points of data.

Catalogers today use the shortened term "MARC" when talking about the latest updated template of MARC21. The Network Development and MARC Standards Office at the Library of Congress and the Standards and the Support Office at the Library and Archives Canada maintain the MARC21 formats with input from libraries, library networks and utilities, and library system vendors around the world.[6]

MARC21 TAGS, FIELDS, SUBFIELDS, AND INDICATORS

Cataloging has a language unto its own with terms and words used in ways that apply specifically to the library setting. When talking about the MARC record, catalogers need to understand and use the terms "tags," "fields," "subfields," and "indicators" properly in order to understand how MARC records are created. MARC vocabulary is also important for library staff to know so they are able to communicate with other catalogers.

Tags

Tags are the three-character codes that begin lines of bibliographic information. Each tag leads a unique line of data in the template. The MARC template tags are arranged in numeric order, beginning with tag 00X and ending with tag 99X. In this chapter we will look at each category of tags and learn their purposes.

Table 4.1.   Examples of MARC Tags

Tag	Description
020	International Standard Book Number (ISBN)
245	Title Statement
337	Media Type
650	Subject Added Entry—Topical Term
856	Electronic Location and Access

When catalogers talk among themselves about a record, they often begin by identifying the issue or concern using the tag number. If told, "Take a look at the 245 tag and be sure it has the LC uniform title," the cataloger would find the 245 line of code in the MARC template of that book record and compare the title of the book with the LC Authorities.

Fields

A **field** contains the bibliographic information of a tag. Fields are made up of subfields, **areas**, and elements. Some fields are **fixed**, meaning the MARC computer application will only allow a specific number of characters. One such example is the Library of Congress Control Number (LCCN), which comprises 12 digits. Most fields, such as the author's name, are **variable**, meaning that a flexible number of characters are allowed. Fields are called areas of bibliographic information in AACR2, the American Library Association's rules for cataloging. Table 4.2 shows some of the field or area information of the e-book *Of Mice and Men*.

Table 4.2. Examples of Tags and Fields for E-book Version of *Of Mice and Men* by John Steinbeck

Tag	Tag Description	Example of Field Data	Type of Field
020	International Standard Book Number (ISBN)	9781436240987	Fixed (every ISBN has 13 characters)
245	Title Statement	|aOf mice and men|h[electronic resource] /|cJohn Steinbeck	Variable (number of characters)
337	Media Type	|acomputer |brdamedia	Variable
650	Subject Added Entry— Topical Term	Cowboys|vFiction	Variable
856	Electronic Location and Access	|uhttp://lion.lib.overdrive.com/	Variable

Source: "Of Mice and Men," Lion Online Catalog, at catalog.lioninc.org/search~S38?/asteinbeck/asteinbeck/1%2C3%2C5%2CB/marc&FF=asteinbeck+john+1902+1968&2%2C%2C2 (accessed December 28, 2015).

Subfields, Elements, Delimiters

A subfield is part of a field of information that relates to the theme of the tag line. For example, in the 245 title statement, the subtitle of a book would require its own subfield in the MARC record. Subfields are also used when there are multiple **elements** that form a related unit of information.

A **delimiter** is the computer code that separates subfields in order to be readable in the computer display. Delimiter codes are either letters or numbers that are placed before the elements in a subfield to separate them. Delimiters are preceded by a vertical line called a pipe. Let's analyze the title and statement of responsibility 245 tag in table 4.2 and inspect its layout using the proper MARC terminology.

Table 4.3.   Analysis of a MARC 245 Tag

245 |aOf mice and men|h[electronic resource]/|cJohn Steinbeck						
Tag	Delimiter	Title	Delimiter	Medium	Delimiter	Author
245	a	Of mice and men	h	electronic resource	c	John Steinbeck

Books and other library resources that have subtitles are cataloged with each part of the title having its own subfield following the main title. The 245 tag for the autobiography written by Agatha Christie is coded here using delimiters and subfields:

TEXTBOX 4.1.

245   10   aAgatha   Christie   :|ban   autobiography

Subfield "a" is the main title: Agatha Christie
Subfield "b" is the subtitle: an autobiography
"a" and "b" are delimiters that separate the subfields.

Beginning by referencing the AACR2 rule for the line of bibliographic information, the cataloger inputs appropriate elements for each of the subfields.

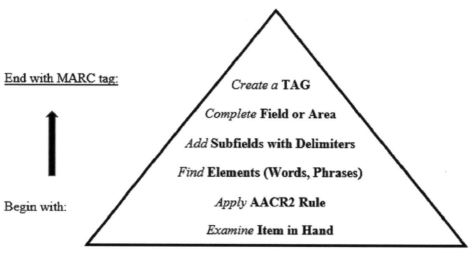

Figure 4.1.   Steps cataloger uses to create a MARC record.

Indicators

Indicators are two numbers that go in the spaces immediately to the right side of the tag. Used in variable fields, these two numeric characters are part of the programming of a MARC field that helps to set up the patron display screen properly. What each indicator means will vary according to the tag. The most commonly used indicators appear in the title and statement of responsibility 245 tag. The first character is either 0 or 1. Zero means there is no title (which is very rare!). A value of 1 means there is a title. The next number character designates whether the title begins with one of the articles: "a," "an," or "the." These words are **non-filing**, which means they do not count in the alphabetical arrangement of titles and should be skipped over. Why nonfiling? AACR2 rule 57C requires librarians to omit an **initial article** from a uniform title.[7] We also ignore initial articles when filing titles in lists and when shelving books. MARC includes the indicator code for the 245 field so that initial articles are ignored when titles are filed in the online catalog. The value of the second indicator is 2 for "a," 3 for "an," and 4 for "the." Wait! Why an extra character for each? The second indicator is a total of the number of characters in the word *plus* an added number for the "space" that comes before the next word in the title.

TEXTBOX 4.2. INDICATOR CODE FOR 245 TAGS

10 = The title does not begin with an article. Begin filing with the first letter of the first word.

12 = The title of the book begins with the article "A." Skip two spaces before filing begins.

13 = The title of the book begins with the article "An." Skip three spaces before filing begins.

14 = The title of the book begins with the article "The." Skip four spaces before filing begins.

MAJOR MARC21 BIBLIOGRAPHIC CODES

The AACR2 guides which bibliographic information is needed in a catalog record. The LC MARC21 template provides the cataloger with a format to create records. The cataloger follows the AACR2 and then codes the information into the template following the LC MARC21 standards. The library's integrated library system provides the cataloger with different MARC templates for each type of resource such as print and e-books, serials, film DVDs, CD audio recordings, and so forth. The remainder of this chapter introduces the fundamental categories of MARC21 bibliographic codes. The third part of this book provides hands-on practice cataloging a variety of materials using the codes of the MARC21 template.

The major MARC21 bibliographic codes are divided here into three categories: the fixed field, variable control fields, and variable data fields. We will use the slightly modified LC MARC record for the book by David McCullough titled *The Wright Brothers* found in the LC online catalog as our example for explaining the codes.

Fixed Field

A fixed field has a predetermined number of characters. The length of the line will always remain the same and occurs at the beginning of the MARC record.

```
000  02298cam a2200421 i 4500
001  18525913
005  20150522093829.0
008  150313s2015 nyuabf b 001 0beng c
010  ___  |a 2014046049
020  ___  |a 9781476728742 (hardcover)
040  ___  |a PSt/DLC |b eng |c PSt |e rda |d DLC
050  00  |a TL540. W7 |b M3825 2015
082  00  |a 629.130092/273 |a B |2 23
100  1_  |a McCullough, David G., |e author.
245  14  |a The Wright brothers / |c David McCullough.
250  ___  |a First Simon & Schuster hardcover edition.
264  _1  |a New York : |b Simon & Schuster, |c 2015.
300  ___  |a 320 pages, 48 unnumbered pages of plates :
          |b illustrations, maps ; |c 25 cm
336  ___  |a text |2 rdacontent
337  ___  |a unmediated |2 rdamedia
338  ___  |a volume |2 rdacarrier
504  ___  |a Includes bibliographical references (pages
          303–308) and index.
505  0_  |a 1. Beginnings–2. The dream takes hold–3.
          Where the winds blow–4. Unyielding resolve–5.
          December 17, 1903–6. Out at Huffman prairie–7.
          A capital exhibit A–8. Triumph at Le Mans–9.
          The crash–10. A time like no other–11. Causes
          for celebration–Epilogue.
520  ___  |a "As he did so brilliantly in THE GREAT
          BRIDGE and THE PATH BETWEEN THE SEAS, David
          McCullough once again tells a dramatic story
          of people and technology, this time about the
          courageous brothers who taught the world how
          to fly, Wilbur and Orville Wright"–Provided by
          publisher.
600  10  |a Wright, Orville, |d 1871–1948.
600  10  |a Wright, Wilbur, |d 1867–1912.
650  _0  |a Aeronautics |z United States |x History
          |y 20th century.
650  _0  |a Aeronautics |z United States |v Biography.
856  41  |3 Sample text |u http://www.loc.gov/catdir/
          enhancements/fy1506/2014046049-s.html
856  42  |3 Publisher description |u http://www.loc.gov/
          catdir/enhancements/fy1506/2014046049-d.html
856  42  |3 Contributor biographical information
          |u http://www.loc.gov/catdir/enhancements/
          fy1506/2014046049-b.html
985  ___  |a PStCIP |d 2015–03–13
```

Leader

The leader information is fixed in length with twenty-four character positions. The leader contains numbers or letters that help process the bibliographic record so that it can be properly viewed in the online catalog.[9] Most of the information in the leader is system supplied—that is, the MARC template has been preprogrammed to generate the codes that will always be the same for the library. An analysis of this leader is shown here:

Table 4.4.   LEADER 02298cam a2200421 i 4500

02298	The record length
cam	**(c)** Record is corrected/revised. (**a**) It is language material. (**m**) It is a monograph.
a	Uses UCS/Unicode
2	The record will use two indicators.
2	Number of characters used to identify a subfield.
00421	Computer-generated, five-character numeric string that indicates the first character position of the first variable control field in a record.
i	Follows *International Standard Bibliographic Description* (ISBD) cataloging and punctuation provisions.
4500	4500 defines where information is positioned in a MARC record.

Variable Control Fields

Variable control fields also process the bibliographic record through letter and number characters. The 001 tag is the control number assigned to the library that is creating the record, which is important in a shared or union catalog. This number is computer generated.

001 18525913

The 005 tag is made up of sixteen characters that identify the record and specify the date and time of the latest record transaction.

005 20150522093829.0

The next line of code, 008, includes the fixed-length data elements. There are forty positions or character spaces that provide coded information about the record. The cataloger methodically goes through these elements, selecting the code that is appropriate for the item in hand. We analyze the 008 tag in table 4.5.

MARC21 VARIABLE DATA FIELDS

Most tags are compilations of multiple or variable fields of data. The remainder of the MARC21 template is made up of variable data fields, which means that any codes and text will change or vary according to the item information. The item in hand to be cataloged determines what the bibliographic information that will be inputted into the record looks like.

Table 4.5.   008 150313s2015 nyuabfb 001 0beng c

008	Tag
150313	Computer-generated six-character numeric string that specifies the date the holdings report was first entered into machine-readable form. Date is given in the pattern *yymmdd*.
s	Single known date of publication
2015	The date specified above
nyu	Place of publication code. See regional code list.[1] "nyu" represents New York.
abf	illustrations, (**b**) maps, (**f**) plates. These are all illustration codes.
e	Target audience is adult (not juvenile)
001	Nature of contents: (**0**) not a conference publication, (**0**) is not a memorial publication, (**1**) the book does have an index.
0beng	book is nonfiction, (**b**) it is a biography, (**eng**) language is English.
c	Cooperative or consortium purchase; will lend hard copy.

1. "MARC Code List for Countries Part 3: Regional Sequence," MARC Standards, Library of Congress, last modified February 13, 2015, at www.loc.gov/marc/countries/countries_regional.html#north (accessed December 29, 2015).

In some ways variable data field cataloging is more straightforward because library staff are familiar with elements such as titles, authors, and copyright dates. In other ways it is more complex because the cataloger must research LC Authorities and create tracings, find FRBR relationships, and create RDA description and access points.

0XX Variable Data

We will examine the remainder of the MARC21 record located in textbox 4.3 in its variable data field number categories beginning with the tag 010. The 0XX variable data are primarily numbers that identify the item, system, record source, or classification.

Table 4.6.   Explanation of the 0XX Variable Data Fields *(Note: delimiters **a**, **b**, **c**, **d**, or **e** that proceed each field or subfield.)*

010	**a** 2014046049	Library of Congress Control Number. It always begins with the year the LC received the book for CIP (2014 was the year for this item).
020	**a** 9781476728742 (hardcover)	The International Standard Book Number is a unique ten- or thirteen-digit global identification number.
040	**a** PSt/DLC |**b** eng |**c** PSt |**e** rda |**d** DLC	(**a**) original cataloging agency code, (**b**) language code, (**c**) code for agency that transcribed record into MARC, (**e**) RDA rules applied, (**d**) agency responsible for modifying MARC record
050	**a** TL540. W7 |**b** M3825 2015	(**a**) LC Classification number, (**b**) item number portion of call number
082	**a** 629.130092/273 |**a** B |**2** 23	Dewey Decimal Classification number (**a**)biography, (**2**) DDC, 23rd edition

Where libraries are members of a consortium, the MARC template may also have a system 035 field to identify the library that created the record that is shared jointly.

1XX Variable Data

The next group of tags, the 100s, are the main entry to authors. Our example is simple as there is only one author with two subfields: (a) and (e):

```
a McCullough, David G., |e author
```

Many records have multiple authors, and RDA rules require all names to be included. The cataloger selects among the three types of author main-entry tags and fields according to the type of author's name:

100—Personal names
110—Corporate names
111–Meeting names

2XX Variable Data

Title, edition, and publication information is recorded in the 2XX variable data fields. It is critical to have the item in hand to examine it closely, as even a slight variation in edition requires its own unique MARC record. Title and publisher information is explained in table 4.7:

Table 4.7.   Explanation of the 2XX Title and Publisher Fields

245 14	**a** The Wright brothers / |**c** David McCullough	**14** are the indicators telling the system to leave four non-filing characters for the initial article "The."
		(**a**) title of book / (**c**) statement of responsibility (Yes, the author's name that occurs in the 100 tag is repeated here!)
250	**a** First Simon & Schuster hardcover edition	edition statement
264	**a** New York : |**b** Simon & Schuster, |**c** 2015	(**a**) city or place of publication, (**b**) name of publisher, (**c**) copyright date

The cataloger should check the LC Title Authority and the LC Names Authority for both the 100 and 200 fields to be sure the uniform name and title determined by the LC are used. If uniform titles are available but are not used, the catalog will contain errors.

3XX Variable Data

The 3XX fields are all about describing the item. The 3XX fields were expanded with RDA rules that encourage catalogers to provide greater description as points of access to the item record. The description varies from item to item, but the cataloger should always aim to complete as much of the template as possible. Sometimes this requires research that goes beyond looking at the item itself. We will analyze the 3XX fields of *The Wright Brothers* in table 4.8.

Table 4.8.   Explanation of the 3XX Physical Description Fields

300	**a** 320 pages, 48 unnumbered pages of plates : **|b** illustrations, maps ; **|c** 25 cm	**(a)** number of pages and plates, **(b)** the book has pictures and maps, **(c)** the book is 25 cm in vertical length
336	**a** text **|2** rdacontent	Content type (text) is the form of communication through which the content of this book is expressed.
337	**a** unmediated **|2** rdamedia	**(a)** In RDA media type term, **(2)** In RDA media type code.[1] The term "unmediated" means the resource can be perceived directly through one or more of the human senses without the aid of an intermediary device.[2]
338	**a** volume **|2** rdacarrier	The carrier type is the format (volume) of the storage medium and housing of the text.

1. "Genre/Form Code and Term Source Codes," Library of Congress, last modified May 14, 2015, at www.loc .gov/standards/sourcelist/genre-form.html (accessed December 29, 2015).
2. Mickey Koth, "Content, Media, and Carrier Type (RDA 6.9, 3.2, 3.3 & MARC 336-338)," Music cataloging at Yale with RDA, last modified March 6, 2015, at www.library.yale.edu/cataloging/music/MARC336338 .htm#unmediated (accessed December 29, 2015).

There are other 3XX MARC fields that support RDA and FRBR that were not used in our example. Catalogers should know about these name attribute fields because they provide access points of information that relate to the author or other aspects of the work or its expression. Table 4.9 lists these new fields.

Table 4.9.   370–388 MARC Fields for Name Attributes

Tag	FRBR/RDA Relationship	Tag	FRBR/RDA Relationship
370	Associated place	380	Form of Work
371	Address	381	Other distinguishing characteristics of work or expression
372	Field of activity	382	Medium of performance
373	Affiliation	383	Numeric designation of musical work
374	Occupation	384	Key (music)
375	Gender	385	Audience characteristics
376	Family information	386	Creator/Contributor characteristics
377	Associated language	388	Time period of creation
378	Fuller form of personal name		

4XX Variable Data

The 400 fields have to do with tracings and series. In our previous chapter on authority control, we learned that the 4XX fields are used to link variant forms of a title to the 245 uniform title field. The data in the 400 through 485 fields tell the computer that these are unauthorized forms of the title and it should "see" the correct or uniform title in tag 245. This convention helps the patron who is using a title that the cataloger identified as a variant form because, by creating a 4XX field, the cataloger commanded the computer to bring the patron to the correct 245 uniform title. In other words, a 4XX field leads from an unauthorized heading to an authorized heading.

400—Traces or connects an unauthorized added entry personal name to the 245 title field.

410—Traces or connects an unauthorized added entry corporate name to the 245 title field.

411—Traces or connects an unauthorized added entry meeting name to the 245 title field.

If the item is part of a series, the series title is data for a 490 field. While our example *The Wright Brothers* neither is a series nor has other variant forms of its title, series and variant forms of titles are points of access that need to be included in 4XX fields. Any added entries associated with the series are recorded in the 800 to 830 fields.

490—Series statement. (See the 800 to 830 fields described below for more information.)

5XX Variable Data

The next set of tags are the 5XX variable data fields. These fields allow content notes and other free text that may help a patron make decisions about the item. There are tag designations for different types of notes the cataloger wishes to express, such as the following:

504—Bibliographic note that tells patron the work has a bibliography and index.

505—Note that provides a list of titles of separate pieces that are included in the book, such as a speech, song, or epilogue.

520—Free space for the cataloger to provide a summary, annotation, or abstract of the work so that patrons have more information about its content.

6XX Variable Data

The cataloger leaves many clues for the patron about the topics or subjects of a library resource. These topics or subjects are filed in the 6XX subject access fields. We learned in chapter 3 that the LC has the final say on which terms should be used and how those terms should be formatted. Catalogers check the LC Authorities before assigning any new topics in order to be sure they use the words or phrases chosen by the LC. Let's analyze the 6XX topics used in our example (see table 4.10).

Table 4.10. Explanation of the 6XX Variable Data Subject Access Fields

600	**a** Wright, Orville, **d** 1871–1948	**(a)** last name, first name of subject of book, **(b)** death date of Orville Wright
600	**a** Wright, Wilbur, **d** 1867–1912	**(a)** last name, first name of subject of book, **(b)** death date of Wilbur Wright
650	**a** Aeronautics **z** United States **x** History **y** 20th century	**(a)** topic, **(z)** location, **(x)** historical work, **(y)** time period
650	**a** Aeronautics **z** United States **v** Biography	**(a)** topic, **(z)** location, **(v)** biographical work

The 651 field is commonly used but is not shown in our example; it is used exclusively for geographic names. Chapter 9 shows how to assign LC and Sears Subject Headings that provide the topics related to an item. These topics are the variable data fields of the 6XX tags. We will also practice assigning subjects in the third section of this book.

7XX Variable Data

Fields in the 7XX are reserved for FRBR and RDA relationships, added entries, or tracings of names that provide additional access to a record. The names could be personal (700), corporate (710), or meeting names (711). In RDA catalogers are required to use the 700 field for names of people who have relationships to the work, author, or even the setting. These relationships become other access points for searching. For example, the 700 fields could name those who contributed to the work or other people who influenced the writer. Because some family members had influence on the author, they could also be named in 700 fields as logical relationships.

The old rule of thumb for pre-RDA cataloging was to limit the number of authors to three. If a work had more than three authors, no one received credit. This was because the old card catalogs could not hold an endless number of cards.

The 7XX fields are also reserved for variant forms of titles. In the previous chapter we learned that when there is a uniform title, other forms of a title that either appear on the spine of the book or have become familiar usages are traced to the 245 field where the LC uniform title is listed. Other versions of the title are listed in 730 uniform title or 740 variant title fields. If the patron searches under a variant title in the 7XX field, similar to a "subject" search, the patron will find the correct computer display that has the uniform title.

8XX Variable Data

Fields 800 to 830 contain unauthorized added entries associated with a series title. These fields are used to trace a series added entry because when the 490 is being used for the proper series title, it cannot also be used for unauthorized added entries. Thus, these added entries are recorded in the 800 to 830 fields as follows:

> **800**—Series Added Entry—Personal Name
> **810**—Series Added Entry—Corporate Name
> **811**—Series Added Entry—Meeting Name
> **830**—Series Added Entry—Uniform Title

The 856 field is used to locate and access electronic information, including URLs to websites that contain e-books, publishers' information, or supplementary information about the topic of the library resource.[10] Even though our example is a print or hardback book, there are three 856 fields of data associated with it:

> **856**—Sample text of the book. **u**http://www.loc.gov/catdir/enhancements/fy1506/
> 2014046049-s.html

856—Publisher information. **u**http://www.loc.gov/catdir/enhancements/fy1506/ 2014046049-d.html

856—Author information. **u**http://www.loc.gov/catdir/enhancements/fy1506/ 2014046049-b.html

9XX Variable Data

The final tags of the MARC21 template are in the 9XX series. The 9XX fields are for local information about the item. These tags are not as commonly used as the other fields and do not show in the patron computer display view. The local information about the item is useful to the cataloger or other library staff but deemed not important to the patron (if it were, it would be put in a 500 contents note). The following information is from our MARC record on *The Wright Brothers*:

$$\text{a PStCIP } | \text{d } 2015\text{--}03\text{--}13$$

The coded information here (remember, it is local to the LC and not particularly meant for others to view) most likely means that the work received Cataloging in Publication (CIP) by the LC catalogers and was entered into the LC catalog on March 13, 2015.

SUMMARY

We have covered a lot of territory in this chapter on MARC21! Chapters 1 through 4 provide fundamental knowledge of the tools and processes for cataloging. A very important tool is the computer coding of MARC21. MARC21 is the standard computer language and code used in libraries in the United States and around the world for inputting the bibliographic information required by AACR2 so it can be processed and retrieved from any online library system. We will continue to develop and use our knowledge of MARC21, AACR2, and LC Authorities for the remainder of this book.

DISCUSSION QUESTIONS AND ACTIVITIES

Discussion Questions

1. Describe the history of MARC to MARC21. When was MARC developed and for what purpose?
2. Explain what the terms "tags," "fields," and "subfields" mean in relation to the MARC template.
3. What is a delimiter and what purpose does it serve?
4. What purpose do indicators serve, and why are they necessary in the 245 title statement field?
5. Explain how RDA has added to the 3XX and 7XX variable fields. Why are these rules an important addition to AACR2 for cataloging items?
6. What is the purpose of the 856 field? Name three ways it can be used.

Activity 1

This activity provides practice using indicators in the 245 field with titles that begin with an article. Write the correct indictor number next to the following book titles. All indicators will begin with the number 1. The second number is the quantity of nonfiling spaces.

Table 4.11. Using Indicators in the 245 Field with Titles That Begin with an Article

Title	Indicator
A Day in the Life of a Teenager	12 (Two nonfiling spaces)
The Adventures of Beekle: The Unimaginary Friend	
A Boy and a Jaguar	
Early Bird	
The Baby Tree	
A Snicker of Magic	
An Apple a Day	
El Deafo	

Activity 2

This activity provides practice using the parts of a MARC record. Copy and paste the bibliographic data from the LC MARC record into the appropriate field. Identify the data type in the second column. See the 008 field as an example.

```
008       150511s2015 nyuab 001 0 eng
010   ___   |a 2015018751
020   ___   |a 9781627792417 (hardcover)
050   00    |a E877.3 |b .O74 2015
082   00    |a 973.927092 |2 23
100   1_    |a O'Reilly, Bill.
245   10    |a Killing Reagan : |b the violent assault that
             changed a presidency / |c Bill O'Reilly and
             Martin Dugard.
250   ___   |a First edition.
264   _1    |a New York : |b Henry Holt and Company, |c 2015.
300   ___   |a 306 pages : |b illustrations, maps ; |c 24 cm
336   ___   |a text |b txt |2 rdacontent
337   ___   |a unmediated |b n |2 rdamedia
338   ___   |a volume |b nc |2 rdacarrier
500   ___   |a Includes index.
600   10    |a Reagan, Ronald |x Assassination attempt, 1981.
651   _0    |a United States |x Politics and government
             |y 1981–1989.
700   1_    |a Dugard, Martin.
```

Table 4.12. Using the Parts of a MARC Record

Tag	Copy Data from Record	Identify Type of Data
008	150511s2015 nyuab 001 0 eng	Fixed Fields
010		
020		
050		
082		
100		
245		
250		
264		
300		
336		
337		
338		
500		
600		
651		
700		

NOTES

1. "Events of the Century," *Library Journal* 124, no. 20 (December 1, 1999).

2. Lynn Blumenstein, "Avram, MARC Pioneer, Dies at 86," *Library Journal* 131, no. 10 (June 1, 2006).

3. "MARC Her Words; an Interview with Henriette Avram," *American Libraries* 20, no. 9 (October 1989).

4. "Events of the Century."

5. "Frequently Asked Questions (FAQ)," MARC21 Standards, Library of Congress, July 12, 2006, at www.loc.gov/marc/faq.html#definition (accessed December 28, 2015).

6. Ibid.

7. Michael Gorman, *The Concise AACR2*, 4th ed. (Chicago: American Library Association, 2004), 134.

8. "The Wright Brothers," LC Online Catalog, at catalog.loc.gov/vwebv/staffView?searchId=1281&recPointer=0&recCount=25&searchType=1&bibId=18525913 (accessed December 29, 2015).

9. "Leader (NR)," MARC21 Bibliographic—Full, Library of Congress, October 2010, atwww.loc.gov/marc/bibliographic/bdleader.html (accessed December 29, 2015).

10. "RDA in MARC Authority Data," Cataloger's Reference Shelf, MARC21 Format for Authority Data, April 2016, www.itsmarc.com/crs/mergedprojects/helpauth/helpauth/rda_in_marc_authority_data.htm (accessed September 15, 2016).

REFERENCES, SUGGESTED READINGS, AND WEBSITES

Blumenstein, Lynn. "Avram, MARC Pioneer, Dies at 86." *Library Journal* 131, no. 10 (June 1, 2006): 18–20.

"Changing the Nature of Library Data." *Library Technology Reports* 46, no. 1 (January 2010): 14–29.

"Events of the Century." *Library Journal* 124, no. 20 (December 1, 1999): 74–75.

Gorman, Michael. *The Concise AACR2*. 4th ed. Chicago: American Library Association, 2004.

Koth, Mickey. "Content, Media, and Carrier Type (RDA 6.9, 3.2, 3.3 & MARC 336–338)." Music cataloging at Yale with RDA, Yale University. Last modified March 6, 2015. Accessed December 29, 2015, at www.library.yale.edu/cataloging/music/MARC336338.htm#unmediated.

Libraries Online. "Of Mice and Men." Online Catalog. Accessed December 28, 2015, at catalog.lioninc.org/search~S38?/asteinbeck/asteinbeck/1%2C3%2C5%2CB/marc&FF=asteinbeck+john+1902+1968&2%2C%2C2.

The Library Corporation. "RDA in MARC Authority Data." Cataloger's Reference Shelf, MARC21 Format for Authority Data. April 2016. Accessed September 15, 2016, at www.itsmarc.com/crs/mergedprojects/helpauth/helpauth/rda_in_marc_authority_data.htm.

Library of Congress. "Frequently Asked Questions (FAQ)." MARC21 Standards. Last modified July 12, 2006. Accessed December 28, 2015, at www.loc.gov/marc/faq.html#definition.

———. "Genre/Form Code and Term Source Codes." Source Code for Vocabularies, Rules, and Schemes. Last modified July 29, 2016. Accessed September 15, 2016, at www.loc.gov/standards/sourcelist/genre-form.html.

———. "Leader (NR)." MARC21 Bibliographic—Full. October 2010. Accessed December 29, 2015, at www.loc.gov/marc/bibliographic/bdleader.html.

———. "MARC Code List for Countries. Part 3: Regional Sequence." MARC Standards. Last modified February 13, 2015. Accessed December 29, 2015, at www.loc.gov/marc/countries/countries_regional.html#north.

———. "The Wright Brothers." LC Online Catalog. Accessed December 29, 2015, at catalog.loc.gov/vwebv/staffView?searchId=1281&recPointer=0&recCount=25&searchType=1&bibId=18525913.

"MARC Her Words; an Interview with Henriette Avram." *American Libraries* 20, no. 9 (October 1989): 860–61.

Penn State University Libraries. "Intro to MARC Tagging." Cataloging and Metadata Services. Accessed December 20, 2015, at www.libraries.psu.edu/psul/cataloging/training/marctaggingintro.html.

Schudel, Matt. "Henriette Avram, 'Mother of MARC,' Dies." *Information Bulletin* 65, no. 5 (May 2006). Accessed December 27, 2015, at www.loc.gov/loc/lcib/0605/avram.html.

CHAPTER 5

Copy Cataloging

LSS are able to explain the value and advantages of cooperative or collaborative cataloging practices to enhance services. (ALA-LSSC Cataloging and Classification Competency #6)

Key Terms

Acquisitions. The processes of reviewing, ordering, purchasing, and receiving library resources.

Bibliographic utility. A source of MARC bibliographic records that a library purchases or to which it subscribes that can be imported to the local catalog. The cataloger searches the utility to find matches of records to the item in hand that needs cataloging.

Call number. The Dewey Decimal or Library of Congress classification number used to organize library collections by topic or subject.

Cataloging module. The software application in an integrated library system (ILS) dedicated to creating, editing, and importing bibliographic records with attached item records into the online catalog.

Circulation parameters. These are the rules for check-in and checkout established by the library for each type of resource.

Consortium. Libraries that form a partnership to share an ILS.

Holding record. Attached to the bibliographic record, this record contains the location information for an item in an individual library.

ISBN. The initialism for International Standard Book Number, a unique thirteen-digit number that identifies a specific edition of a book.

ISSN. The initialism for International Standard Serial Number, a unique eight-digit number that identifies a specific title (not volume) of a magazine, newspaper, or journal.

Item record. Attached to the bibliographic record, this second record contains local information, unique to a specific library, about the resource being cataloged such as its circulation rules, call number, barcode, replacement cost, and collection type.

Itype. A code that identifies the location or ownership of a specific type of library resource, such as DVDs, in a shared online catalog.

XML. An initialism for Extensible Markup Language, a type of code recommended for posting data or information on the Internet and used to code and edit new websites.

Z39.50. An international information retrieval standard that enables one computer to speak to another in order to find and obtain information.

INTRODUCTION

In this chapter we will learn how catalogers may transfer and use some or all of the information of a bibliographic record for their own cataloging work. The process of using other libraries' information is called copy cataloging, and it is perfectly acceptable in the library profession.

Library staff who have copy cataloging skills are essential for moving new items or catalog donations from the box to the shelf in a timely manner and for making other changes to keep the online catalog accurate. Copy catalogers must have a strong knowledge of the rules and standards of cataloging because they make evaluative decisions about what information to copy and how to use it appropriately in their records.

LSS CATALOGERS

Many professional tasks, such as copy cataloging, can be performed by support staff. Managers may delegate copy cataloging to staff because of the large volume of materials to be processed, the lack of professional catalogers, library staff's language and subject expertise, and cost savings.[1] As budgets are stressed and professional librarians must increasingly allocate their time to numerous mandates, it makes sense that skilled staff catalogers can reduce backlogs and take on more responsibility and complexity with cataloging training. However, good training takes time and can be intense. Copy catalogers also must be willing to learn the theory of cataloging practices in order to engage in the accurate work that contributes to the library catalog.[2]

Staff catalogers are versatile employees and may enhance their career opportunities and job security. Every library needs accurate and productive catalogers, and this need will only grow as new technologies allow libraries to share their holdings both locally and globally.

When staff have the skills to engage in more complex, professional cataloging, backlogs are decreased and patrons' access to materials is enhanced. Staff likewise benefit from the opportunity to acquire new skills and expertise. With decreased budgets, the work of staff catalogers has become increasingly more valuable, and they should be recognized for their important contributions.[3]

Table 5.1. Become a Staff Cataloger

Express	your interest with your manager and cataloger.
Ask	if you can spend part of your time supporting the cataloger.
Use	a text such as this to learn the fundamental tools of catalogers. Practice using the LC Authorities, LC MARC standards, and AACR2 rules. By reading this book, answering the discussion questions, and performing the activities at the end of each chapter you are off to a great start!
Share	with a cataloger your own interests, such as knowledge of a global language, music, art, or other talents and other subject-area expertise because a cataloger may need help with items in these disciplines.
Enroll	in courses, workshops, or webinars in cataloging processes and procedures.
Make	a point of continuing your professional learning. Cataloging is in an exciting period of change, and even the most experienced cataloger must learn new practices.
Practice	creating many different cataloging records.
Learn	from your mistakes—we all do! Remember, cataloging is an exacting science!
Accept	challenge and responsibility. More and more will come your way once you have proven yourself to be knowledgeable about the basics of cataloging!

THREE TYPES OF CATALOG RECORDS

Bibliographic Records

So far in this book, the only type of catalog records discussed has been bibliographic. A bibliographic catalog record contains the unique information specific to a book or resource. The information does not change regardless of where the resource is located. Bibliographic records contain such information such as the title, author, publisher, copyright date, edition, ISBN, LCCN, and subjects. A resource's bibliographic record is ubiquitous, which means that no matter where the resource or copies of the resource are located, even if a duplicate copy is in a library on the other side of the world, the bibliographic information will not change.

Holding Records

Each library resource has its own MARC holdings record. **MARC holdings records** contain the holdings information—which copies are owned and where they are held—for bibliographic items in both physical and electronic forms. The holding record is brief and is where the cataloger supplies the **call number** of the item and its physical location in his or her library. Holding records are unique to each individual library, as call numbers and locations can vary depending on how an institution classifies materials and assigns items to collections. Holdings records are created so that materials can be found.

When the item is a serial such as a magazine, journal, or newspaper that is published at regular intervals, the holding record also has fields for the publication dates and issue numbers. The record also provides a place for notes where the cataloger can add specific information about the serial, such as where it can be used or circulated.

The MARC holding record template appears for the cataloger after the bibliographic record is created or accepted into the **cataloging module** of the integrated library system (ILS). After the bibliographic record is created, the next step is to identify where the item can be found by its call number and collection location.

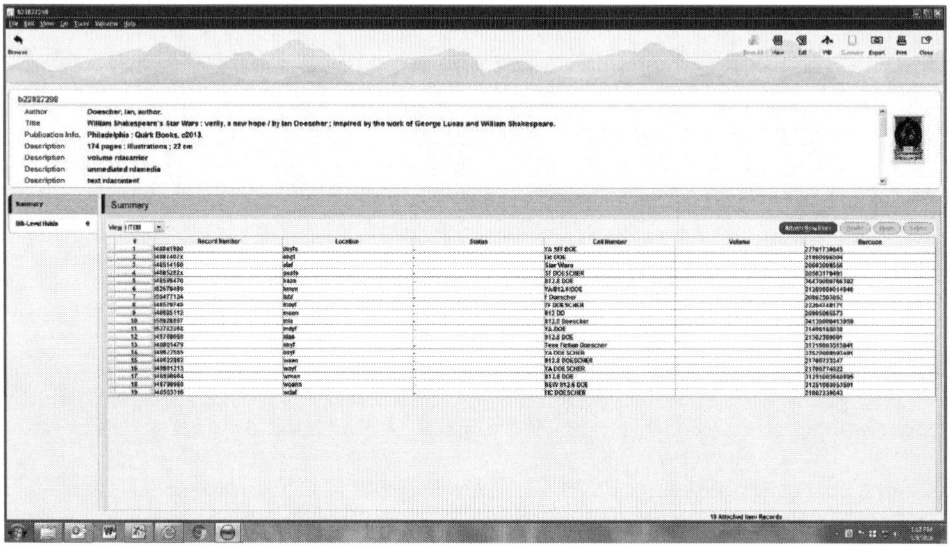

Figure 5.1.   Screen Shot of a Holding Record. Ledyard Public Libraries, Library Catalog.

Item Records

The third type of cataloging record, in addition to bibliographic and holding records, is the **item record**. Similar to holding records, item records are unique to a particular library—they contain additional information that is determined by the local institution that is helpful to both patrons and staff. Item records have many fields of information, and the library can choose which ones to use. The information in an item record often has to do with **circulation parameters**, collection types, **acquisitions**, and other information needed to manage the item. Some of this information, such as the copy number and loan rules, are supplied by the cataloger. Other fields, such as check-in location and status (whether the item is currently on the shelf or somewhere else), are supplied by the ILS and change with the item's circulation activity.

Like holding records, item records contain fields of information specific to the individual item and library. Item records are not typically suitable for copy cataloging in their entirety, but some fields tend to be linked. For example, a public library may allow adult patrons to borrow an adult fiction book for three weeks, renewable for another three weeks. The fields of loan rule, item type, collection type, and number of renewals for this library should always contain the same information, and the cataloger will supply them automatically.

Table 5.2. Typical Fields of an Item Record with Explanations

Cataloger-Supplied Information	ILS-Supplied Information
Copy number: number of duplicate copies	Check-in location: library where the item is returned and checked in
Collection code: identifier code by library and type of item, such as MDFIC for Middletown's (MD) adult fiction collection (FIC)	Checkout date: month, day, and year a patron borrows the item
Purchase date: month and year when an item was acquired	Checkout location: library where the item is borrowed
Location: where the item can be found	Due date: month, day, and year the borrowed item must be returned without penalty
Loan rule: the amount of time and type of patron, and dues associated with item	Year-to-date circulation: number of times the item was borrowed in a year
Item type: the kind or form of the library resource, such as book, serial, DVD, audio, e-book, and so forth	Last patron: person who most recently borrowed the item
Price: actual cost of the item or the discounted cost to the library	Patron number: barcode of the patron who borrowed the item
Number of renewals: the number of times the item may be renewed by the patron before bringing it back to the library	Total renewals: cumulative number of times the item has been renewed
OPAC message: free text for a note about the item that provides patrons additional information	Last checkout date: last time the item circulated
Status: cataloger wands barcode and sets the status to on shelving cart or available	Status: various standings are supplied as item is checked out, available, in repair, or missing
Vendor: Information about the company that sold item to library	Total checkouts: number of times item has been borrowed

Source: "Item Records: Fixed Length Fields," AskTico, University of California, at www.lib.berkeley.edu/asktico/procedures/item-records-fixed-length-fields?destination=node%2F8 (accessed January 12, 2016).

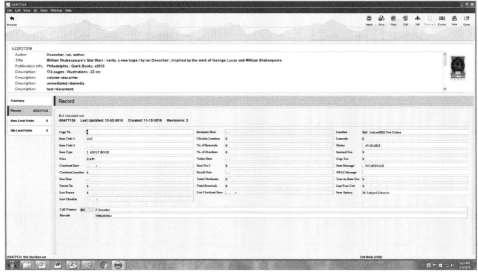

Figure 5.2. Screen Shot of an Item Record. Ledyard Public Libraries, Library Catalog.

LEVELS OF COPY CATALOGING

There are many different levels of copy cataloging. At all levels the cataloger determines if the fields of information match the item in hand. It takes a solid understanding of MARC standards and AACR2 rules to know if the information available
to copy is appropriate for the record.

The first level of copy cataloging is the exact match. This occurs when the library
obtains a second or duplicate copy of an item already in the collection. The bibliographic records can be copied in their entirety, and the item record needs only
the slightest modification for its copy number and purchase date (assuming that the
vendor and price remain the same).

If the cataloger finds an exact match for the bibliographic information of the
item, she or he may either modify the item record or create an entirely new one, depending on the source of the record. If the bibliographic record is found in a shared
consortium catalog, then only a modified item record is needed, as OPAC message
and perhaps even the circulation parameters may be shared. If the bibliographic
record is not from a shared consortium or district catalog, then an entirely new item
record will be needed.

Sometimes only small modifications are needed to both the bibliographic record
and item record. An example of this would be a second edition of a resource that
has only slight changes. Most of the bibliographic information is the same for both
editions. The cataloger would copy the first edition record and then make appropriate line or field changes so that the new record now reflects the second edition. The
author, title, and publisher would remain the same. Other elements, like the edition,
copyright date, and number of pages, would be different. If this record were in a
consortium catalog, the item record could also be copied and modified as needed.

Finally, the bibliographic record may need to be modified and a new item record
may need to be created. Item information would not be appropriate if the cataloger
is copying from outside the library or consortium. Table 5.3 compares these different options for copy cataloging.

Ultimately, it is the cataloger's decision to determine when and how much to
copy catalog. The resources available to the cataloger should be used to save the time
and expense of original cataloging whenever possible.

SOURCES OF BIBLIOGRAPHIC RECORDS

The sources of bibliographic records for copying will vary depending on the size,
type, and budget of the library. There will also be additional sources of records if the
library belongs to a consortium and if there is a statewide union catalog. All libraries have access to Library of Congress records, but some may also purchase records
from national or international sources. The cataloger should become familiar with
all of the sources of bibliographic records the library has access to and should learn
how to transfer MARC records from each.

The cataloger's initial or first search for bibliographic records is in the local library
catalog, the most basic and closest source of records. If the library already owns a
copy, it is a simple process to attach another item record for this second copy to the
one bibliographic record. The cataloger calls up the record and attaches a new item
record representative of the duplicate copy.

Table 5.3. Levels of Copy Cataloging

Type of Copy Cataloging	Example of When to Use
Exact match for bibliographic and item records	Use when library acquires a second or duplicate copy. Modify copy information only.
Exact match for bibliographic record. Item Record can be copied and modified.	Use when a library item is a duplicate of another in the shared system. Modify item record with individual library circulation rules and other information.
Exact match for bibliographic record. Item record is not useful.	Use when a library item is a duplicate of another in an outside system. Create a new item record with individual library circulation rules and other information.
Similar but not an exact match for bibliographic record. Item record could be useful for some information.	Use when a library item is a second or third edition that does not have substantive changes. The bibliographic record is found in the shared system. Slight modifications are needed to both the bibliographic and item records.
Similar but not an exact match for bibliographic record. Item record does not contain useful information.	Use when a library item is another edition or a title that has been published many times with slight variations by the same publisher. Create a new item record with individual library circulation rules and other information.

Two Items Attached to One Bibliographic Record

Figure 5.3. Two items attached to one bibliographic record.

SHARED CATALOGS

Shared catalogs came about primarily for the purposes of interlibrary loans. A secondary benefit is that the work of the cataloger was enhanced with the ability to copy catalog from other member libraries.

The majority of academic, public, and school libraries share their catalogs. For example, according to the 2014 statistics report from the Ohio State Library, only 60 of the 260 public libraries in the state were not members of a cooperative shared catalog for interlibrary loan.[4] Academic libraries share a common catalog among all of the campuses of an institution, and many also form **consortia** with universities and colleges nearby or with similar degree programs. K–12 libraries often have a shared catalog for the schools in the district, and many public libraries have either created small consortia with neighboring libraries or belong to regional organizations. Rhode Island, a small state where all public libraries are within driving distance, has one shared catalog for all of its public libraries.[5]

Increasingly, libraries find that sharing provides both cost savings and patron access to much larger collections than a single library can provide. Shared catalogs are a valuable asset of the member libraries and are governed by common rules and policies to maintain the highest-quality catalog records.

Consortium catalogers search for a match in the common catalog to see if another member library is already using the bibliographic record. If so, the bibliographic record simply needs another item record attached to it with the specific information of the member library.

ITEM TYPES

Every item in the library is classified by type. The item-cataloging process groups similar items into collections or item types with an accompanying code such as adult fiction (FIC), films (DVD), juvenile easy books (JE), e-books (EB), mysteries (MYS), and so forth. When a library is a member of a consortium, an item type, sometimes called an **itype**, is often preceded with a two- or three-letter alpha code that identifies library ownership.[6] For example, the itype for any item in the Valley Library Consortium, whose headquarters is located in Saginaw, Michigan, is preceded by two letters that represent the name of the library such as "RR" for River Rapids Library or "DC" for Delta College Library.[7] The itype code is rarely seen in the public catalog. The code is translated via the cataloguing module so that patrons read the library name, the collection, and where the item is located.

Table 5.4.   Examples of IType Codes

Code	Collection
ELHSC	East Lyme High School Science Fiction Collection
NLNDVD	Public Library of New London DVD Collection
STCJE	Stony Creek Library Juvenile Easy Books
WSBB	Westbrook Public Library Biography
IVYJBCD	Ivoryton Library Children's Book on CD Fiction

Source: "Appendix I—LION cataloging codes," Bibliographic Manual, Libraries Online, at www.lioninc.org/committees/bibliographic-2/bibliographic-manual/appendix-i-lion-cataloging-codes/ (accessed January 21, 2016).

STATEWIDE UNION CATALOGS

Catalogers should know what resources are offered through their state library. All of the fifty state libraries have online catalogs available via the Internet for anyone to search and view records. Minimally, the catalogs provide access to the collections housed in the state libraries, which are often of historic or legislative nature, and almost all states offer digital journals, e-books, and other online databases.

Some states, including Alaska and Indiana, offer online catalogs of a portion of the state's public, school, and college libraries. Evergreen Indiana is a growing consortium of 107 public, school, and institutional libraries located throughout Indiana whereby patrons of member libraries can borrow materials from the other member libraries.[8] In Alaska, residents may search and borrow over one million books, music, and movies from the state catalog that comprises all types of member libraries found throughout the southcentral and southeast parts of the state. Rhode Island's Ocean State Libraries and Connecticut's researchIT CT are examples of true statewide catalogs that have all of the academic, public, and K–12 school catalogs, as well as many of its special and private school libraries, accessed through one portal.[9]

How do catalogers access the MARC records from their state library union catalogs? With **Z39.50** connections, library catalogs can transfer MARC records electronically from one to another. Z39.50 is an international information retrieval standard that enables one computer to speak to another in order to find and obtain or transfer information.[10] Information from any Z39.50 compliant database can be searched and retrieved using a Z39.50 compliant system. The advent of Z39.50 opened up a new way for catalogers to retrieve and copy records from each other. A copy of the MARC bibliographic record from the state library catalog will transfer using Z39.50 to the local library catalog so that the cataloger can accept or modify it and attach item and holding records for use in the local catalog.

LIBRARY OF CONGRESS ONLINE CATALOG

Another great resource catalogers have is the Library of Congress Online Catalog. The catalog contains eighteen million catalog records for books, serials, manuscripts, maps, music, recordings, images, and electronic resources in the Library of Congress collections.[11] Because most publishers in the United States provide the Library of Congress with a prepublication copy for cataloging purposes so that the Cataloging in Publication (CIP) information is created for the item's title page or accompanying material, this is a comprehensive catalog for finding and copying MARC records.

The Library of Congress Online Catalog Gateway uses Z39.50 connections, and it invites libraries to access its records using this gateway.[12] Consortiums and statewide catalogs take advantage of this opportunity to expand the resources catalogers have to share and copy excellent bibliographic records. Even a cataloger in a small or medium library that does not have any other resources should talk with the library director and IT specialists to see if they have or can obtain Z39.50 so that they can access the records of the Library of Congress catalog.

OCLC—WORLDCAT

So far we have looked at local, regional, state, and national library catalogs as means for copying bibliographic records. OCLC is an international commercial vendor of over 2.3 billion item records and over 360 million MARC bibliographic records.[13] Academic, research, special, government, and large public libraries around the globe, as well as library consortia, subscribe to OCLC to interlibrary loan items and to obtain and share MARC bibliographic records. OCLC also provides many up-to-date tools and resources for catalogers. OCLC WorldCat is the online catalog that member libraries have access to via Z39.50 connections; it provides MARC bibliographic records, authority files, and item records. A library that joins OCLC is expected to contribute its own catalog records to be shared in WorldCat.

All of these resources can save time and resources for cataloging departments. Catalogers always search for high-quality MARC bibliographic records to copy before creating original records. Most consortia and libraries with large volumes of cataloging connect with several of these resources via Z39.50 to make use of the best available records found in libraries.

PROCEDURES FOR COPY CATALOGING

Catalogers should be methodical in following the procedures set forth by their supervising catalogers to search, select, evaluate, upload, and edit records from other sources. If the support staff *is* the library cataloger and is working in a shared catalog, it is important the procedures be followed exactly as prescribed by the bibliographic committee of the consortium. If the cataloger is working in a stand-alone catalog, such Fas ollett Destiny, he or she may work with a product called Alliance Plus that is used by many K–12 schools to download MARC records into their local systems.[14] The single-site cataloger should follow the steps suggested by the software vendor and use online help to fully understand the recommended procedures. If steps are not followed, the imported records could be incomplete or inaccurate. There are some general steps to follow in any copy cataloging process.

Search and Match Records

The first question to ask is whether the item already exists in the local library catalog. In order to obtain accurate search results, the best access point is the item's **ISBN**, or International Standard Book Number. If the item is a serial such as a magazine, newspaper, or journal, it will have an **ISSN**, or International Serial Number. These numbers are clearly identified with either "ISBN" or "ISSN" preceding them. Currently, an ISBN has thirteen digits, but the ISBN of an older book may have ten digits. There are eight digits in a serial ISSN.

The cataloger may have to perform several searches before a match is determined. If an ISBN cannot be found for a book, then the title and author should be searched. Be careful because there may be multiple editions. The edition, publisher, and physical description (copyright, pages, size of book, and the like) will also have to match before the bibliographic record is accepted.

Each item type has its own key points for searching. See table 5.5 for the recommended order of matching item data.

Select and Evaluate Records

Depending on the size of the bibliographic source and the number of records used, the cataloger may find several that may look promising. Even with the ISBN

Table 5.5. Order of Matching Key Data to Records in a Bibliographic Source

Books	1. ISBN
	2. Author
	3. Title
	4. Edition *If all of the above matches, you may also look for the following:*
	5. Publisher
	6. Physical Descriptions
Serials	1. ISSN
	2. Title
	3. Dates
	4. Publisher *If all of the above matches, you may also look for the following:*
	5. Physical Description
E-books or Audiobooks	1. ISBN
	2. Author
	3. Title
	4. Edition *If all of the above matches, you may also look for the following:*
	5. Publisher
	6. Physical Description
	7. Narrator
Music	1. Title
	2. Lyricist
	3. Composer
	4. Performer
	5. Physical Description (format and the like)
Film	1. Title
	2. Screenwriter
	3. Director
	4. Actors
	5. Producer
	6. Physical Description (format and the like)

Source: John Sandstrom and Liz Miller, *Fundamentals of Technical Services*, ALA Fundamentals Series (Chicago, IL: Neal-Schuman, 2015), 93.

as the match point, the quality of records may vary. Some catalogs do not require full MARC records, and work will be needed to upgrade them. Go slowly here and compare and contrast the records.

What makes a good record? Compare the item in hand to the record. Even if the title and author match, are there any discrepancies in the physical attributes? If the record says the book is 18 cm in length but the book you have in hand is 22 cm, then this is not an exact match even if the publisher, date, and pictures are the same. If there is doubt, look for things like exact matches of print layout on pages, number of pages, and front and back matter. For items that are not books, the labels, packaging, and other attributes like the length of the film or the accompanying orchestra should be matched.

The reliability of records should be questioned. A consortium that employs a cataloger to review records to ensure the quality of the database will have more accurate records than one that does not. The Library of Congress is always a dependable source, even if the cataloger in the small library has to reenter the record into his or her stand-alone system. Remember: "garbage in" is "garbage out," and our work is immediately displayed in our online public catalogs for the world to see!

Import Records

Sources of MARC records are also referred to as **bibliographic utilities**. Some bibliographic utilities, such as OCLC, are very large. Others may be as small as a publisher's database of MARC records for the resources they sell. Consortiums or very large catalogs may purchase and import batches of records at one time. The bibliographic records that are not needed will be discarded later. The process of discarding bibliographic records that do not have attached item records is often referred to as cleaning up the database. This is a necessary task that should be done periodically because without an item record attached, only the bibliographic information will show in the online public catalog. In such cases, patrons could become confused or even frustrated because such records will not have location information and patrons will not be able to place a hold on the item as no library has claimed to own it by attaching an item record!

Importing MARC records into the local catalog can be a simple as one or two clicks when a library uses Z39.50 to connect with bibliographic utilities. If the library is purchasing records from a commercial source such as Baker & Taylor, Follett, or individual publishers, the cataloger may seek support from IT staff who could communicate with the vendor to be certain that the files and formats of the MARC records are compatible and transferable.

If the library does not have Z39.50 connections to bibliographic sources, the cataloger should still use the online public access catalogs of academic institutions, states, and the Library of Congress to find matches. The ILS vendor may have templates available to the cataloger within the system to import and edit outside records. There are also options to work with many free or commercial third parties to edit and import records. The Library of Congress provides a list of these specialized sites and tools.[15]

Table 5.6.   Free Specialized Tools to Import and Edit MARC Records

MARCBreaker and MARCMaker	MARCMaker, developed by the Library of Congress, generates the MARC record structure from preformatted text. MARCMaker accepts files from most text editors and word processors if the text is formatted according to the simple input file rules. This MARC utility runs on PCs using Windows platform.
MarcEdit	MarcEdit provides users with new flexibility when working with and crosswalking MARC data. Features include a MarcEditor with numerous, built-in MARC editing functions.
MARC/Perl	MARC/Perl is a tool for reading, manipulating, outputting, and converting bibliographic records in the MARC format.
USEMARCON Plus (Universal MARC Record Convertor)	USEMARCON facilitates the conversion of catalog records from one MARC format to another.
MARC to XML / XML to MARC Conversion Utilities	MARC to XML / XML to MARC utilities are free programs that permit conversion between the MARC and XML structures.

Edit Records

Once a record has been matched to an item, the cataloger often has to edit the record to comply with local bibliographic policies. For example, the 040 tag that codes library ownership always needs to be changed. The library that imported the record into the system needs to identify itself in case changes or upgrades need to be made. Typically, other libraries do not change the bibliographic record unless granted permission.

The consortium Libraries Online, or LION, requires when editing a bibliographic record that the subfield "d" is added to an 040 tag followed by the library that is creating, or editing and importing, the record three-digit code.[16] Suggested examples of editing from LION's bibliographic policy manual include the following:

TEXTBOX 5.1. EXAMPLES OF EDITING A MARC RECORD

Correct misspellings

Adding subtitles or performers

Changing the title and subtitle when the "item-in-hand" differs from what is in the system and there has been no edition change

Adding missing information such as the 300 tag

Adding other pertinent information

We will now look at one of the specialized tools the Library of Congress endorses for editing and importing MARC records.

MARCEdit

If a match is found in an outside bibliographic utility or source, most likely the record will be in a file format that is incompatible with the local ILS cataloging module. In order to change the file format, edit the record, and import it into the ILS, a specialized software tool must be used. We will look at one tool from table 5.6 called MarcEdit to see how it supports the work of catalogers.

MARC records are viewed in bibliographic utilities in various data file formats, such as DAT. MarcEdit[17] is a tool the cataloger uses to do the following:

1. Download and save the record from the bibliographic utility in DAT or other file formats to the workstation.
2. Change the file format of the record to a mnemonic MRK format ready for editing.
3. Convert the edited record to the MRC file format so that it can be imported from the workstation to the local ILS.

In this process MarcEdit uses the Library of Congress utilities MARCBreaker and MARCMaker to move MARC data into a friendly mnemonic file format. The

MarcEditor is MarcEdit's built-in metadata editor.[18] It includes a number of global editing functions, such as add/delete fields, edit subfields, swap field data, copy field data, edit indicators, generate call numbers, validate records, generate reports, find/replace, and so forth. MarcEdit has many helpful tutorials, including "MarcEdit 101: I Have a MARC Record, Now What?"[19] This tutorial clearly explains the process of downloading, editing, and importing records to the local ILS. If the library does not have built-in editing tools, catalogers should explore MarcEdit as an option; it is extremely easy to use and will save an enormous amount of time and expense.

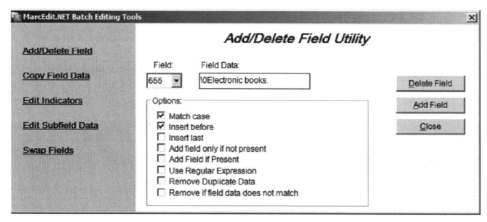

Figure 5.4.   Edit Subfield Screen in MarcEdit. MarcEdit.

EXAMPLE FROM UNITED STATES
COAST GUARD ACADEMY (USCGA) LIBRARY

The USCGA Library imports MARC bibliographic records from OCLC and the Library of Congress to their local SIRSI system. Using a government document as an example, the cataloger demonstrated the process as shown in table 5.7.[20]

Table 5.7.   Copy Cataloging a Government Document from OCLC to USCGA

1	Searches OCLC by title for "Antarctic Minerals Policy" 1990 Hearing (this item does not have an ISBN). Narrows search by title and year.
2	Looks at the 050 tag and accepts the LC call number. Reviews record for RDA tags and fast subject headings (that will be deleted on the USCGA side).
3	Copies the OCLC number of the bibliographic record and pastes it into USCGA–SIRSI. Record comes over from OCLC to SIRSI. Record is matched to item in hand and loaded into local system.
4	Searches and finds government documents online and adds the 856 field because an electronic version is available. This information is added to the bibliographic record that is now in the USCGA catalog.
5	Completes item and holding record. Exports holding information to OCLC so that USCGA can be shown as a holding and lending library.

Another cataloger demonstrated batch copy cataloging between the local USCGA SIRSI system and OCLC.[21] In a similar way she scanned in several ISBN numbers as a "batch," and matches or close matches were returned from OCLC. She evaluated each return until she was satisfied she had exact matches. Using an off-line work-space on her desktop, she slightly modified the bibliographic records and added item records. When she was finished working off-line with her "batch," she up-loaded the work to SIRSI. By working in batches, she was able to do repetitive work, such as adding a local code or note, efficiently and quickly.

Photo 5.1. United States Coast Guard Academy Library, New London, CT.

As a branch of the Department of Homeland Security, the USCGA library limits its access to other university and government collections to OCLC and the Library of Congress catalog for MARC records.

SUMMARY

Catalogers copy, edit, and import outside bibliographic records as part of their work. In the United States, bibliographic sources with millions of MARC records are available for use. The value of cooperative or collaborative cataloging practices cannot be overstated, as such practices save inordinate amounts of time and money for libraries. Staff catalogers must be knowledgeable about the content and purpose of bibliographic, holding, and item records so that they can appropriately integrate them into their ILS. Cataloging is not a solitary activity but rather one that calls on the cataloger to interface with local, regional, state, national, and even global resources to enhance library services.

DISCUSSION QUESTIONS AND ACTIVITIES

Discussion Questions

1. Discuss ways support staff can learn more about the work of a cataloger on the job.
2. What are the three types of cataloging records, and how does each inform or relate to the others?
3. What are the main differences between a bibliographic record and an item record?
4. Describe the different bibliographic sources of MARC records. Which sources does your library cataloger use? Why does he or she use these and not others?
5. List the steps of copy cataloging in the order they should be completed. Describe each step and why it is important to the goal of importing accurate records into the local catalog.
6. What is MarcEdit and why should catalogers consider using it?

Activity 1: Changing Records from Patron to Staff or MARC Display

Many public access online catalogs can switch between patron and MARC display with the click of a button. Beginning catalogers can learn a lot by comparing and contrasting how the information of a MARC record is formatted in the patron view of the catalog.

1. Go to www.lioninc.org and select "Catalog."
2. Search the title "The Hunger Games."
3. Select any title that is listed.
4. Look above the search boxes and find "Staff View." Click to see the MARC record of this item. Look at the record and find key access points such as its title, author, subjects, and so forth.
5. Click on "Regular View." Locate the access points in the regular patron view to see how the MARC information is displayed for patrons. Repeat this process with other titles.

Activity 2: Practice Using the Editing Tool MarcEdit

MarcEdit is a free editing cataloging tool and can be downloaded to a Windows or Macintosh computer. Using the tutorials and instructions found on the MarcEdit website, do the following:

1. Download and install the MarcEdit 6.2 application appropriate for your computer from marcedit.reeset.net/downloads.
2. Using the Library of Congress catalog at catalog.loc.gov, search a record on your favorite Star Wars episode.
3. Using the instructions found in the "MarcEdit 101: I Have a MARC Record, Now What?" tutorial located at marcedit.reeset.net/tutorials, download and save a MARC record from the Library of Congress onto the desktop of your computer.

4. Using the MarcEdit software, delete a field, add a subfield, copy field data, edit indicators, generate call numbers, and generally become comfortable editing the record.

5. When done, you may delete the record and remove the MarcEdit program from your computer.

NOTES

1. Natalie Gelber and Irina Kandarasheva, "Notes on Operations PCC Training for Copy Catalogers," *Library Resources and Technical Services* 55, no. 3 (July 2011): 163–71.

2. Ibid.

3. Elizabeth Cox and Ann K. D. Myers, "What Is a Professional Cataloger? Perception Differences between Professionals and Paraprofessionals," *Library Resources and Technical Services* 54, no. 4 (October 2010): 212–26.

4. "2014 Ohio Public Library Statistics," State Library of Ohio, at library.ohio.gov/documents/2014-ohio-public-library-statistics/ (accessed January 16, 2016).

5. "OSL Fact Sheet," Ocean State Libraries, at oslri.org/home/about-osl/fact-sheet/ (accessed January 16, 2016).

6. "Item Records," Bibliographic Database Standards and Procedures Manual: Procedures, Valley Library Consortium, at www.vlc.lib.mi.us/ii-item-records (accessed January 19, 2016).

7. Ibid.

8. "The Evergreen Indiana Open-Source ILS Initiative," Evergreen Indiana, at www.in.gov/library/evergreen.htm (accessed January 21, 2016).

9. "OSL Fact Sheet"; "researchIT CT," CT State Library, at researchitct.org (accessed January 21, 2016).

10. "What is Z39.50?," Libraries Australia, at www.nla.gov.au/librariesaustralia/services/search/z3950/ (accessed January 21, 2016).

11. "Library of Congress Online Catalog," Library of Congress, at catalog.loc.gov/ (accessed January 21, 2016).

12. "About the Z39.50 Gateway," Gateway to Library Catalogs, Library of Congress, last modified October 2, 2015, at www.loc.gov/z3950/gateway.html#about (accessed January 21, 2016).

13. "WorldCat Facts and Statistics," OCLC, at www.oclc.org/worldcat/catalog.en.html (accessed January 21, 2016).

14. "Alliance Plus Online, Alliance AV," Follett Software Company, at www.follettsoftware.com/_file/File/pdf/Alliance_and_AV_10544A.pdf (accessed January 21, 2016).

15. "MARC Specialized Tools," MARC Records, Systems, and Tools, Library of Congress, at www.loc.gov/marc/marctools.html (accessed January 22, 2016).

16. "Libraries Online (LION) Bibliographic Policy Manual," Libraries Online, at www.lioninc.org/committees/bibliographic-2/bibliographic-manual/ (accessed January 22, 2016).

17. "Current News," MarcEdit—Your Complete Free MARC Editing Utility, MarcEdit Development, at marcedit.reeset.net/ (accessed January 22, 2016).

18. Ibid.

19. "MarcEdit 101: I Have a MARC Record, Now What?" MarcEdit Development, at marcedit.reeset.net/tutorials (accessed January 22, 2016).

20. Elisa Graydon, interview, United States Coast Guard Academy Library, New London, CT, January 29, 2016.

21. Janet Whitty, interview, United States Coast Guard Academy Library, New London, CT, January 29, 2016.

REFERENCES, SUGGESTED READINGS, AND WEBSITES

Alaska State Library. "Alaska State Library Catalog." Accessed January 21, 2016, at jlc-web.uaa
.alaska.edu/client/en_US/asl/.

Connecticut State Library. "ResearchIT CT." CT State Library. Accessed September 15, 2016,
at researchitct.org.

Cox, Elizabeth, and Ann K. D. Myers. "What Is a Professional Cataloger? Perception Differences between Professionals and Paraprofessionals." *Library Resources and Technical Services*
54, no. 4 (October 2010): 212–26.

Follett Software Company. "Alliance Plus Online, Alliance AV." Brochure. Accessed January
21, 2016, at www.follettsoftware.com/_file/File/pdf/Alliance_and_AV_10544A.pdf.

Gelber, Natalie, and Irina Kandarasheva. "Notes on Operations PCC Training for Copy Catalogers." *Library Resources and Technical Services* 55, no. 3 (July 2011): 163–71.

Graydon, Elisa. Interview. United States Coast Guard Academy Library, New London, CT.
January 29, 2016.

Indiana State Library. "The Evergreen Indiana Open-Source ILS Initiative." Evergreen Indiana.
Accessed January 21, 2016, at www.in.gov/library/evergreen.htm.

"Item Records," in *Bibliographic Database Standards and Procedures Manual: Procedures*. Valley
Library Consortium. Accessed January 19, 2016, at www.vlc.lib.mi.us/ii-item-records.

Libraries Online. "Appendix I—LION cataloging codes." Libraries Online (LION) Bibliographic Policy Manual. Accessed January 21, 2016, at www.lioninc.org/committees/
bibliographic-2/bibliographic-manual/appendix-i-lion-cataloging-codes/.

———. "Libraries Online (LION) Bibliographic Policy Manual." Last modified May 1, 2014.
Accessed January 22, 2016, at www.lioninc.org/committees/bibliographic-2/bibliographic
-manual/.

Library of Congress. "About the Z39.50 Gateway." Gateway to Library Catalogs. Last modified
October 2, 2015. Accessed January 21, 2016, at www.loc.gov/z3950/gateway.html#about.

———. "Library of Congress Online Catalog." Accessed January 21, 2016, at catalog.loc.gov/.

———. "MARC Specialized Tools." MARC Records, Systems, and Tools. Accessed January 22,
2016, at www.loc.gov/marc/marctools.html.

———. "What Is a MARC Holdings Record and Why Is It Important?" Understanding MARC
Holdings Record. Last modified January 28, 2011. Accessed January 13, 2016, at www.loc
.gov/marc/umh/UMHpt1–6.html.

MarcEdit Development. "Current News." MarcEdit—Your Complete Free MARC Editing Utility. Accessed January 22, 2016, at marcedit.reeset.net/.

———. "MarcEdit 101: I Have a MARC Record, Now What?" Tutorials, MarcEdit—Your Complete Free MARC Editing Utility. Accessed January 22, 2016, at marcedit.reeset.net/tutorials.

National Library of Australia. "What is Z39.50?" Libraries Australia. Accessed January 21,
2016, at www.nla.gov.au/librariesaustralia/services/search/z3950/.

Ocean State Libraries. "OSL Fact Sheet." Accessed January 16, 2016, at oslri.org/home/about
-osl/fact-sheet/.

OCLC. "About OCLC." Accessed January 21, 2016, at www.oclc.org/en-US/home.html.

———. "WorldCat Facts and Statistics." Accessed January 21, 2016, at www.oclc.org/worldcat/
catalog.en.html.

Regents of the University of California. "Item Records: Fixed Length Fields." AskTico. Accessed January 12, 2016, at www.lib.berkeley.edu/asktico/procedures/item-records-fixed
-length-fields?destination=node%2F80.

Sandstrom, John, and Liz Miller. *Fundamentals of Technical Services*. ALA Fundamentals Series.
Chicago: Neal-Schuman, 2015.

State Library of Ohio. "2014 Ohio Public Library Statistics." Accessed January 16, 2016, at
library.ohio.gov/documents/2014-ohio-public-library-statistics/.

Whitty, Janet. Interview. United States Coast Guard Academy Library, New London, CT. January 29, 2016.

CHAPTER 6

Metadata

LSS know the basics of standard metadata formats and cataloging rules to select, review, and edit catalog records, and to generate metadata in various formats. (ALA—LSSC Competency #3)

Key Terms

BIBFRAME. An acronym for the term "Bibliographic Framework," this Library of Congress initiative will replace MARC record cataloging in the future. Cataloging standards are changing to include more description and metadata that will be accessed universally through search engines rather than proprietary MARC record systems. MARC records will transfer to BIBFRAME. The Library of Congress will determine when to abandon the MARC standard.

HTML. An initialism for hypertext markup language, the computer code most commonly used to create websites. It permits text and images to be linked to internal and external web pages. Many digital library resources, such as websites, articles, e-books, and documents, can contain hyperlinks because they are written in HTML.

Metatag. A top line of computer code on a web page for inputting searchable subjects that will enhance the page's ranking. Such lines of code influence search engine results by matching the user's search terms with the subjects found in the code. Library programmers can influence the ranking of their websites by using metatags.

RDA. The initialism for Resource Description and Access, the new cataloging standard that replaced the *Anglo-American Cataloguing Rules* (AACR2). RDA fields require the cataloger to provide more information than previous versions of MARC about the description, authority, and relationships to creators and users of an item being cataloged.

URI. The initialism for Uniform Resource Identifier. In the future, cataloging records will be created in BIBFRAME and each line of code will be a URI or web address pointing to linking descriptive or authority information stored on the servers of the Library of Congress and other libraries.

XML. An initialism for Extensible Markup Language, a type of code recommended for posting data or information on the Internet and used to code and edit new websites. XML works with HTML so that relationships between lines of code can be made. It has become a common language for programming websites to enhance searching and is the coding language of BIBFRAME.

INTRODUCTION

When librarians catalog library materials, they currently use the Library of Congress MARC record. MARC records are the uniform standard for cataloging adopted by libraries more than fifty years ago so that bibliographic data could be computer readable and shared.

In this chapter we will compare cataloging books to cataloging digital collections and objects in order to explain the concept of metadata and how it can be used. Because libraries are rapidly becoming centers for creating, storing, and promoting digital objects that are cataloged with metadata, it is important to be able to use metadata to help patrons find and locate digital objects.

WHAT IS METADATA?

Let's begin this chapter with an understanding of the word "metadata." Metadata as it relates to technology is commonly defined as "data about data."[1] This definition confounds and confuses; it appears to be more doublespeak than helpful. Let's break down the word into its two component parts, *meta* and *data*, to understand what metadata is. The prefix "meta-" has several meanings, but the one that best applies to library materials means "beyond" or "going beyond." Metadata *goes beyond data.* Going one step further, metadata goes beyond the obvious and straightforward data presented by the item to be cataloged.

"Data" is a word that is used frequently. Everyone seeks data to help make decisions. Data can be such things as the following:

1. facts
2. statistics (numbers)
3. basic, obvious, or common information

Data are used in education, business, and of course libraries for reference, learning, and analysis. Statistics are one type of data. Each month my town library board receives circulation and usage statistics from the previous month. These are interesting numbers on their own, but real meaning occurs when we compare data from the same month of the previous year. We can make meaning from the differences in the data. Data permeate our world and are used to understanding, predict, judge, and evaluate ideas.

MARC21

Adopted by the Library of Congress over fifty years ago, MARC became the national standard for cataloging. In 1998 MARC was replaced by MARC21, a significant revision. Since then, ongoing changes, such as the adoption of **RDA** rules and the 856 field for linking websites, have kept the cataloging process relevant to libraries and their users.

Library books and other materials are described by bibliographic data used to create the MARC21 record, which consists of tags and fields. Each tag and its field identify unique data about the library material. Three of the more common tags and fields are as follows:

Tag: 100; Field: Author Personal Name
Tag: 245; Field: Title Statement
Tag: 300; Field: Physical Description of item such as pages, illustrations, and dimensions (**a**40 p. :$bill ;$c20 cm.)

The tags and fields in the example above (100, 245, and 300) require straightforward data or facts. These facts can be found by looking on the title page, thumbing through the book to see if it has illustrations, and measuring the vertical length of the book with a metric ruler. The record in the online catalog of the author, title, pages, illustrations, and size provides patrons the basic information they need to select and locate the book. The data speak for themselves but provide no further insights into relationships or the authority of the item to other works or objects.

MARC21 is much more robust than this simple example of three tags and fields. There are many other tags and fields in MARC21 that require additional knowledge or research by the cataloger to complete a full record. The cataloger selects metadata—descriptions, subjects, annotations, personal relationships, and so forth—throughout the record that patrons will use to conduct searches. Consider the MARC21 record template for a book. Library staff who are not familiar with cataloging will need much further training to fully understand and use MARC21. However, the template shows us the various pieces of bibliographic information, including metadata, that is searchable through online catalogs to help patrons select and locate books from library collections.

METADATA FOR DIGITAL OBJECTS

The data that describe library books and materials in MARC21 are fairly standard and often come directly off the title page of the book or credits of the item. In order for books and media to be copyrighted, the Library of Congress requires basic bibliographic data of title, author, publisher, date, and the like. This is not the case with digital objects or collections. Objects are not copyrighted because copyright is for fixed written, musical, or visual expression.

Objects are unique and do not conform to standardized physical attributes or formats like books do. Therefore it is difficult, if not impossible, to use the library MARC cataloging system to catalog digitized objects. Digitized objects, other than works of art, rarely have formal titles. When I introduce my students to metadata, I ask them to pretend they have become so famous that a museum wants to preserve and digitize their shoes. What would the metadata title of their shoes be? They create different titles for the same object—*sandals, beach shoes, Mary's flip-flops*—because there is no definitive title! In fact, it may make sense for an object to be assigned several synonymous titles. While in MARC21 it is rare to have even one alternate title, in metadata there can be multiple titles, as many as make sense for future Internet searching!

Creating metadata—going beyond the basic facts of the object—requires the cataloger to research the digital object. Basic data about the object are needed, but information about such things as important relationships should also be included in the metadata record. The metadata cataloger has more freedom than the MARC21 cataloger to go beyond the basics to develop search terms and keywords about the digital object. Library staff can ask the following three questions about the digital object to help them begin to create metadata:

1. What is it?
2. How is it made?
3. What is it used for?

The first question addresses the content or purpose of the object. It helps us understand what the object is about. The second question is about the form and physical features of the object. The third question reaches out to the relationship the object has to people, events, time periods, places, or other things. Most of the metadata to answer these questions go beyond what is presented by holding or touching the object. Library staff who gather and create metadata may see themselves in the role of detective, historian, archaeologist, or even forensic investigator!

FRBR and RDA

The standards of cataloging work are rapidly undergoing change. Underlying this change is the fundamental problem that MARC21 has not kept up with Internet search engines. In other words, the records of MARC21 do not hand off cleanly to Google, Yahoo, or Bing. The Library of Congress is committed to **BIBFRAME**, which will replace MARC21 records that work in online catalogs with **XML** records that extensively link all bibliographic data to **URI** (Uniform Resource Identifiers).

Two new revisions to cataloging MARC21 that will carry over to BIBFRAME are FRBR and RDA. In order to understand metadata better, a short description of each of these rules is necessary.

Photo 6.1. Book with Audio and Text Features.

FRBR is an initialism for Functional Requirements for Bibliographic Records. It is a system that has been in place for many years. Basically, it is model for how to think about and approach cataloging. Table 6.1 shows the four entities in FRBR.

Table 6.1. The Four Entities of FRBR

Work	A distinct artistic or creative concept
Expression	The realization of the expression (in text, song, and so forth)
Manifestation	The layout of the publication, how a DVD is recorded, and specific editions
Item	The physical book, DVD, or other material owned by the library to be cataloged

In table 6.1, *work* and *expression* have to do with the concept. The terms *manifestation* and *item* have to do with the physical item owned by the library. When we think about objects we can distinguish between the artistic concept and the physical item. Breaking down our cataloging in this way allows us to think of all the possibilities of metadata for an object.

RDA is another important guideline for catalogers. RDA stands for Resource Description and Access. In the MARC21 Template, the 300, 600, and 700 tags were expanded. Instead of limiting our description of a book to its illustrations, pages, and size, with RDA we now provide information about the author's professional occupation, gender, and language. In the subject fields of the 600 and 700 tags catalogers are required to provide more subjects, such as all authors who are affiliated with the work. FRBR and RDA require catalogers to think about themselves as recorders of metadata rather than suppliers of basic information about library items.

METADATA STANDARDS

The two most common metadata standards are MODS and Dublin Core. In the future, BIBFRAME will be the standard for both the Library of Congress library cataloging and metadata. Following this section on standards we will look at a few of the collection management systems libraries and museums use to create online catalogs of the objects in their digital collections. As in MARC21, metadata standards are tags for specific fields of information.

XML—eXtensible Markup Language

HTML is the language of web design and Internet searches. Most web pages are written in the computer code of HTML. Metadata describes the *relationships* of the object to other data, whether people, events, time, or place. XML is code that describes relationships between data. Metadata uses HTML to present information, but XML tags that describe the relationships are also required. Collection management systems have XML embedded in the HTML code so that related data can be properly linked.

MODS—Metadata Object Description Standard

Unfortunately, there is no quick and easy way today to convert a MARC21 record to a metadata standard record. There are too many differences between the fields of information for the two standards to neatly overlap. Another problem with conversion is the loss of data, especially around relationships fields. However, becoming familiar with MODS (Metadata Object Description Standard) may be the easiest way for staff, especially those who catalog in MARC21, to begin to learn about and work with metadata.

MODS is supported by the Library of Congress, which provides many good resources for beginner MODS catalogers.[2] Guidelines are provided that help new metadata catalogers to create original MODS records and to convert MARC21 records to MODS. MODS and MARC21 use tags differently. MODS and other metadata standards use XML coding language that requires that line information be preceded with metatag information:

Table 6.2. Comparison of Title Entry between MARC21 and MODS

MARC21—Title Tag and Field	MODS—XML Coded Title
245 (a) Trophy won by sailboat *Moondyne* in 1889.	**<mods:titleInfo> <mods:title>** Trophy won by sailboat Moondyne in 1889**<mods:/title> </mods:titleInfo>**

The text between <mods:title> and <mods:/title> is the title of the trophy. The HTML code </mods:titleInfo> *that appears before and after* the title in the MODS

Photo 6.2. Sailing trophy.

example is necessary to demark the title information so that the program will slot the information in the title line.

Let's compare MARC21 and MODS. Coding the title of the sailboat trophy *Moondyne* in MARC and coding its metadata require different sets of skills and information. However, the title could be copied and pasted from MARC21 into the title element metadata line of MODS. This process of transferring data is called mapping. Mapping is taking one set of data and bringing it to another place where it makes sense. Mapping or transferring data from MARC21 is an efficient way to learn and use metadata because some of the elements of MODS are the same as the tags and fields of MARC21.

Some of the common elements of MODS that can be mapped to MARC21 (or vice versa) are the following:

1. Title
2. Name
3. Language
4. Physical Description
5. Note
6. Subject
7. Date

Elements that cannot be neatly mapped between the two because MARC21 does not provide a place for this information are the following MODS standards:

1. Related items
2. Identifier
3. Access condition
4. Extension
5. Part
6. Record Info

TEXTBOX 6.2. PRACTICE

Print a simple MARC21 record from a library online catalog and try mapping as many data as possible to MODS elements. Congratulations! If you are a novice, you created your first of many metadata records!

Dublin Core

A second common metadata standard is Dublin Core. The standard is named for the city of Dublin, Ohio, where OCLC is headquartered and where the standard was initiated to catalog objects on the web in 1995. Over the past twenty years Dublin Core has been adopted as the standard for metadata by museums and libraries over the world.

As is the case with MODS, Dublin Core element data are inputted in XML computer code. Also similar to MODS, Dublin Core consists of a handful of elements that may be mapped from MARC. Unfortunately, catalogers cannot retrieve enough descriptive and relationship data about how an object was made and what it was used for from a MARC record, even with the additional RDA requirements. They need to conduct research about the item or use the outside resources to create complete elements records in Dublin Core. There are currently fifteen elements of data that describe a digital object or resource in Dublin Core as shown in table 6.3:[3]

Table 6.3.   Dublin Core Metadata Elements

Contributor	Person, an organization, or a service that contributes to the resource
Coverage	A named place, location, period, date, or jurisdiction that applies to the resource
Creator	Responsible for creating the resource
Date	Point or period of time associated with the resource
Description	Descriptive information about the resource or primary source
Format	The file format, physical medium, or dimensions of the resource
Identifier	Classification or other information that formally identifies the resource
Language	Language of the resource
Publisher	Responsible for making the resource available
Relation	Related resource to this object
Rights	Information about rights held in and over the resource
Source	May be derived from the related resource in whole or in part
Subject	The topic of the resource
Title	Name given to the resource
Type	Nature or genre of the resource

Each element may be used more than once, and some elements may not be used at all. For example, the famous digital image of Neil Armstrong landing on the moon in 1969 may have multiple relations, such as to the other Apollo 11 astronauts Buzz Aldrin and Michael Collins, the Navy, NASA, Armstrong's family members, his academic career, and so forth. Dublin Core leaves clues of relationships of the item to another person, place, time period, material type, or event. Our national libraries, museums, and other institutions with sizable digital collections use the Dublin Core system of metadata to classify and catalog resources.

Table 6.4.   Creating Metadata

Dimensions	Approximately 3" tall × 2.75" wide × 2" long
Material	Plastic
Color/Style	Blue, Green, Orange, Pink, Yellow
Instructions and More Details	Runs on sunlight via the solar cell on the upper front of the base.
WARNING	CHOKING HAZARD: Small parts. Not for children under 3 yrs.

The University of Mississippi provides a good approach to begin cataloging with Dublin Core. They suggest that the elements can be broken into two categories: mandatory elements and recommended elements.[4] Of course, all elements should be found if possible. But if it is not possible, staff can create a basic record using the mandatory elements of title, creator, subject, description, date, format, identifier, and rights management. Rights management is important because it describes copyright, property rights, and how the digital item may or may not be reproduced or used.

Dublin Core Activity

With practice we all can become proficient catalogers of metadata! Gather the metadata of personal or family objects. Table 6.4 shows the artifact of a solar desk ornament (photo 6.3). Let's create its metadata! (Note that there can be more than one entry for each element.)

Table 6.5.   Identifying Metadata by Dublin Core Elements

Title	Solar Dancing Flower
Creator	Office Playground
Subject	Toys
	Solar Toys
Dimensions	Approximately 3" tall × 2.75" wide × 2" long
Date	2014
Format	Plastic, solar collector
Identifier	http://www.officeplayground.com/solar-dancing-flower-smile-face-mini-p5091.html?gclid=CPaMxp3i8swCFUQehgodt1UHLg
Relation	Toy is powered by solar. It is used for amusement or as a stress reliever.

Because Dublin Core is coded in XML, metadata records are available through keyword searches on the Internet.

Photo 6.3. Solar Dancing Flower.

BIBFRAME

BIBFRAME was introduced earlier in this chapter as the future replacement for MARC21. We should also be aware that the URI, or linking of each element line of BIBFRAME, has the potential to be hyperlinked to websites and other authority data that will further describe the digital object.

Because BIBFRAME is also coded in XML, libraries will need only one system for cataloging and metadata, not the multiple systems required today. In summary, important benefits of BIBFRAME are as follows:

- BIBFRAME links data elements about an object to websites and other information sources on the web.
- The Internet will be the one place for library patrons to search both traditional library materials and digital objects.
- Catalogers will have one standard for their work that incorporates all rules and practices for creating records.
- BIBFRAME will provide the means for library staff to catalog and create metadata for digital objects that, in turn, will spur libraries to invest in creating local digital collections that may be shared worldwide.

Library staff can prepare for future changes in national cataloging standards by following the Library of Congress website on BIBFRAME found at www.loc.gov/

bibframe. In addition to providing general information, the website also has links to new vocabulary catalogers will need to know and a description of what the BIBFRAME model will ultimately be. Updates on implementation and testing are also found here. Catalogers, particularly those who work in library technical services, should learn about BIBFRAME now and participate in cataloging workshops. The Library of Congress will soon be making decisions about when BIBFRAME will replace MARC21. We all need to be prepared!

METADATA MANAGEMENT SYSTEMS

There are many options for libraries and museums to host and use metadata for staff and patrons. All systems use embedded XML code and are potentially searchable on the Internet. We will examine a few of the options libraries and museums have today for displaying and managing metadata.

PastPerfect

One of the most common collection management systems is PastPerfect.[5] This Windows-based application is one of the most affordable systems, making it an attractive option for small museums and libraries to manage their digital collections. The templates of PastPerfect are user-friendly. Metadata can be created for such things as lace and other objects of clothing from the nineteenth century. PastPerfect can also manage metadata for scanned journals, letters, and diaries. Data from Excel can be uploaded into PastPerfect. PastPerfect is an excellent choice for any library or museum to manage and display metadata of digital objects.

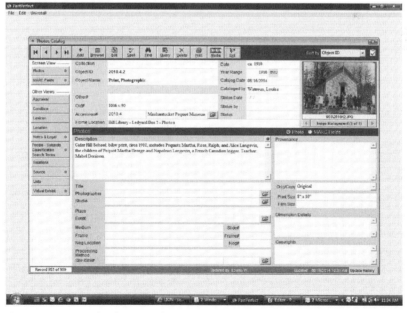

Figure 6.1. Example of a PastPerfect Record.

Greenstone Digital Library Software—Open Source

Greenstone Digital Library Software is open-source, multilingual software available at little or no cost to the user. It was developed in cooperation with UNESCO and Human Info NGO. UNESCO, the educational arm of the United Nations, is committed to sharing educational, scientific, and cultural information throughout the world. Creating and sharing digital resources, particularly among third world and developing countries, is a way for UNESCO to use technology to support educational standards and goals. Human Info NGO is located in Belgium and provides data processing and dissemination services to the United Nations and developing countries using open-source software and websites. The creation of digital libraries is a way Human Info NGO can

- facilitate access to information
- create new ways for education dissemination
- assist developing countries in the fight against poverty
- provide solutions for current global issues[6]

Library staff who work with organizations that increase awareness of and help people in developing countries may be interested in digital collection projects that could be shared using Greenstone Digital Library Software. The software is compatible with Windows, Macintosh, and Linux platforms, and the Greenstone website has much documentation on how to download the software and get started.

Web Publishing Sites

Two examples of web publishing sites are Gallery Systems and WordPress. Gallery Systems eMuseum works with metadata templates.[7] A library or museum that desires a website with a seamless "look" can customize the collection management side to match the display of the library website. Library staff would refresh and publish new data locally to keep the site current. WordPress is used by the Connecticut Digital Archive hosted by the University of Connecticut.[8] An open-source project, it is free for anyone to use and has a history of reliability. WordPress is used to host 17 percent of the web, and it is run on larger platforms (not local computers). In addition to supporting websites, blogs, and other communications, WordPress works with metadata systems including Dublin Core.

In this section you have been introduced to several options for managing and hosting digital collections metadata. However, there are many other fine products and solutions. Look at the Collection Management Systems/Software chart for additional vendor products and descriptions.[9]

SUMMARY

You may be asking, "How can I help my library get started on creating and hosting metadata?" Here are some of the issues for librarians:

1. Libraries are vested in integrated library systems (ILS) that require cataloging in MARC and display the labeled format of MARC. Taking on a second system for cataloging metadata and collection management can be daunting!
2. MARC tags and fields do not align neatly with metadata fields, so full migration of metadata to MARC is not possible.
3. A second online catalog for digital collections could be confusing for patrons and costly for the library to purchase and maintain.
4. Until BIBFRAME becomes our national standard, there is no perfect integration of metadata and MARC systems.

Library staff can support the digitization of local library collections by becoming familiar with metadata. Learn the basics and do not be afraid! Have fun creating metadata at home or using common objects. Once you have gained confidence, begin creating metadata for library "treasures" that patrons do not see. Ask your supervisor if you can digitize the object and then create metadata records similar to those for the solar dancing flower artifact. Is it possible for the library to acquire PastPerfect? PastPerfect is a great solution for a small project or library. If you cannot immediately obtain a license, download the free trial and demonstrate to your supervisor and other library staff its great potential. Library staff who know the role of technology in creating, identifying, retrieving, and accessing information resources and demonstrate facility with appropriate information discovery tools can successfully lead others to adopt digitization of important resources as a key library service.

DISCUSSION QUESTIONS AND ACTIVITY

Discussion Questions

1. What is metadata?
2. What are the similarities between metadata and MARC tags? What are some differences?
3. How has technology increased the use of metadata in libraries? In what ways?
4. Why is it important for LSS to learn about metadata and be able to use it at work?
5. In what collections in your library would you recommend the cataloger use metadata rather than MARC? Why?

Activity: Metadata Grab Bag

Collect a brown bag of odds and ends from around the house and office and create Dublin Core metadata about them. Use the Internet and other reference sources to find out more about the object to enable full metadata.

- Objects can be such things as a ruler, egg timer, small statue, small toy, and so forth. Test your own skills by creating metadata about objects you encounter in your home. Think of having a contest on a mundane day with other library staff, seeing who can create the most metadata on the oddest things.

- A most unusual metadata experience could be with a vegetable, such as a potato. Find as many points of data (metadata) as you can about its size, shape, buds, marks, and the like.

Remember: practice, practice, practice will hone your metadata skills!

NOTES

1. Karen Coyle, "Understanding Metadata and its Purpose," *Journal of Academic Librarianship* 31, no. 2 (2005): 160–63, available at kcoyle.net/jal-31-2.html.

2. "MODS: Metadata Object Description Schema," Library of Congress, last modified February 1, 2016, at www.loc.gov/standards/mods/ (accessed September 15, 2016).

3. "Using Dublin Core—The Elements," Metadata Innovation, last modified November 2005, at dublincore.org/documents/usageguide/elements.shtml (accessed December 31, 2014).

4. "University of Mississippi Users' Guide for Dublin Core Metadata Cataloging," Digital Accounting Collection, University of Mississippi, at www.olemiss.edu/depts/general_library/dac/files/user_guide.html (accessed December 31, 2014).

5. "Museum Software," PastPerfect Museum Software, at www.museumsoftware.com/ (accessed December 31, 2014).

6. "About Us," Human Info NGO, at humaninfo.org/about_us.html (accessed December 31, 2014).

7. "TMS 2014," Gallery Systems, at www.gallerysystems.com/tms-2014-new-features (accessed December 31, 2014).

8. "About WordPress," WordPress, at wordpress.org/about/ (accessed December 31, 2014).

9. Bob Schmidtt, "Collection Management Systems/Software, Ver. 1.2," Car Collections and Digital Technology, at carlibrary.org/CMS-Table.htm accessed December 27, 2014).

REFERENCES, SUGGESTED READINGS, AND WEBSITES

Coyle, Karen. "Understanding Metadata and Its Purpose." *Journal of Academic Librarianship* 31, no. 2 (2005): 160–63. Available at kcoyle.net/jal-31-2.html.

Dublin Core Metadata Initiative. "Using Dublin Core—The Elements." Metadata Innovation. Accessed December 31, 2014, at dublincore.org/documents/usageguide/elements.shtml.

Gallery Systems. "TMS 2014." Accessed December 31, 2014, at www.gallerysystems.com/tms-2014-new-features.

Gill, Tony, Anne Gilliland, Maureen Whalen, and Mary S. Woodley. *Introduction to Metadata*. Online version, 3rd ed. Los Angeles: Getty, 2008. Available at www.getty.edu/research/publications/electronic_publications/intrometadata/index.html.

Human Info NGO. "About Us." Accessed December 31, 2014, at humaninfo.org/about_us.html.

LeBlanc, Jim, and Martin Kurth. "An Operational Model for Library Metadata Maintenance." *Library Resources and Technical Services* 52, no. 1 (January 2008): 54–59.

Lee, Seungim, and Elin Jacob. "An Integrated Approach to Metadata Interoperability: Construction of a Conceptual Structure between MARC and FRBR." *Library Resources and Technical Services* 55, no. 1 (January 2011): 17–32.

Library of Congress. "MODS: Metadata Object Description Schema." Last modified November 24, 2014. Accessed December 31, 2015, at www.loc.gov/standards/mods/.

New Zealand Digital Library Project. "About Greenstone." Greenstone Digital Library Software. Accessed December 31, 2014, at www.greenstone.org/.

PastPerfect Software. "Museum Software." Accessed December 31, 2014, at www.museum software.com/.

Schmidtt, Bob. "Collection Management Systems/Software, Ver. 1.2." Car Collections and Digital Technology. Accessed December 27, 2014, at carlibrary.org/CMS-Table.htm.

University of Mississippi Libraries. "University of Mississippi Users' Guide for Dublin Core Metadata Cataloging." Digital Accounting Collection. Accessed December 31, 2014, at www.olemiss.edu/depts/general_library/dac/files/user_guide.html.

WordPress. "About WordPress." Accessed December 31, 2014, at wordpress.org/about/.

PART 2

Classification of Library Materials

CHAPTER 7

Dewey Decimal Classification System

LSS know and can apply the basics of classification and organization schemes for collections. (ALA-LSSC Cataloging and Classification Competency 4)

LSS know and can explain the value and purpose of cataloging and classification to help users find the resources that they seek. (ALA-LSSC Cataloging and Classification Competency 7)

Key Terms

Abridged Dewey. A shortened version of the Dewey Decimal Classification System used by small libraries.

Call number. The Dewey Decimal or Library of Congress classification number used to organize library collections by topic or subject.

DDC23. The abbreviation for the twenty-third edition of the Dewey Decimal classification system.

Fixed location. Prior to Dewey, a new book was assigned a designation, such as an accession number, that set its permanent location at a specific place on a shelf.

Relative index. An alphabetical listing of the topics of knowledge found in DDC23, with associated call numbers.

Relative location. Location of an item with or near other books on the same topic or subject using the Dewey classification system, but not located in a permanent or fixed place on a shelf. Item locations will shift or change shelves according to how a collection grows.

Topics of knowledge. Another name for all possible subjects known to humankind and able to be classified by Melvil Dewey's system.

Unabridged Dewey. The full version of the Dewey Decimal classifications recommended for libraries with more than twenty thousand items in their collections.

INTRODUCTION

Up until now we have discussed cataloging in terms of the data or processes used in creating bibliographic, holding, and item records. In this and the next two chapters, our focus will shift to the classification of library materials. Classification is a unique arm of cataloging that involves establishing Dewey or LC **call numbers** and LC subject headings that describe the contents of the item. In this chapter we will learn about and enhance our skills using the Dewey Decimal call number system.

CLASSIFICATION

Classification is the process of assigning items into groups based on ways they are alike. Classification can also be the arrangement or organization of things that are similar.[1] Catalogers do both with library resources. We assign items a call number based on their subject content so that materials on the same topic will be grouped together. The call number also serves to organize items on library shelves so that collections of similar genre, format, or level will be housed together. Within each collection, such as nonfiction, YA (young adult), or media, the call number will further function to group items by common subject content and author.

050 and 082 Fields

Within the MARC bibliographic record there are fields for classification. The 050 field is for the Library of Congress call number. The 082 field is for the Dewey Decimal call number. Textbox 7.1 shows the 082 field, and textbox 7.2 demonstrates how the call number for *The Encyclopedia of Volcanoes* (Academic Press, 2000) is constructed.

TEXTBOX 7.1. 082 FIELD

082—DEWEY DECIMAL CLASSIFICATION NUMBER (R)
Indicators
First—Type of edition
#—No edition information recorded (BK CF MU VM SE) [OBSOLETE]
0—Full edition
1—Abridged edition
2—Abridged NST version (BK MU VM SE) [OBSOLETE]
7—Other edition specified in subfield $2
Second—Source of classification number
#—No information provided
0—Assigned by LC
4—Assigned by agency other than LC
Subfield Codes
$a—Classification number (R)
$b—Item number (NR)
$b—DDC number—abridged NST version (SE) [OBSOLETE]
$m—Standard or optional designation (NR)
$q—Assigning agency (NR)

Here is an example of the construction of a Dewey call number:

TEXTBOX 7.2. CALL NUMBER FOR *THE ENCYCLOPEDIA OF VOLCANOES*

```
082 00 551.21/03|2 21
082     MARC Field
0       Full edition
0       Assigned by Library of Congress in CIP
551.21  Dewey number for Volcanoes
03      3 volume set Encyclopedia
2       subfield 2
21      LC used twenty-first edition of Dewey Decimal
        Classifications
        (in year 2000 when published)
```

When a prepublication item is accepted by the Library of Congress for Cataloging in Publication (CIP), the item is assigned both a LC call number and a Dewey Decimal call number. While catalogers often accept the call number given in CIP, there are numerous times when the number does not work within the local library collection. The cataloger has the option to modify or change the call number. Remember, cataloging is both an "art" and a "science," and the classification of materials allows local discretion.

For the remainder of this chapter we will focus on the Dewey Decimal system, beginning with its history.

MELVIL DEWEY

Melvil Dewey was born in Adams Center, New York, in 1851 and lived to be eighty years of age. As a young person he was influenced by many social and religious reform movements that were popular in upstate New York in the nineteenth century, including those seeking equal educational, religious, and economic rights for women and minorities. His parents taught him social responsibility and the value of education. While attending Amherst College in the early 1870s, he worked in the library for pocket money and became frustrated with the inefficient way books were catalogued and shelved chronologically in the order they were purchased and received. Dewey studied the problem by comparing the Amherst system to the systems used by other libraries to arrange their shelves. And then, in Dewey's words, "After months of study, one Sunday during a long sermon [in church] . . . the solution flasht over me so that I jumpt in my seat and came very near to shouting, 'Eureka!'"[2]

What came to Dewey was an idea for representing all **topics of knowledge** with numbers, using decimals for specificity. Rather than using acquisitions, item size, book cover color, author's name, or other common methods of classification, Dewey decided that any subject content could slot into one of ten broad knowledge categories. Thus he chose the "decimal"—the number ten. "Decimal" in simple terms means relating or pertaining to tenths or the number ten. The numbers within the ten categories of knowledge expanded or became longer as the topic or content of the book became more specific. One of the great benefits of the Dewey Decimal system is that there is always room for new topics in any of the broad ten categories because call numbers can be expanded from the general topic numbers for more specificity or for related new ideas.

From being a college student with a new way of classifying library books, Dewey went on to become one of the most highly regarded professional librarians in the world. In 1876 he was elected the first secretary of the American Library Association and twice served as its president. He was hired as a librarian for Columbia College in New York City; while there, he established the Columbia School of Library Economy (the first of its kind in the nation), which admitted women as students. Dewey was an early advocate of training and employing women as librarians and can be credited with opening the library profession to women.[3] Dewey continued his career as director of the New York State Library. Always on the edge of recalcitrance, his was a life not without controversy—he even changed his first name "Melville" to "Melvil." But Dewey always remembered his roots, was committed to reform, and was passionate about helping others succeed.

Photo 7.1. Melvil Dewey. Library of Congress.

Libraries Use the Dewey or LC Classification Systems

Libraries have a choice between using Dewey Decimal call numbers or the Library of Congress call numbers for their collections. In the United States, most public, school, and small academic libraries use Dewey as a method for organizing books so that books on the same subject are near each other on the shelves.[4] Public libraries as prestigious as the New York Public Library and the Los Angeles Public Library use Dewey. Dewey is expandable, and, being based on the number ten, it is a logical system that library staff and most patrons can understand. Dewey works very well for collections where there are a limited number of items on any one subject. For example, if a high school library has fifty books on manned space flight, patrons can readily make their selection from within the fifty books, located next to each other on the shelf, that are classified with the Dewey number for this topic (629.45).

On the other hand, most research institutions and larger colleges and universities use the Library of Congress Classification (LCC) system that was created in 1891 specifically to meet the needs of the Library of Congress collection. It is based on twenty-one classes designated by a single letter and further divided into subclasses.[5] Purdue University has a School of Aeronautics and Astronautics with an extensive collection of materials on manned space flight.[6] Purdue's most famous alumnus is Neil Armstrong, who took the first steps on the moon on July 20, 1969. The university graduated twenty-three astronauts, and forty-seven alumni have flown on forty-seven space shuttle missions. With numerous materials dedicated to manned space flight, Purdue requires the extensive designations provided by the Library of Congress call numbers to classify its materials. It would be an impossible task to locate a specific item if thousands and thousands of materials all had the same Dewey call number (629.45). The LCC system provides extensive collections many more subtopics with greater specificity.

Photo 7.2.   Neil Armstrong Moon Landing. Library of Congress.

Most public, school, and small to medium-sized academic libraries use the Dewey Decimal classification system because they do not have large collections in just a few concentrated topics of knowledge. When the materials of library collections are diverse and come from all topics of knowledge, the subdivisions of Dewey work well for classification.

DEWEY DECIMAL CLASSIFICATION (DDC)

Prior to Melvil Dewey, libraries numbered books according to their locations on the shelves, which was often by accession or order of purchase. This was called a **fixed location** because once the book had a shelf designation, it did not change regardless of how many books were acquired after it. New books were added after the last book on the shelf, receiving their own fixed location. Dewey introduced two new features: **relative location** and **relative index**.[7] Books receive call numbers in terms of their relationship to one another without regard for the shelves or rooms where they are placed. Relative location allows indefinite intercalation; books can be moved about in the library without altering their call numbers.

The relative index shows the connection between subjects and the disciplines in which they appear. Subjects are listed alphabetically. Under each subject, the disciplines in which the subject is found are listed alphabetically. In the print version of the DDC, the disciplines are indented under the subject. In the electronic version, the disciplines appear as subheadings associated with the subject.[8]

Tools

There are many places a cataloger can find the Dewey Decimal tools. Just as the American Library Association takes responsibility for cataloging rules and the Library of Congress has assumed authority for MARC standards, OCLC has responsibility for the Dewey Decimal Classification (DDC).

OCLC provides many resources for catalogers. It sells both print and electronic or web versions of the DDC. The DDC is updated regularly by OCLC as world events, cultural changes, the arts, literature, and even patterns of life spur new publications. New knowledge and advances in areas such as law, education, science, medicine, and technology require new Dewey classifications so that libraries have a place in their collections for new items. OCLC and the LC consult with each other to revise DDC to keep it current and responsive to today's materials.

Print

Since Melvil Dewey there have been twenty-three **unabridged** editions of the DDC. Libraries with collections over twenty thousand items should consider the unabridged version that comprises four volumes.

Libraries with collections of fewer than twenty thousand items may consider using the **abridged** version of DDC. The abridged version has been revised fifteen times and is aptly titled DDC15. This one-volume text is more affordable for small libraries where subdivisions of knowledge areas are not as specific. For example, a small library with ten books on paranormal phenomena may give all of the books

Table 7.1. Unabridged Dewey Decimal Classifications (DDC)

Volume 1	Introduction, features, glossary, manual for using DDC, and tables with notations for adding greater specificity to DDC
Volume 2	DDC summaries: the top three levels of the DDC Schedules: the organization of knowledge from 000 through 599
Volume 3	Schedules: the organization of knowledge from 600 through 999
Volume 4	Relative index: an alphabetical list of subjects with the disciplines in which they are treated arranged alphabetically under each entry

Source: "Dewey Services," OCLC, www.oclc.org/dewey/features.en.html#print (accessed January 29, 2106).

the DDC number 130, whereas a library with a larger collection would subdivide the paranormal collection into groups of books on apparitions or ghosts (133.1), witches (133.4), or astrology (133.5).

WebDewey

The resources of DDC23 are available in an online subscription called Web-Dewey. This database provides catalogers with quick and easy way to build call numbers because, in addition to the relative index, it provides many other topic or access points to the call numbers.[9] It also has many prebuilt numbers for specific topics, such as a time and place in history that catalogers would typically have had to compile on their own using multiple sources in the four-volume print DDC23. Library catalogers who are also members of OCLC WorldCat can check Dewey numbers in OCLC automatically with WebDewey. WebDewey can also help catalogers with subject authority control because LC subject headings are associated with Dewey class numbers. With quarterly updates, catalogers do not have to wait for the next print edition to have the most recent version.

Library directors have to weigh the cost of purchasing the print version of DDC23, which will not be replaced for a few more years, against the annual subscription fee of WebDewey, which is always updated and takes much less time for a cataloger to use. Prices are available from OCLC, and subscriptions to WebDewey can be had according to the number of catalogers licensed to use it per library.

TEXTBOX 7.3. ENHANCED WORKFLOW WITH WEBDEWEY[10]

WebDewey provides the following:

- Flexible searching of the WebDewey database.
- Browsing of indexes of DDC23 numbers, the relative index, and Library of Congress Subject Headings.
- Hierarchical displays that show the position of each class number in relation to broader and narrower classes.
- Extensive use of hyperlinks for convenient access to related records.
- Links from Library of Congress Subject Headings listed in a record to the corresponding subject authority records.
- Displays of the ten main classes and the DDC23 tables that enable top-down navigation through the DDC23.

HOW DEWEY WORKS

To create a Dewey number, a cataloger may use one or more of the three tools provided in the four volumes of DDC23 or the databases of WebDewey. The more general the topic of knowledge, the less a cataloger may have to do to create the call number. The three main tools found in DDC23 are the relative index, schedules, and tables.

Relative Index

The relative index in the print version of DDC23 is found in volume 4, the last in the set. However, for many catalogers volume 4 is where they begin to determine the call number. In WebDewey, browsing the relative index can occur at any time because it is linked to schedules, tables, and the LC catalog.

Dewey Decimal Classification

Disabled veterans	362.408 697	Disciples of Christ (continued)	
legal status	343.011 6	religious group	T7—266
social welfare	362.408 697	seminaries	207.116 6
Disadvantaged workers		theology	230.66
public administration	350.836	Discipline	
central governments	351.836	armed forces	355.13
local governments	352.943 6	law	343.014
Disarmament	327.174	education	371.5
ethics	172.4	home child care	649.64
religion	291.562 4	labor economics	331.259 8
Christianity	241.624	labor unions	331.873
see also Political ethics		legislators	328.366
international politics	327.174	personnel management	658.314
law	341.733	public administration	350.147
military science	355.03	central governments	351.147
social theology	291.178 7	local governments	352.005 147
Christianity	261.87	prisons	365.643
Disassembling tools	621.93	Disco dancing	793.33
Disaster insurance	368.122	Discoglossidea	
see also Insurance		paleozoology	567.8
Disaster nursing		Discoglossoidea	597.84
medicine	610.734 9	Discographies	011.38
Disaster relief	363.348	Discount	332.84
law	344.053 4	Discount rates	332.84
Disasters	904	economics	332.84
international law	341.766	central banking	332.113
law	344.053 4	macroeconomic policy	339.53
management aspects	658.477	Discount stores	381.149
personal safety	613.69	management	658.879
psychology	155.935	see also Commerce	
social effects	303.485	Discourse analysis	
social services	363.34	linguistics	401.41
public administration	350.754	specific languages	T4—014 1
central governments	351.754	rhetoric	808 001 4
local governments	352.935 4	Discoveries in geography	910.9
Disc recordings		Discoveries in natural history	508
sound reproduction	621.389 32	Discoveries in science	509
Discarding		Discovery	
library collections	025.216	archaeological technique	930.102 82
museology	069.51	Discovery (Law)	347.072
Discarnate spirits	133.9	criminal law	345.072
Discharge (Military personnel)	355.114	Discrete-time systems	003.83
Discharged offenders	364.8	Discriminant analysis	519.535
labor economics	331.51	Discriminants	
Discifloral plants	583.2	number theory	512.74
Disciples of Christ	286.6	Discrimination	305
biography	286.609 2	ethics	177.5
church government	262.066	see also Ethical problems	
parishes	254.066	social theology	291.178 34
church law	262.986 6	Christianity	261.834
doctrines	230.66	Discrimination (Psychology)	152.1
catechisms and creeds	238.66	quantitative studies	152.82
guides to Christian life	248.486 6	Discrimination in education	370.193 4
missions	266.66	law	344.079 8
moral theology	241.046 6	Discrimination in employment	331.133
public worship	264.066	labor unions	331.873 2
religious associations	267.186 6	law	344.011 33
religious education	268.866	Discrimination in housing	363.51

184

Figure 7.1.   Example of a Relative Index Page. Internet Archive.

The index in the back of a book is used to find a specific topic within the text. Likewise, the purpose of the relative index is to locate specific Dewey numbers. The topics of knowledge are arranged alphabetically, and next to each topic is its corresponding Dewey call number. For example, the general topic of medicine corresponds to 616. But if a type of medicine is specified, such as home remedies (616.024) or emergency medicine (616.025), the call number gets longer as the topic becomes more specific. The relative index pinpoints an exact call number without having to search the schedules. The downside of the relative index may be that the term a cataloger is searching in the index may not be the best or only topic of the item content.

Vocabulary

There is a vocabulary to use in order to clearly discuss how the Dewey system works. Table 7.2 contains the important terms catalogers need to know.

Table 7.2. Vocabulary

Class	A group of objects exhibiting one or more common characteristics.
Main Class	One of the ten major groups of the DDC, numbered 0 through 9, represented by the first digit of notation.
Division	The second level of subdivision in the DDC, represented by the first two digits in the notation, such as 81 in 810 American Literature.
Section	The third level of subdivision in the DDC, represented by the first three digits in the notation, such as 812 in 812 American Poetry.
DDC Summaries	A listing of the first three levels (main classes, divisions, and sections) of the Dewey Decimal Classification system.
Subdivision	Notation that may be added to other numbers to make a class number appropriately specific to the work being classified.
Summary	A listing of the chief subdivisions of a class that provides an overview of its structure.
Schedules	Listings of subjects and their subdivisions arranged in a systematic order with notation given for each subject and its subdivisions. The series of DDC numbers 000 through999, along with their headings and notes.
Tables	In the DDC, lists of notation that may be added to other numbers to make a class number appropriately specific to the work being classified. The numbers found in a table are never used alone.
Standard Subdivisions	Subdivisions found in table 1 that represent frequently recurring physical forms (dictionaries, periodicals) or approaches (history, research) applicable to any subject or discipline.

Source: "Dewey Decimal Classification glossary," OCLC, at www.oclc.org/support/documentation/glossary/dewey.en.html#_R (accessed January 29, 2016).

Main Classes

Assigning all topics of knowledge to one of ten classes illustrates the brilliance of Melvil Dewey! Linking any topic to one of the ten main classes still works, even with the explosion of information in the twenty-first century. Table 7.3 lists the ten main classes and what they represent. Once the main class is selected, the next digit or notation is called the division.

Table 7.3.   Main Classes of DDC

000	Computer science, information, & general works
100	Philosophy & psychology
200	Religion
300	Social sciences
400	Language
500	Science
600	Technology
700	Arts & recreation
800	Literature
900	History & geography

Divisions

The second notation is the first step in subdividing the classes. The division digit expands ten options to a hundred. Also called the "hundredths," the second notation or division is very important in categorizing information. The hundred divisions of Dewey can be found in Table 7.4. As shown, the second digit divides broad classes into areas of concentration. For example, within Natural Sciences and Math (500) there are several divisions, each a unique discipline of study.

Table 7.4.   Dewey 100 Divisions

000	**General reference, information & computers**	180	Ancient, medieval, oriental philosophy
		190	Modern western philosophy
010	Bibliography		
020	Library & information sciences	**200**	**Religion**
030	General encyclopedic works	210	Natural theology
040	Special topics	220	Bible
050	General serials & their indexes	230	Christian theology
060	General organizations & museums	240	Christian moral & devotional theology
070	News media, journalism, publishing	250	Christian orders & local churches
080	General collections	260	Christian social theology
090	Manuscripts & rare books	270	Christian church history
		280	Christian denominations & sects
100	**Philosophy & psychology**	290	Other & comparative religions
110	Metaphysics		
120	Epistemology, causation, humankind	**300**	**Social sciences**
130	Paranormal phenomena	310	General statistics
140	Specific philosophical schools	320	Political science
150	Psychology	330	Economics
160	Logic	340	Law
170	Ethics (moral philosophy)	350	Public administration

360	Social problems & services	680	Manufacture for specific use
370	Education	690	Buildings
380	Commerce, communications, transport	**700**	**Arts & Recreation**
390	Customs, etiquette, folklore	710	Civic & landscape art
		720	Architecture
400	**Language**	730	Sculpture
410	Linguistics	740	Drawings & decorative arts
420	English & Anglo-Saxon languages	750	Paintings & painters
430	Germanic languages (German)	760	Graphic arts (Printmaking & prints)
440	Romance languages (French)	770	Photography
450	Italian, Romanian, Rhaeto-Romanic	780	Music
460	Spanish & Portuguese languages	790	Recreational & performing arts
470	Italic languages (Latin)		
480	Hellenic languages (Classical Greek)	**800**	**Literature**
490	Other languages	810	American literature in English
		820	English literature
500	**Natural science & mathematics**	830	Literature of Germanic language
510	Mathematics	840	Literatures of Romance language
520	Astronomy & allied sciences	850	Italian, Romanian, Rhaeto-Romanic Literatures
530	Physics	860	Spanish & Portuguese literatures
540	Chemistry & allied sciences	870	Italic literatures (Latin)
550	Earth sciences	880	Hellenic literatures (Classical Greek)
560	Paleontology & Paleozoology	890	Literatures of other languages
570	Life sciences		
580	Botanical sciences	**900**	**History & geography**
590	Zoological sciences	910	Geography & travel
		920	Biography, genealogy, insignia
600	**Technology (applied sciences)**	930	History of the ancient world
610	Medical sciences (Medicine, Psychiatry)	940	General history of Europe
620	Engineering	950	General history of Asia (Far East)
630	Agriculture	960	General history of Africa
640	Home economics & family living	970	General history of North America
650	Management	980	General history of South America
660	Chemical engineering	990	General history of other areas
670	Manufacturing		

Source: "Dewey 100 Divisions," Dewey Decimal System: 100 divisions, last modified December 8, 2015, at semo.libguides.com/c.php?g=292234&p=1947032 (accessed January 29, 2016).

Sections

If the division classification is not specific enough to classify an item—and most often it is not—the cataloger moves to the third notation, called the section. The third digit expands the unit of ten to one thousand distinct topics of knowledge. Examples of sections are shown in table 7.5.

Table 7.5.   Examples of Sections

Main Class	300	Social sciences
Division	320	Political science
Section	326	Slavery and emancipation
Main Class	500	Natural sciences
Division	550	Earth sciences
Section	551	Geology, hydrology, meteorology
Main Class	700	Arts and recreation
Division	780	Music
Section	784	Ensembles with one instrument

The section is very important because it narrows the path for classification. For example, as you look at the three sections that were selected above, each is a subtopic of the division. But often the section topic is not enough, as a library would not want to place all of its books about musical instruments together. It would be better if each type of instrument—such as strings, keyboard, and percussion—had its own call number. And even better, within each type of instrument there could be a specific classification, such as for violin, guitar, and harp. We move to the schedules to find these deeper classifications.

Schedules

The bulk of the classification scheme is found in the schedules. In the unabridged DDC23, the schedules take up volumes 2 and 3. Volume 2 goes from 000 through 599. Volume 3 picks up with 600 through 999.

Libraries either purchase the print version of DDC23 or subscribe to WebDewey to have and use the most current schedules. For our purposes, older editions of the schedules, DDC19 and DDC20, are available on the web. We will use DDC20 to learn about schedules. However, if you have access to DDC23, please use it instead. Volume 3 of DDC20 can be found at archive.org/stream/deweydecimal cla03dewe#page/54/mode/2up. Find the other volumes of DDC20 by using the back arrow once, scroll down to the bottom of the screen, and click to use another volume.

The schedules are arranged by main classes, divisions, sections, and then subdivisions. All subdivisions follow the decimal point after the division. The call number 333.918 represents wetlands, a controversial social topic today. Textbox 7.4 shows how this number is constructed from the schedules and how it builds on the general concept of social sciences.

TEXTBOX 7.4. DEWEY CLASSIFICATION FOR WETLANDS

```
300 Social Sciences
330 Economics
333 Land Economics
333.91 Water
333.918 Wetlands
```

Catalogers have the authority to assign Dewey call numbers. They examine the item in hand and select the best match using DDC23 schedules. The decision is not always clear-cut, particularly if the item has more than one topic. If it does, the cataloger may have to go back "up the ladder" and select a more general call number.

The only way to become familiar with DDC is to use it, to peruse library collections organized with Dewey call numbers, and to study how items on the same subject end up next to each other.

Summaries

At regular places in the schedules, there are summaries of the upcoming main sections of the call number. Figure 7.2 shows a page from the beginning schedule and summary on the topic of psychology.

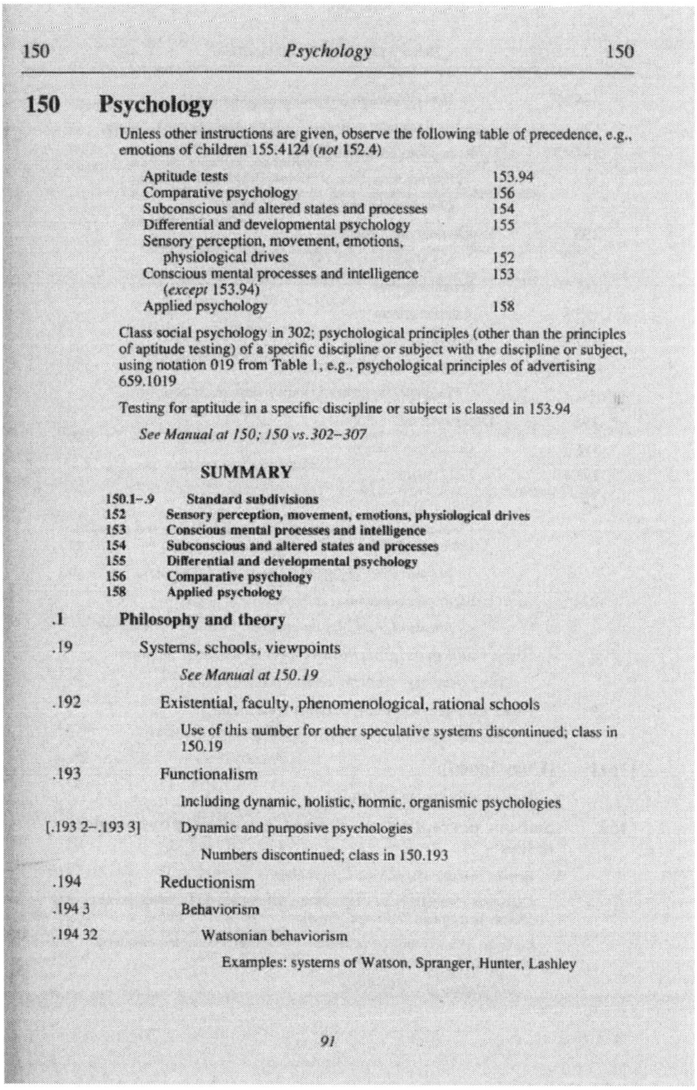

150 *Psychology* 150

150 Psychology

Unless other instructions are given, observe the following table of precedence, e.g., emotions of children 155.4124 (*not* 152.4)

Aptitude tests	153.94
Comparative psychology	156
Subconscious and altered states and processes	154
Differential and developmental psychology	155
Sensory perception, movement, emotions, physiological drives	152
Conscious mental processes and intelligence (*except* 153.94)	153
Applied psychology	158

Class social psychology in 302; psychological principles (other than the principles of aptitude testing) of a specific discipline or subject with the discipline or subject, using notation 019 from Table 1, e.g., psychological principles of advertising 659.1019

Testing for aptitude in a specific discipline or subject is classed in 153.94

See Manual at 150; 150 vs. 302–307

SUMMARY

150.1–.9	**Standard subdivisions**
152	**Sensory perception, movement, emotions, physiological drives**
153	**Conscious mental processes and intelligence**
154	**Subconscious and altered states and processes**
155	**Differential and developmental psychology**
156	**Comparative psychology**
158	**Applied psychology**

.1 **Philosophy and theory**

.19 Systems, schools, viewpoints

See Manual at 150.19

.192 Existential, faculty, phenomenological, rational schools

Use of this number for other speculative systems discontinued; class in 150.19

.193 Functionalism

Including dynamic, holistic, hormic, organismic psychologies

[.193 2–.193 3] Dynamic and purposive psychologies

Numbers discontinued; class in 150.193

.194 Reductionism

.194 3 Behaviorism

.194 32 Watsonian behaviorism

Examples: systems of Watson, Spranger, Hunter, Lashley

91

Figure 7.2. Example of a Schedule Page with Summary. "Dewey Decimal Classification and Relative Index," Internet Archive, archive.org/details/dewey decimalcla02dewe (accessed January 29, 2016).

If the summary division is not sufficient for classification, a cataloger will look further into the schedule for more exact number assignment. In figure 7.2 we can see that 151.1943, Behaviorism, identifies a specific theory of psychology and that books about the behaviorist John Watson would have the number 2 added to classify the collection of psychology books by specific scientist.

Tables

In addition to the schedules, there are several tables in DDC23 that catalogers use to add to or build call numbers. Some tables, such as 1, 2, and 4, are used more frequently. Tables for catalogers are found in textbox 7.5:

TEXTBOX 7.5. TABLES IN DDC

Table 1 Standard Subdivisions (for dictionaries, encyclopedias, and other formats)
Table 2 Geographic Areas, Historic Time Periods
Table 3 Individual Literatures
Table 4 Individual Languages
Table 5 Racial, Ethnic, and National Classes
Table 6 Languages
Table 7 Groups of Persons

Tables are found in volume 1 of DDC23 and are linked in WebDewey. The numbers found in a table are never used alone but rather are added or embedded into the regular call number. Subdivisions found in table 1 represent frequently recurring physical forms (dictionaries, periodicals) or approaches (history, research) applicable to any subject or discipline.[11] For example, the call number of *The Dictionary of Twentieth-Century History* has the dictionary designation of "03" added. Twentieth-century history would normally have the number 909.82 for history between 1900 and 1999. However, "03" is added from table 1 because of the dictionary format of the book.

Table 2 is used frequently for assigning geographical or historical significance. *Native Trees of Palau*, by Ann Kitalong, may begin with the call number 582.16 for trees but would have "966" (found in table 2) added to designate the country of Palau, an island in Micronesia in the Pacific Ocean, and thus would be classified as 582.16966.

Working with tables takes practice. There are rules catalogers are to follow when using the tables. Sometimes, for instance, digits are overlaid rather than repeated. Work carefully with tables and seek help from professional catalogers when in doubt.

ASSIGNING CALL NUMBERS

There are several steps a cataloger may take before digging into the schedules to find the correct call number. It is always good to look in these places. However, the final decision about any call number rests within the library, as local libraries have autonomy in deciding where an item best resides in a collection. Call numbers can be—and are—modified to fit the way library patrons will locate and use the resource.

TEXTBOX 7.6. ASSIGN DEWEY CALL NUMBERS

1. If the item is preprocessed, does the assigned call number from the vendor agree with where the items should be in your collection?
2. Look on the reverse side of the title page and find the Dewey number that was assigned by the LC in the CIP process.
3. If copying a MARC bibliographic record, look at the 082 tag for the Dewey number that was assigned either by the LC, OCLC, or your state or local union catalog.
4. Look at your own collection to see if there are other items on the topic.
5. If doubt persists or no call number can be found in these places, use DDC23 to construct the number.

Trust your judgment. If you have doubts about the classification, continue to examine the item to understand its contents and subject more fully.

Sometimes a cataloger will use all of these steps to find the correct call number, as classification is truly an art and a science!

Nonprint Library Resources

The Dewey Decimal Classification System is meant to classify all types of library materials in addition to books. Regardless of the resource's format—e-books, serials, manuscripts, pamphlets, software, film, images, audio, or any combination of media—the item can be classified by its topic and assigned a Dewey call number. While these items do not have title pages like books and will not have gone through the CIP prepublishing program, catalogers have the tools with DDC23 to assign numbers. Depending on the library, some media are classified by local systems that do not require Dewey numbers. However, many libraries integrate media with their regular bookshelves and thus need to classify those resources using Dewey call numbers.

ADDITIONAL RESOURCES

This chapter is meant to give library staff a working overview of the Dewey Decimal Classification System. There are many resources available online and from commercial vendors to assist catalogers, among them are a WebDewey subscription and the print version of DDC23. In addition, the following online resources in table 7.6 are among many that are available to enhance our learning.

Table 7.6. Web Resources for Dewey

OCLC Resources	Tutorials, updates, glossary, instructional guides	www.oclc.org/dewey/resources.en.html
OCLC Resources	Third-level summaries of DDC23	www.oclc.org/dewey/resources/summaries
University of Illinois	"Anatomy of a Call Number"	www.library.illinois.edu/circ/tutorial/anatomy.html
OCLC Classify	Experimental classification web service	classify.oclc.org/classify2/

Library staff can learn about cataloging using these additional resources along with the many mentioned in this chapter.

SUMMARY

In this chapter we were introduced to the art and science of classifying materials using the Dewey Decimal Classification, which is the oldest and most-used system by libraries in the United States. Using Dewey we can apply the basics of classification and organization schemes for any type of library resource collection or format. Library staff who know DDC can explain the value and purpose of cataloging and classification to help users find the resources that they seek.

DISCUSSION QUESTIONS AND ACTIVITIES

Discussion Questions

1. Why did Melvil Dewey develop his own classification system?
2. Explain the meaning of ten or "decimal" in the Dewey Decimal System.
3. Explain the purpose and differences between the Relative Index and the Schedules in DDC23.
4. Explain the meaning and differences between "main classes," "divisions," and "sections."
5. How are tables applied and used in creating a Dewey call number?
6. What steps does a cataloger take in making the final selection or creation of a Dewey call number?

Activity 1: Create Original Call Numbers

1. Use either DDC23 or WebDewey if you work in a Dewey library or, if you do not have access to current Dewey sources, use the older edition of DDC20 found at archive.org/details/deweydecimalcla04dewe.
2. Create Dewey numbers for items on the following topics of knowledge using the schedules and tables of DDC (for your own practice and learning, do not look up numbers in other sources).
3. Write down your call numbers next to each item and justify how you developed them.

TEXTBOX 7.7.

1. A book on kittens and puppies
2. A film on the Beatles
3. A computer game on space aliens
4. A book on dream interpretation
5. A book on block scheduling in high schools
6. A food-and-drink travel guide on the country of Belize
7. A biography of Taylor Swift
8. A history of the first railroads in Asia
9. A book of Cuban poetry in Spanish
10. A film on immigrants who passed through Ellis Island

Activity 2: Use the Experimental Classification Service of OCLC

1. Now that you have practiced creating original call numbers, try the experimental service of OCLC. It can be found at classify.oclc.org/classify2.
2. Using the same list of topics from Activity 1, try to locate Dewey numbers through this service by title or subject.
3. How similar were the numbers you created in Activity 1 to the results of your searches here?

NOTES

1. "Simple Definition of Classification" [Merriam-Webster Dictionary], Merriam-Webster, Incorporated, last modified 2015, at www.merriam-webster.com/dictionary/classification (accessed January 24, 2016).

2. Sarah Prescott, "If You Knew Dewey. . . ," *School Library Journal* 47, no. 8 (August 2001): 51–53.

3. Alden Whitman, ed., *American Reformers* (Bronx, NY: H. W. Wilson, 1985).

4. Jill Wiercioch, ed., "Basic Cataloging: Intro to Call Numbers," IPL2, last modified 2013, at ipl2server-2.ischool.drexel.edu/div/farq/deweyFARQ.html (accessed January 26, 2016).

5. Ibid.

6. "Our Role in the History of Spaceflight," Purdue in Space, www.purdue.edu/space/history.html (accessed January 26, 2016).

7. "Biography of Melville Dewey," Dewey Decimal in the UIUC Bookstacks, www.library.illinois.edu/circ/tutorial/biography.html (accessed January 29, 2016).

8. "Dewey Decimal Classification Glossary," Dewey Decimal Classification glossary, OCLC, at www.oclc.org/support/documentation/glossary/dewey.en.html#_R (accessed January 29, 2016).

9. Ibid.

10. Ibid.

11. "Dewey Decimal Classification Glossary."

REFERENCES, SUGGESTED READINGS, AND WEBSITES

Internet Archive. "Dewey Decimal Classification and Relative Index." Accessed January 29, 2016, at archive.org/details/deweydecimalcla02dewe.

Kent Library Research Guides. "Dewey 100 Divisions." Dewey Decimal System: 100 divisions. Last modified December 8, 2015. Accessed January 29, 2016, at semo.libguides.com/c.php?g=292234&p=1947032.

Library of Congress. "About Melvil Dewey (1851–1931)." Accessed January 24, 2016, at www.loc.gov/aba/dewey/about-dewey.html.

Online Computer Library Center (OCLC). "Dewey Decimal Classification Glossary." Accessed January 29, 2016, at www.oclc.org/support/documentation/glossary/dewey.en.html#_R.

———. "Dewey Services." Accessed January 29, 2016, at www.oclc.org/dewey/features.en.html#print.

———. "Introduction to the Dewey Decimal Classification." Accessed January 29, 2016, at www.oclc.org/content/dam/oclc/dewey/versions/print/intro.pdf.

Prescott, Sarah. "If You Knew Dewey. . . ." *School Library Journal* 47, no. 8 (August 2001): 50–53.

Purdue University. "Our Role in the History of Spaceflight." Purdue in Space. Accessed January 26, 2016, at www.purdue.edu/space/history.html.

University of Illinois. "Anatomy of a Call Number." Dewey Decimal in the UIUC Bookstacks. Accessed January 30, 2016, at www.library.illinois.edu/circ/tutorial/anatomy.html.

———. "Biography of Melville Dewey." Dewey Decimal in the UIUC Bookstacks. Accessed January 29, 2016, at www.library.illinois.edu/circ/tutorial/biography.html

Whitman, Alden, ed. *American Reformers*. Bronx, NY: H. W. Wilson, 1985.

Wiercioch, Jill, ed. "Basic Cataloging: Intro to Call Numbers." IPL2. Last modified 2013. Accessed January 26, 2016, at ipl2server-2.ischool.drexel.edu/div/farq/deweyFARQ.html.

CHAPTER 8

Library of Congress Classification System

LSS know and can apply the basics of classification and organization schemes for collections. (ALA-LSSC Cataloging and Classification Competency 4)

LSS know and can explain the value and purpose of cataloging and classification to help users find the resources that they seek. (ALA-LSSC Cataloging and Classification Competency 7)

Key Terms

Depository. A library or government facility where copies of works are kept and preserved. A depository does not necessarily circulate items.

Enumeration. A complete order or listing, usually by number such as the assignment of numbers to represent specific topics in the Library of Congress Classification System.

Expansion. A system of classifying books and other materials whereby main classes of subjects are further subdivided for specificity.

Main class. This is the broadest, most general division of topics.

Notation. Numerals, letters and symbols are used to represent the main and subordinate divisions of a library classification scheme. In the Dewey Decimal classification system, Arabic numbers are used to represent all topics or subjects. In the Library of Congress system, letters represent the main classes and divisions, and numbers and punctuation are used for greater specificity.

Repository. A building, usually in a central location, such as a library, where things may be stored.

Schema. A representation or plan, such as the Library of Congress classifications, that represent all topics of knowledge or the placement of books in the LC.

Subclass. A second or more specific division of general knowledge in a subject area.

INTRODUCTION

In the previous chapter we learned about the Dewey Decimal classification system. The second library classification system used in the United States is the Library of Congress Classification (LCC) system.

U.S. copyright law was established under the direction of Librarian of Congress Ainsworth Rand Spofford in 1870.[1] With this law, the Library of Congress (LC) became the **repository** for books, pamphlets, maps, music, prints, and photographs copyrighted in the United States. The LC used the Cutter Expansive Classification for organizing its materials, but it soon became clear neither it nor the Dewey Decimal system provided the flexibility to classify the largest library collection in the world.

Shortly after the opening of the new Library of Congress, a decision was made to develop an entirely new classification system specifically for the collections of the Library of Congress.[2] Based on the Cutter Expansive system, the LCC begins with a list of predetermined subjects listed in its classification tables.

CUTTER EXPANSIVE CLASSIFICATION

Charles Ammi Cutter created Cutter numbers and the Cutter Expansive Classification system. Later in this chapter Cutter numbers, used by many libraries today, will be explained.

Cutter was a graduate of both Harvard University and Harvard Divinity School, but he chose not to be ordained. Instead, he worked as a librarian at Harvard libraries from 1860 to 1868. While there, he experimented with the idea of a dictionary catalog that would be arranged on notecards for easy alphabetization rather than accession. Later, as librarian of the Boston Athenaeum, he experimented with the novel idea of adding subject headings to the notecards. His experiment later served as the basis of the Library of Congress Subject Headings. Cutter thought the Dewey Decimal system did not offer enough broad categories of classification for all of the Athenaeum's books, so he developed his own system called the Cutter Expansive Classification that was based on a broad **notation** of classes.[3]

TEXTBOX 8.1. CUTTER'S MAIN CLASSES[4]

A General works (encyclopedias, periodicals, society publications)
B–D Philosophy, Psychology, Religion
E, F, G Biography, History, Geography and travels
H–J, K Social sciences, Law
L–T Science and technology
U–VS Military, Sports, Recreation
VT, VV, W Theatre, Music, Fine arts
X Philology (the branch of knowledge that deals with the structure, historical development, and relationships of a language or languages)
Y Literature (expanded by language, and in English form)
Z Book arts, Bibliography

Expansions were made for more specific subjects within a class. Cutter published schedules for the first six expansions from 1891 through 1893. Portions of the seventh expansion were published from 1896 through 1911, but Cutter died before finishing work on it; most notably, the technology section remained unfinished. Textbox 8.2 shows an example of the Cutter Expansive system on the subject of medicine.[5] At the time Cutter created this table, he had expanded his system to four notations. Note that under "Remedies Other than Drugs," "Q" represents medicine, "QD" represents therapeutics, "QDO" represents remedies other than drugs. Taking the notations to the fourth expansion, "QDQI" represents vegetarianism, and "QDQU" represents a milk-and-grape cure.

TEXTBOX 8.2. THE CUTTER EXPANSIVE SYSTEM ON THE SUBJECT OF MEDICINE

QDO	Remedies Other than Drugs	QD6
QDP	Massage	QD61
QDQ	Alimentation, Diet	QD62
QDQA	Hygienic cookery	QD621
QDQE	Manuals for invalids	QD622
QDQI	Vegetarianism	QD623
QDQO	Graham cure	QD624
QDQU	Milk-and-grape cure	QD625
QDR	Metallotherapy, Perkin's Tractors	QD63
QDS	Pneumatic Aspirations	QD64
QDT	Rest cure	QD65
QDU	Bloodletting, Leeches, Cupping Scarification	QD66

Because Cutter had made no provision for the continuation of his system, the Library of Congress deemed the Cutter Expansive Classification unsuitable for its ever-growing collections. However, there are still a few libraries today that update Cutter and classify their materials with Cutter Expansive; one of them is Forbes Library in Northampton, Massachusetts.[6]

LIBRARY OF CONGRESS CLASSIFICATION SYSTEM

The Cutter Expansive System was the foundation the LC used to create its own classification **schema.**

LCC Vocabulary

Like Dewey, LCC has its own vocabulary about its structure. Before we can discuss the LCC system, we need to be comfortable with its special vocabulary.

Table 8.1.   LCC Vocabulary

Main Class	One of the twenty-one major groups of the LCC. Letters A through Z (except I, O, W, X, and Y) represent the first digit of notation. For example, **H** represents **Social Sciences**.
Subclass	The second level of division in the LCC is the **subclass**. It is represented by a second letter in the notation. For example, **HV** represents the subclass of **Social pathology. Social and public welfare**.
Enumeration or Numbers	The third level of division in the LCC is the **enumerative or number** classification. Numbers that represent common concepts are found in the LCC schedules or tables. After the subclass of **HV**, the number **547** represents **self-help groups**. Thus, to classify works about self-help programs, the LCC cataloger would use **HV547**.
Subdivision Schedules	**Subdivision** schedules with the alpha and enumeration codes are free and available from the Library of Congress Classification Outline.[1] The Classification Web is a subscription database with full specificity.[2]
Cutter Number	The Cutter Number follows the LCC classification to further distinguish the book. The Cutter Number indicates the author's last name or first word of the title of the book.
Edition / Year of Publication	The edition of a volume is the next part of the call number. The year of publication follows the Cutter number to indicate the edition.

1. "Library of Congress Classification Outline," Cataloging and Acquisitions, last modified 2016, accessed February 5, 2016, https://www.loc.gov/catdir/cpso/lcco/.
2. "World Wide Web access to Library of Congress Classification and Library of Congress Subject Headings," Classification Web, accessed February 5, 2016, https://classificationweb.net/.

The LCC system is, in some ways, less complicated than the Dewey Decimal system because there are fewer components needed to construct a call number. However, because the LCC is meant for much larger collections that require deeper and more specific classification, it may seem more complex. That is the case because the enumeration and assignment of Cutter numbers are distinct activities and do not necessarily logically follow the same alpha system of the main system and subclass system. In other words, the cataloger constructs the LCC call number from three different types of data—alpha, numeric, and Cutter Number.

Main Classes

Library items are grouped together on similar subjects by their call numbers. In a way that is similar to the Cutter Expansion Classification, the LCC begins with a one-letter alpha notation. The LCC was developed with just one collection—its own—in mind, so the classes are created for the Library of Congress resources. Its collection was primarily developed to be a **depository** of the items vetted through U.S. copyright law. A depository is an indefinite place of storage where items are archived. A depository is not necessarily a circulating library.

The LC was originally established to provide library service to both the House and the Senate, and it continues to do so. Because of this mission, many of its collections are in the areas of law, politics, military, and administration; its collections are less strong in the arts, science, and technology.[7] The twenty-one **main classes** reflect these collection biases. For example, there are two main classes for the history of America (E and F), but only one class for science (Q). Moreover, the U.S. Army (U) and U.S. Navy (V) have their own main classes.

Photo 8.1. Algebra Books with LCC "QA" Classification for Mathematics. Donald R. Welter Library, Three Rivers Community College, Norwich, CT.

Photo 8.2. "E" for History of the Americas. Donald R. Welter Library, Three Rivers Community College, Norwich, CT.

Subclasses

Once the main class is determined, the second division is the subclass. The **subclass** allows for more topics within the main class. Subdivisions begin to align the topic of the book with the call number. For instance, the main class of science (Q) has eleven subclasses:

TEXTBOX 8.4. SUBCLASSES OF SCIENCE "Q"[9]

QA Mathematics
QB Astronomy
QC Physics
QD Chemistry
QE Geology
QH Natural History / Biology
QK Botany
QL Zoology
QM Human Anatomy
QP Physiology
QR Microbiology

Each main class has its own listing of subclasses. Each subclass with its codes can be found online at the Library of Congress Cataloging and Acquisitions website. The coding, while simple, does not represent words. Thus, the subdivision codes do not follow any clear logic. For example, QC represents physics and not chemistry. QA is mathematics, not astronomy. QB is astronomy and not biology. Carl Sagan's popular book *Cosmos* would be classified in subclass QB (see figure 8.1). Over time, you'll become familiar with the codes, but the LC does not build in logical cues or shortcuts to our learning!

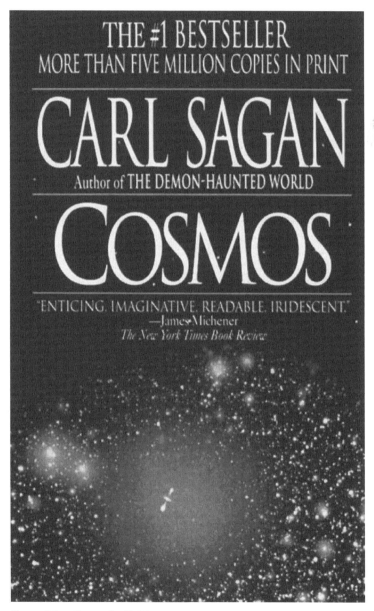

Figure 8.1. *Cosmos* by Carl Sagan.

History and Geography

The numbers 125 through 174.6 represent the time period of the tenth through the sixteenth centuries. The number 174.6 specifically represents the medieval period up to 1519. Thus, DD174.6 is the LC call number for items on German history during the Middle Ages through 1519.

LIBRARY OF CONGRESS CLASSIFICATION OUTLINE

 CLASS D - WORLD HISTORY AND HISTORY OF EUROPE, ASIA, AFRICA, AUSTRALIA, NEW ZEALAND, ETC.

(Click each subclass for details)

Subclass D	History (General)
Subclass DA	Great Britain
Subclass DAW	Central Europe
Subclass DB	Austria - Liechtenstein - Hungary - Czechoslovakia
Subclass DC	France - Andorra - Monaco
Subclass DD	Germany
Subclass DE	Greco-Roman World
Subclass DF	Greece
Subclass DG	Italy - Malta
Subclass DH	Low Countries - Benelux Countries

(Continued on next page)

Figure 8.2. Subclasses of D—World History. Library of Congress.

The numbers 201 through 257.4 represent the time period of the nineteenth and twentieth centuries. The number 228.8 specifically represents the period of World War I, from 1914 through 1918. Thus, DD228.8 is the LC call number for items on German history during World War I from 1914 through 1918.

Subclass DD

DD1-(905)	History of Germany
DD1-21	General
DD21.5-43	Description and travel
DD51-78	Antiquities. Social life and customs. Ethnography
DD84-257.4	History
DD84-96	General
DD99-120	Military, naval, and political history. Foreign relations
DD121-257.4	By period
DD121-124	Earliest to 481
DD125-174.6	Early and medieval to 1519
DD126-155	Medieval Empire, 481-1273

Figure 8.3. Enumerations of Subclass DD. Library of Congress.

Look at the time divisions and geographic divisions in main classes D, E, F, and G. There are thousands of **enumerations** under these main classes that have to do with time and place. The cataloger should be as inclusive as possible about the time periods or regions represented in the item at hand.

Enumeration

After selecting the alphabetical class and subclass, the next step is adding numbers or enumeration. The purpose of the numbers is to provide more specificity or options for classification within the subdivision. While the numbers do follow a hierarchy within the subdivision, they do not necessarily carry over from one main division to another, as they do in the Dewey Decimal system. Thus, catalogers must rely heavily on the LCC Outlines and check them each time for updates or changes.[10] Because this classification system is created for and maintained by the LC, the LC can arbitrarily make changes to its own schema at will.

Enumeration works like this:

1. Determine that the book *The Mystery of Fortune-Telling* by Carl R. Green belongs in main class B (Religion, Philosophy, Psychology).
2. Click the main class B link from the LCC Outlines.[11] Find on the Adobe PFD table that BF, or Psychology, is the closest match in the subdivisions.
3. Open the document next to the link for main class B. In this document, find the enumerations that most closely match the book. Occult sciences range from 1404 through 2055.
4. Fortune-telling is represented by the enumeration range of 1845 to 1891. In order to find precise specificity (which would be needed in a very large collection on fortune-telling), use the subscription tool of Classification Web to find the exact LC call number.[12]

TEXTBOX 8.5. ENUMERATIONS FOR OCCULT SCIENCES

BF1404–2055	Occult sciences
BF1444–1486	Ghosts. Apparitions. Hauntings
BF1501–1562	Demonology. Satanism. Possession
BF1562.5–1584	Witchcraft
BF1585–1623	Magic. Hermetics. Necromancy
BF1651–1729	Astrology
BF1745–1779	Oracles. Sibyls. Divinations
BF1783–1815	Seers. Prophets. Prophecies
BF1845–1891	Fortune-telling
BF2050–2055	Human-alien encounters. Contact between humans and extraterrestrials

---

While this process can be tedious, there is a work-around for catalogers. Remember, the LC has the Cataloging in Publication (CIP) program.

Cataloging in Publication

Publishers are encouraged to send a copy of prepublication books to the LC for their CIP program. A complete MARC record with LC call number is created for each new book. The LC call number appears in the 050 field. By searching the book in a union or other shared catalog, a cataloger would discover the LC call number assigned in the 050 field:

050 00 BF1861|b.G74 2012

Because the number **1861** was assigned directly by the LC CIP service from the enumeration range of 1845 to 1891, the cataloger can be assured it is correct.

Figure 8.4. *The Mystery of Fortune-Telling* by Carl R. Green and William R. Sanford..

CUTTER NUMBERS

Rather sadly we left Charles Cutter and his Expansive Classification System in an almost defunct state earlier in this chapter, with just a few libraries continuing its use. But Mr. Cutter would be pleased to know that over 125 years later, his Cutter number system for authors and titles is alive and well. It is an important part of LCC.

The Cutter number is primarily used to encode the author's last name in a way that distinguishes it from other authors who write on the same topic. The Dewey Decimal system simply encourages the cataloger to add an author code of the first three letters of the author's last name under the Dewey number. Because the LCC is meant for vast collections, it is necessary to classify the author as well. The Cutter number is the third important component of the LCC. Cutter numbers are created using the Cutter conversion table or chart.

Table 8.2.   Constructing Cutter Numbers

1. After initial **vowels**

for the second letter:	b	d	l–m	n	p	r	s–t	u–y
use number:	2	3	4	5	6	7	8	9

2. After initial letter **S**

for the second letter:	a	ch	e	h–i	m–p	t	u	w–z
use number:	2	3	4	5	6	7	8	9

3. After initial letters **Qu**

for the second letter:	a	e	i	o	r	t	y
use number:	3	4	5	6	7	8	9

4. For initial letters **Qa–Qt**

use numbers:	2–29

5. After other initial consonants

for the second letter:	a	e	i	o	r	u	y
use number:	3	4	5	6	7	8	9

6. For further expansion of the last name

for the letter:	a–d	e–h	i–l	m–o	p–s	t–v	w–z
use number:	3	4	5	6	7	8	9

Source: "Cutter Table," Cataloger's Reference Shelf LC Cutter Tables, at www.itsmarc.com/crs/mergedProjects/cutter/cutter/basic_table_cutter.htm (accessed February 5, 2016).

Let's take my own last name, Shaw, as an example. Because it begins with the letter *S*, we use the second option. "Shaw" in Cutter is S539. After *S*, select the number 5 from the second chart to represent the second letter in my name, *h*. But there are many people named Shaw! Expand the Cutter number by next using the sixth chart. To represent the *a* in Shaw, select number 3 from the sixth chart, followed by number 9 from the same chart for *w*. Go ahead and try your own last name, using the appropriate first through fifth charts, then expand to the fourth letter by using the sixth chart.

There are free Cutter generators available online—and they work just fine! Try the Cataloging Calculator; as quickly as you type in the last name, the Cutter number is generated.[13] While it is beneficial to understand what is behind the construction of the Cutter number, it is inefficient to create them using charts when there are calculators.

Edition or Year

If the book is a revised or new edition, the year of the edition follows the Cutter number. If the book is the only or first edition, the year of publication follows the Cutter number.

INTERPRETING A LC CALL NUMBER

The LCC is made up of three major parts. The first part uses letters for the main class and subclass. The second part is the enumeration or number that further specifies the subtopics of the subclass. The Cutter number, the third part of the LCC, follows the LC number. It is often preceded by a period. There may be a fourth component, such as a volume number, followed by the edition or publication date. Textbox 8.6 breaks down the construction of KF 801 .C65 v.3A1960.

TEXTBOX 8.6. INTERPRETING A LC NUMBER

K is the main class for law
F is the subclass for United States law
801 is the enumeration for general works on the law
.C65 is the Cutter number representing that last name of the author Corbin[14]
v.3A is the volume number
1960 is the year of publication

LIBRARY OF CONGRESS CLASSIFICATION USERS

The LCC was designed by the Library of Congress for its own collection.[15] It was not designed to be a national cataloging system for general use by all libraries, and it still maintains a primary focus on its own collections.

Libraries Use LCC

The LCC system is so vast that it is not well-suited for the small or medium-sized collections found in schools and most public libraries. Rather, it has become the standard for large university and academic libraries and research centers, as well as special collection libraries. When libraries have thousands of books concentrated in one area of study, they need to segregate items in the collections by more subdivisions and enumerations than DDC offers. Research libraries use the LCC because their entire collection may be devoted to a limited number of subjects that are important to the work and study of the patrons. A medical library, for instance, could have the majority of its collections begin with the main class R for medicine, but the books would be appropriately separated by subdivision and enumeration with the many options for classification the LC provides.

Because the LCC is found today in many academic and special libraries as well as cooperative cataloging projects such as OCLC's WorldCat and the LC Online Catalog, the Library of Congress is receptive to suggestions for changes and new classes.[16] But the ultimate decisions about adding, deleting, or modifying subdivisions and enumerations rest with the LC.

Some university library systems, such as the University of Illinois libraries, split their classifications between the DDC and the LCC.[17] Most of the libraries at the University of Illinois use the DDC because the library staff feel it is easier for students to browse and find books with this system. They use the twenty-one classes of the LCC for the subject libraries of music, law, and Asian studies because the LCC provides more combinations and greater specificity of topics.

Patrons Use LCC

Most patrons do not encounter the LCC until they are in college, and the system can be confusing. Even librarians who do not work regularly with the LCC may need to review how to locate materials. There is no crossover between Dewey and LCC to help patrons make sense of either arrangement.

Neither scholarship nor historic preservation are the objectives of the LC collection development, and thus the LCC system has not developed to fully address these issues. The LC has been the leader of MARC standards shared by English-speaking countries, but its classification system has been created and managed to suit its own collection needs. Not until the onset of digitization technology did the LC strive to share its resources, including its tools for classification, with all citizens.

How to Locate an Item in an LC Library

Most patrons do not want to know the nuances of the classification system. They just want to locate library resources in the most efficient manner. Use the following steps to locate LCC books:

1. Observes the main classes arranged by section alphabetically around the room, beginning with A and ending with Z.
2. Within each class, the subclasses are arranged alphabetically by the second letter. AE comes before AG, TR would come after TM, and so forth.
3. Within each subclass, the books are arranged by enumeration or number. To determine the arrangement of the call numbers on the shelves, read these numbers the way you would count: 50 comes before 500, which comes before 5000.
4. Next follows the Cutter number. To determine the arrangement on the shelves, read Cutter numbers the way you would read a decimal, looking at

and evaluating the placement of the digits within the number: .7 comes before .701 which comes before .71.

LC Tools for Catalogers

Unlike the DDC, where the library must purchase either the print or online subscription to the classification data, the LC makes the majority of its resources free and available online. The Library of Congress Classification Outline is the primary tool catalogers use to identify main classes, subclasses, and enumerations.[18] If a library needs even more specificity, it should purchase an online subscription to Classification Web.[19] The LC no longer prints its classifications in catalogs, having decided that sharing all updates online is more cost efficient and provides more current information. Catalogers also benefit from using the LC records found through the CIP process in the LC Online Catalog to locate the 050 field.[20] Charles Cutter's tables for creating Cutter numbers are freely available on the web, as are Cutter calculators that will use an algorithm to transform the first four characters of an author's last name into a Cutter number.

Materials Format

Regardless of the format of the library material—print, e-book, audio, media, serial, photograph, and so on—it can be classified by the LCC. In all cases, the cataloger examines the item to come up with the best understanding of its content. In the MARC record, the LCC is entered in the 050 field. In the item record, it is also entered in the location field so that patrons will be able to find the item on the shelf.

As with all cataloging, classifying items by the LCC becomes easier with practice. Approach the classification in the three steps or parts suggested: (1) class and subclass, (2) enumeration, and (3) Cutter number. Patrons will also be more proficient and confident in locating materials when they understand these three parts.

SUMMARY

When library staff know and can apply the basics of LCC classification and organization schemes to their work, they become essential contributors for maintaining collections. Those who are able to use the LCC proficiently and confidently can explain the value and purpose of cataloging and classification to others and help users find the resources they seek. While many library staff did not grow up using LC libraries, learning about and using the LCC system is important for interacting with an academic or research library.

DISCUSSION QUESTIONS AND ACTIVITIES

Discussion Questions

1. Explain the similarities between the Cutter Expansive System and the Library of Congress Classification system. Why are the similarities important to librarians?

2. What are the three parts of an LCC call number? Explain what each part represents.
3. Why is the LCC more useful to research and academic libraries? Why is it not so useful for small to medium school and public libraries?
4. What is a Cutter number, and why are they still used today?
5. What are the LCC tools a cataloger uses to create a full LC call number?

Activity 1: Cutter Numbers

Using the Cutter Tables (do not use the calculator!), create Cutter numbers for the following authors: Suzanne Collins, Stephen King, J. K. Rowling, John Green, Stephenie Meyer, and Veronica Roth. Now create your own Cutter number!

Activity 2: Create LCC Numbers

Using the LC Classification Outline, create LCC numbers for the following titles with expanded Cutter numbers and dates:

1. *Just Mercy* by Bryon Stevenson
2. *A Brief History of Time* by Stephen Hawking
3. *Last Night I Dreamed of Peace: The Diary of Dang Thuy Tram* by Dang Thuy Tram
4. *Everyone is Italian on Sunday* by Rachael Ray
5. *Killing Lincoln* by Bill O'Reilly

Once you have created the LCC numbers, check your work by going to the LC Online Catalog, looking up each title, and changing the record to MARC view. Compare the 050 tag and field to your work.

NOTES

1. "History of the Library," Library of Congress, at www.loc.gov/about/history-of-the-library/ (accessed February 1, 2016).
2. Vanda Broughton, *Essential Classification*, 2nd ed. (Chicago: Neal-Schuman, 2015), 162.
3. Conrad R. Winke, "The Contracting World of Cutter's Expansive Classification," *Library Resources and Technical Services* 48, no. 2 (2004): 122–29.
4. "Charles Ammi Cutter," in *New World Encyclopedia* (New York, NY: Paragon House, 2011), last modified July 22, 2013, at www.newworldencyclopedia.org/entry/Charles_Ammi_Cutter (accessed February 5, 2016).
5. "Expansive Classification," Cornell University Library, at archive.org/stream/ cu31924092476252#page/n11/mode/2up (accessed February 5, 2016).
6. "The Expansive Classification," Cutter Classification, Forbes Library, at forbeslibrary.org/ research/cutter-classification/ (accessed February 5, 2016).
7. Broughton, *Essential Classification*, 164–65.
8. "How to Read a Library of Congress Call Number," University Library, University of Illinois at Urbana-Champaign, last modified October 2, 2015, at www.library.illinois.edu/ugl/ howdoi/lccallnumber.html (accessed February 5, 2016).

9. "Library of Congress Classification Outline," Cataloging and Acquisitions, Library of Congress, at www.loc.gov/catdir/cpso/lcco/ (accessed February 5, 2016).

10. Ibid.

11. Ibid.

12. "World Wide Web Access to Library of Congress Classification and Library of Congress Subject Headings," Classification Web, Library of Congress, at classificationweb.net (accessed February 5, 2016); Lori Robare, Steven Arakawa, Paul Frank, and Bruce Trumble, eds. *Fundamentals of Library of Congress Classification* (Washington, DC: Library of Congress, Cataloging Distribution Service, 2008), available at www.loc.gov/catworkshop/courses/fundamentalslcc/pdf/classify-trnee-manual.pdf.

13. Kyle Banerjee, "The Cataloging Calculator," at calculate.alptown.com/ (accessed September 15, 2016).

14. "How to Read a Library of Congress Call Number."

15. Broughton, *Essential Classification*, 163.

16. Ibid., 165.

17. "How to Read a Library of Congress Call Number."

18. "Library of Congress Classification Outline."

19. "World Wide Web Access to Library of Congress Classification and Library of Congress Subject Headings."

20. "Library of Congress Online Catalog," Library of Congress, atcatalog.loc.gov/legacy.html (accessed February 5, 2016).

REFERENCES, SUGGESTED READINGS, AND WEBSITES

Banerjee, Kyle. "The Cataloging Calculator." Accessed September 15, 2016, at calculate.alp town.com/.

Broughton, Vanda. *Essential Classification*. 2nd ed. Chicago: Neal-Schuman, 2015.

"Charles Ammi Cutter." In *New World Encyclopedia*. New York: Paragon House, 2011. Last modified July 22, 2013, Accessed February 5, 2016, at www.newworldencyclopedia.org/entry/Charles_Ammi_Cutter.

"Expansive Classification." Cornell University Library. Available from the Internet Archive at archive.org/stream/cu31924092476252#page/n11/mode/2up.

Forbes Library. "The Expansive Classification." Cutter Classification. Accessed February 5, 2016, at forbeslibrary.org/research/cutter-classification/.

Intner, Sheila S., and Jean Weihs. *Standard Cataloging for School and Public Libraries*. Westport, CT: Libraries Unlimited, 2007.

Library Corporation. "Cutter Table." Cataloger's Reference Shelf, LC Cutter Tables. Accessed February 5, 2016, at www.itsmarc.com/crs/mergedProjects/cutter/cutter/basic_table_cutter.htm.

Library of Congress. "History of the Library." Accessed February 1, 2016, at www.loc.gov/about/history-of-the-library/.

———. "Library of Congress Classification Outline." Cataloging and Acquisitions. Accessed February 5, 2016, at www.loc.gov/catdir/cpso/lcco/.

———. "Library of Congress Online Catalog." Accessed February 5, 2016, at catalog.loc.gov/legacy.html.

———. "World Wide Web Access to Library of Congress Classification and Library of Congress Subject Headings." Classification Web. Accessed February 5, 2016, at classificationweb.net/.

Robare, Lori, Steven Arakawa, Paul Frank, and Bruce Trumble, eds. *Fundamentals of Library of Congress Classification*. Developed by the ALCTS/CCS-PCC Task Force on Library of Congress Classification Training. Washington, DC: Library of Congress, Cataloging Distribution Service, 2008. Available at https://www.loc.gov/catworkshop/courses/fundamen talslcc/pdf/classify-trnee-manual.pdf.

University of Illinois at Urbana-Champaign. "How to Read a Library of Congress Call Number." University Library. Last modified October 2, 2015. Accessed February 5, 2016, at www .library.illinois.edu/ugl/howdoi/lccallnumber.html.

Winke, R. Conrad. "The Contracting World of Cutter's Expansive Classification." *Library Resources and Technical Services* 48, no. 2 (2004): 122–29.

CHAPTER 9

Subject Classification

LSS know and can apply the basics of classification and organization schemes for collections. (ALA-LSSC Cataloging and Classification Competency 4)

LSS know and can explain the value and purpose of cataloging and classification to help users find the resources that they seek. (ALA-LSSC Cataloging and Classification Competency 7)

Key Terms

Collections. These are groupings of library materials, often assembled by genre, material format, age, reading level, historic value, or some other useful demarcation.

Controlled vocabulary. The words and phrases chosen by the Library of Congress to be included in or excluded from its subject authority database.

Folksonomies. An alternative classification system generated through social media to share suggestions of library resources without having to know library cataloging terminology.

Genre. Categories of literature, music, or art that further define a broader category such as fiction, nonfiction, poetry, drama, and so forth.

Inversion. Some Library of Congress subject headings transpose or reverse the order of the noun and verb because it is more logical to search by the noun.

Main heading. The key topic, term, name, place, or other concept that is the subject of a library resource.

Natural language. Not computer code or artificial programming commands, this is the ordinary day-to-day speaking and writing used by humans to communicate with each other in their native tongues, such as in English, Spanish, or Mandarin Chinese.

Reserves. Temporary collections of books or other library resources set aside at the circulation desk or other accessible location for students in a specific class to use for a set amount of time inside of the library.

Status code. The term or abbreviation used in the ILS cataloging program to describe the current state or location of a library item, such as available on the shelf, checked out to a patron, on display, or in use in other ways. A code is also used if the item is missing, in storage, or lost.

Subfields. The MARC coded locations for subdivision information in a 6XX field that further clarifies the LC main subject heading such as its subtopic, form, chronological setting, or geographic information.

Tagging. The actual process of creating one or more keyword labels (tags) and associating them with a library catalog record. A folksonomy is the classification system that arises from these tags.

INTRODUCTION

In previous chapters the assignment of call numbers was discussed. Call numbers are letter and number codes representing the topic or subject of an item and establishing its location on the shelf. In this chapter we will learn about other aspects of classification: the designation of collection codes and the assignment of subject headings to library resources.

LIBRARIES ORGANIZED BY COLLECTIONS

All of a library's resources are organized and subdivided into **collections**. A collection is a group of materials that have a purpose for being located together. The purpose for most collections is to make it easy for patrons to find a specific type of literature or material. Collections created by material type or **genre** are meant to be permanent, with dedicated floor space and ample shelving. Fiction is a genre collection that may comprise anywhere from one third to half of the books of a school or public library. Nonfiction is the predominant collection type in an academic or research library.

Photo 9.1.   Children with books from Juvenile Collection.

Reference, a key collection for libraries, provides materials that have a structured approach to useful information in one place. Today, print reference collections are being downsized as they are replaced by databases, but there are still reasons to keep some materials apart from regular circulating nonfiction because of the abundance of ready information they provide or other unique demands.

Libraries offer many other types of collections that combine fiction and nonfiction materials, such as age-appropriate collections of young adult and children's books. They also may preserve important artifacts and writings in local history or genealogical collections that often have special circulation rules. Most libraries also have collections designated for biography and pleasure reading such as mystery, romance, or science fiction.

Libraries create collections around media, e-books, and other formats. Patrons expect to find DVDs, magazines, newspapers, audio files, and software located in separate collections to make browsing easier. Differing circulation rules can also be more easily set when formats are in their own collections. School media specialists were once urged to shelve all items, regardless of format, on the same shelf organized by Dewey Decimal so that students could find all information in one place. But librarians found this impractical because standard library shelving could not reasonably or efficiently accommodate or display so many different shapes, sizes, and materials. Locating items was actually more difficult when all formats were all together on the same shelf.

Collections may be created to serve a temporary purpose. Items are culled from the permanent collection and then returned once the need is met. Temporary collections could be created for new books, course **reserves**, or displays. For example, for Banned Books Week, an ALA event that happens each fall, librarians may want to bring attention to our freedom to read by creating displays of materials that have been frequently challenged in libraries across the country.[1] These items could come from both the nonfiction and fiction collections. For this display the cataloger changes the collection and **status codes** in the item record. Once Banned Books Week is over, the cataloger will change the collection code and item status back to its original designation.

Library collections are primarily created because of genre or content, item format, or a temporary need. Each item in a library is classified into a collection. Most common genre or content collections are as follows:

TEXTBOX 9.1. EXAMPLES OF COMMON GENRE OR CONTENT COLLECTIONS

Fiction. Adult novels and stories, arranged by author's last name

Nonfiction. Adult content that is true or real, classified by Dewey Decimal or LC call numbers

Reference. Sources that are used for information

Children. Subdivided by fiction, nonfiction, juvenile, reading levels, easy books, or other

Teen. Subdivided by fiction, nonfiction, special area topics, and media

Serials. Magazines, newspapers, journals

Biography. Real stories about people

Popular Genre. Mystery, science fiction, historical fiction, romance, and so on

History or Genealogy. Local history, documents, letters, and artifacts

Collection Codes

Catalogers deal with collection codes. The purpose of a collection code is to classify an item into the appropriate group of materials for its location. Some integrated library systems (ILS) refer to the collection code as the "location" field in the item record. Each of the collections listed in textbox 9.1 will have its own code that designates the location information of the item searched by the patron in the public display of the online catalog. Libraries that have a shared catalog will have another level of designation. For example, the Libraries Online consortium has a two-letter name code for each library. "EH" is the name code for East Lyme High School, and the Public Library of New London code is "NL."[2] Both libraries have fiction collections. The collection code for East Lyme High School is EHFIC, which indicates EH for East Lyme High School and FIC for fiction collection. NLFIC is the collection code for the Public Library of New London.

TEXTBOX 9.2. EXAMPLES OF COLLECTION CODES USED AT MCGILL UNIVERSITY LIBRARIES[3]

BIRK REF	Reference—Birks Reading Room
BLDR RES	Reserves—Blackader-Lauterman
EDUC CRLAB	Curriculum Lab—School of Education
ICC FILM	Film—University Archives
LAW STOR	Storage—Nahum Gelber Law
ISLM RARE	Rare books—Islam Studies

The codes of BIRK, BLDR, EDUC, and so forth correspond to campus libraries or departments at the university, and by looking at the code students would know which building houses an item. The collection code, preceded by its building designation, is entered in each library resource item record. If items physically move from one collection to the next, their item records will be adjusted.

Status Codes

The status of an item correlates closely with the collection code. The status tells in real time what is going on with the item. Is it on order or is it on the shelf and available? Is it checked out in circulation? Could it be lost or missing? An item could also be on extended loan, in repair, or noncirculating because of displays, its condition, its location on reserve, its rarity, its fragility, or reference importance.

Some status changes occur automatically through the ILS. When a book goes through the acquisitions process and receives a barcode, with the first wand its status changes from "on order" to "available" or "new book," depending on the library. When the barcode is read at checkout, the status immediately and automatically changes from "available" to "checked out."

However, library staff do have to manually change the status when an item is temporary moved to a display or placed on reserve. Staff may also have to change status when the item goes into repair, has missing parts, or is considered lost or missing.

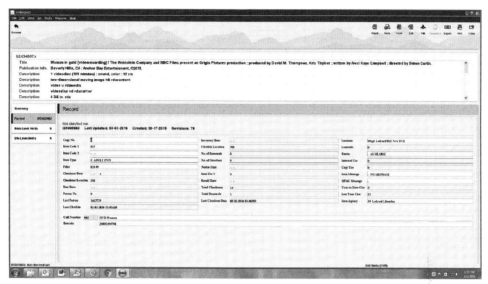

Figure 9.1. Item Record with Collection and Status Codes. Ledyard Public Libraries. Library Catalog.

Digital Collections

For years catalogers only thought about items they could touch, lift, carry, or otherwise manipulate. Libraries today acquire access to digital content for their patrons in the form of e-books, e-journals, sound files, and websites. Regardless of whether the library owns or leases the content, catalogers must integrate the content of the digital library into the online catalog so that patrons are aware of and can make choices about information offered by the library but not housed on its shelves. When a patron locates in the Libraries Online catalog a copy of *Go Set a Watchman* by Harper Lee, for instance, he or she can make the choice between print, audio file, and e-book formats because the collection code in each's item record designates its format type.[4] The patron finds that the e-book or e-audio is located in "Downloadable Overdrive," the company that leases the digital content to the Libraries Online consortium members.

We are in the initial stages of being able to import full MARC records for e-books and e-journals from subscription databases. It would be impossible for individual catalogers to catalog thousands and thousands of e-books and e-journal articles. Large companies that own the digital content, such as Overdrive and EBSCO, have the MARC records and want to sell them to the subscribing libraries. The technology is there, but most school and public libraries cannot afford to purchase the MARC records of digital content on their own. However, for academic and research libraries, and those school and public libraries in consortia, it is becoming a necessity rather than a luxury to have an integrated catalog with the MARC records of digital content.

Alternate Classification Systems

A few libraries in the United States choose to place such strong emphasis on classifying within their collections that they either do not use call numbers at all or have their own variation. These libraries are often special libraries, such as the National Library of Medicine (NLM), that have such a concentration of materials in one area that neither Dewey Decimal nor Library of Congress call numbers provide the subdivisions needed to identify and segregate materials.

The NLM uses the Library of Congress schedules QS–QZ and W–WZ.[5] These LC schedules supplement the NLM's own classification system for medicine. It is a somewhat complicated system that is part LC, part its own. The numerals 1 through 49 are used to classify materials by publication type, such as dictionaries, atlases, laboratory manuals, and so on. QS–QZ, W–WY, and WZ are used to classify works published after 1913; the nineteenth-century schedule is used for works published from 1801 to 1913; and WZ 220–270 is used to provide century groupings for works published before 1801 and Americana. Geographic subdivisions are provided for certain subjects in the NLM. Catalogers who may work for or with NLM materials learn this unique classification system that classifies what we know now and will continue to learn about the health of and medicine for the human body.

Some libraries choose not to use call numbers. Because they have created so many subcollections within the topics of nonfiction works, they feel call numbers are confusing and unnecessary.

A few public libraries have made the bold decision to forgo classifying with call numbers and to rely solely on collection subdivisions. The Maricopa County Libraries in Arizona use Book Industry Standards and Communications (BISAC) to classify and display their books with the subdivisions used in commercial bookstores.[6] They call their system ShelfLogic; rather than using numbers, it relies on subject and genre to aid patrons in finding the materials.[7] BISAC creates over fifty divisions or categories of knowledge as opposed to the ten main divisions of Dewey or the twenty-one main classes of the LC. Within each of the BISAC divisions, there are equally as many—if not more—subdivisions. For example, the subject category of "games" has subdivisions for coloring books, card games, chess, magic, and trivia, to name a few. The Maricopa County Libraries use BISAC subject headings to group books into small collections on shelves, not unlike a bookstore.

The Colorado Rangeview Library District also uses BISAC. Calling themselves the Anythink Libraries, they use a modified classification system that is a combination of BISAC and additional narrower terms.[8] Their system, which they call "WordThink," has the broad BISAC category placed on book spine labels, with a narrow term such as "Art" or "Drawing" placed below the broad category.[9] Other libraries, such as Darien Library in Connecticut, forgo call numbers and organize their children's collections by subjects, color codes, age, or reading levels when browsing is the primary means to gain access and to select books.

Folksonomies

Folksonomies are systems through which social media users rather than professional catalogers tag items with keywords as an alternative to standard library classification systems.[10] Anyone can tag, and tags are shared across social media. Tagging is the actual process of creating one or more keyword labels (tags) and associating them with a digital information object, such as a website, picture, video, or even a library catalog record. A folksonomy is a classification system that arises from these tags. Users of tags may feel they can describe a book, film, or other resource more directly than through the vocabulary used by libraries. For some people, the library online catalog is confusing, and the structure of subject headings does not make sense to them. Users of folksonomies want items described in more familiar and comfortable terms. Folksonomies are being used with such social media as Flickr, LibraryThing, and Pinterest where people can make recommendations for library resources in real time and in real language.

LibraryThing is a subscription database that uses the technology of folksonomy so that individuals or libraries can have a social media forum for sharing their ideas and recommendations for library books and media.[11] Participants share their perceptions of materials and tag accordingly. The more often an item is tagged with a particular word, the larger the word will appear—in other words, it is ranked based on its frequency or popularity.

Figure 9.2. Folksonomy Tagging Example from LibraryThing. LibraryThing.

While folksonomy tagging and ranking does not have the precision of professional cataloging, it undoubtedly will grow because it is popular with millions of online users around the globe. Tagging is a way to use metadata or descriptive information about an item. Folksonomies can complement library catalogs, and many individual library catalogs and consortium catalogs subscribe to LibraryThing or similar products that help patrons make decisions about selecting library resources. Folksonomies also provide patrons an avenue for sharing their opinions about materials. Folksonomies are a form of reader advisory service that is easy to use and has growing appeal.

LIBRARY OF CONGRESS SUBJECT HEADINGS

Collections group resources together in an area of the library because of commonality in content, format, or unique or temporary purpose. Call numbers, whether they Dewey or LC, provide a specific placement of an item on the shelf within its collection. Both of these processes are immensely helpful when a patron has time and a general idea about what she or he is looking for.

The subject heading is the third and perhaps most important tool for finding a needed library resource when the title or author is unknown. Each subject heading represents a single object or idea. Most of the time. library patrons do not know the title or author of the book they want to use or will check out. What they do know, however, is the topic or subject they are interested in. As with names and titles, the Library of Congress takes ownership and responsibility for the rules and creation of subject headings. It is accepted practice in libraries in the United States to use LC subject headings in their cataloging.

Though libraries once had to purchase *LC Subject Headings* (LCSH) as printed volumes, today LCSH is available at no cost through the LC Authorities website.[12] The LC Subject Headings database is the primary database of main headings. The LC also offers a smaller database of children's subject headings, which is primarily used by catalogers of elementary or primary school libraries and collections for children in public libraries. The LC Children's Subject Headings database is designed to complement LCSH when LCSH does not provide suitable terminology, form, or scope for children.[13]

Subject Search

Subject headings are another tool for sorting library materials into common topics. Prior to online catalogs, catalogers were mostly limited to three subject cards per item so as not to overfill the drawers of the wooden card catalogs. Catalogers were challenged to determine the three most likely subjects that described the book.

Today catalogers are not limited to a set number of subjects; in fact, with RDA, we are encouraged to use as many subjects as we think patrons will need to learn about or locate the item. Subject searches provide us a list of both the terms to use and also other associated subheadings with the term, such as we see in figure 9.3 with Attention-Deficit/Hyperactivity Disorder. This ordered alphabetical list of links to items expands the term to alternative treatments, case studies, diet therapy, fiction, genetic aspects, and many other subtopics.

The concept of being able to find books by topic through an online catalog is grounded in the tradition of subject cards. By providing multiple individual subject lines (or cards), catalogers in the past enabled patrons to locate any item by any or all of the main topics contained within them. Catalogers did their best to standardize the terms or topics they used for subjects.

The Copyright Act of 1870 required that two copies of every book, map, engraving, photograph, musical composition, periodical, and other material submitted for copyright be brought to the Library of Congress.[14] When the Library of Congress expanded into their new building in the late nineteenth century, it established a call number system to manage and locate the numerous materials in its repository. In 1898 the LC also established the LC Subject Heading list for its cataloging; that

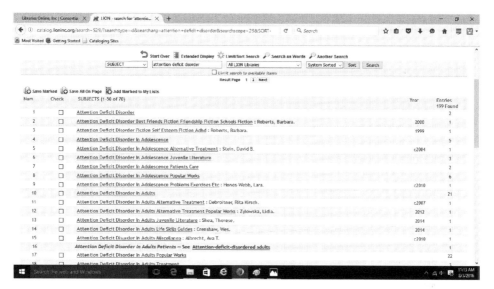

Figure 9.3. Example of a Subject Search for Attention-Deficit Hyperactivity Disorder. Libraries Public Online, Middletown, CT.

list is today collaboratively shared with all libraries to provide standardized subject access to their collections.[15]

Subject Heading Structure[16]

Text in the English language is constructed and read from left to right. LC subject headings are also constructed from left to right beginning with the **main heading**, or most likely term for the concept. Following the main heading, the subject can be subdivided further by such things as subtopic, designation, date, or geographic region.

When an LC main heading is one word, it is a noun—that is, a person, place, concept, or thing. When the LC main heading is constructed of more than one word, it typically is a noun and an adjective. Formerly, the noun always came first, followed by a comma and then the adjective, such as "mushrooms, edible." In recent years, subject main headings have been written in **natural language**. This main heading is now "edible mushrooms" because that is the natural way we speak.

Inversion of the noun and adjective is common with adjectives describing language or nationality, such as "Poetry, German"; "Automobiles, French"; or "Patents—Taiwan." A subject heading may also be inverted if there is greater importance placed on the noun, such as "fowl, wild" instead of "wild fowl." It would be more logical to look under the word "fowl" than "wild" for birds that live freely in the open spaces.

Most names are also inverted with the surname coming first because we usually search for people under the last name, or surname. The name is followed by the birth and death date. Rather than "Taylor Swift," the LC subject heading is "Swift, Taylor, 1989."

Another construction that is used less often is the parenthetical qualifier, which is used to remove ambiguity or make an obscure word or phrase more explicit.[17] For example, the subject heading "COBALT (Video game)" distinguishes how the word "cobalt" is used as a subject heading because cobalt has many meanings, including as a chemical element.

Subdivisions[18]

A multiple-concept subject heading contains two or more otherwise individual or independent concepts coordinated or related through linking devices such as the conjunction "and."[19] Multiple-concept subject headings may be further clarified with subdivisions, and these are commonly found throughout the LCSH database. Subdivisions are frequently used to combine multiple concepts into one subject heading and are often segmented with a dash between the two independent concepts. Examples of these kind of subject headings are "Men and Women at Work" or "Children—1800–1840." The first example indicates that *both* men *and* women work. In the second example, the noun "Children" is further delineated by *when they lived* during a specific time period in the nineteenth century. Only a small number of all possible subdivision combinations are represented in the LCSH database. The four key subdivisions used in LC subject headings are shown in table 9.1.

Table 9.1.   Four Main Library of Congress Subdivisions

Subdivision	Description	Examples
Topical	Topical subdivisions are used under a main heading or other subdivisions to create a specific subtopic.	Actors—Employment Soccer—Equipment Video games—Adverse effects
Form	Form subdivisions describe the format of the material or how the material is organized. When form is used, it is the last subdivision.	Natural history—Encyclopedias Divorce—Proceedings Fashion—19th century—Periodicals
Geographic	A geographic subdivision indicates the location of the topic.	Hurricanes—North Carolina United States History—Pennsylvania Skiing—Colorado—1950–1960
Chronological	Chronological subdivisions limit the main heading to a specific time period. Chronological subdivisions can be used with topical, geographic, or historic subdivisions and, when used, follow those subdivisions.	United States—History—Revolution, 1775–1783 Schools—Arizona—1870–1880 Surgery—History—15th century

Sears Subject Headings

Minnie Earl Sears was a cataloger for the New York Public Library at the turn of the twentieth century. She then went to work for the H. W. Wilson Company, a publisher of professional library materials. While there she was responsible for creating a list of LC subject headings that would be most appropriate and used for small to medium-sized libraries. First published in 1923 and now in its twenty-first edition, this one-volume handbook is still popular today with K–12 school and small public library catalogers who rely on the Sears List of Subject Headings to provide them with the most useful LC subject headings for small collections.

Figure 9.4. Sears List of Subject Headings Published by H. W. Wilson. "Sears List of Subject Headings," H. W. Wilson Collections, accessed February 16, 2016, http://www.hwwilsoninprint .com/sears.php.

The Sears List of Subject Headings follows the same rules for construction and subdivisions as LCSH. When the list of LC Subject Headings was only available in print and not online, Sears was much more affordable. Today, the twenty-first edition of the Sears List of Subject Headings is available in print from H. W. Wilson as well as online as a subscription database from EBSCO.

LIBRARY OF CONGRESS SUBJECT AUTHORITY

Why is the use of standardized LC subject headings important when we have keyword searching? First, when libraries use uniform subjects, patrons become familiar with the terms, and the terms are portable from library to library. Because all libraries use the LC subject headings, patrons apply their knowledge of terminology from one library catalog to another. Second, today few libraries stand alone. Our libraries are members of shared school districts, academic institutions, public library consortiums, and state union catalogs. When all libraries use the LC subject headings to classify the content of their works, searching is focused and results are narrower than if librarians relied on keywords.

Third, LC subject headings are used to create bibliographies and lists. In the online catalog, subject headings in an item record are often active links that will provide immediate access to bibliographies of other library materials on the same topic.

TEXTBOX 9.3. REASONS TO USE LIBRARY OF CONGRESS SUBJECT HEADINGS

1. Patrons maximize their knowledge and skills
2. Subject headings are universal among libraries
3. Bibliographies of materials on similar subject content can be readily created

---

In chapter 3 we were introduced to Library of Congress (LC) authority control and learned there are three types of authorities: name, title, and subject. Authority control—that is, the agreement that libraries use a single and standardized form of names, titles, and subjects—is essential for maintaining the efficiency of searching and the functionality of library catalogs. Without subject authority control there would be much wasted time running similar searches to find books, films, and other library resources.

The Library of Congress determines the words and phrases (nouns and adjectives) used to create main subject headings for its materials. The words it chooses are a **controlled vocabulary**. In other words, the LC makes a conscious determination of the words and terms that will and will not be used. While there are many perfectly good words and terms that could be used, the LC controls the vocabulary of its subject headings to maintain focus and structure. In its controlled vocabulary, the LC determines if it is more natural to use the singular or plural form of the subject main heading.

The LC also establishes the rules and procedures to expand into subdivisions. All of the LC subject headings are compiled and updated in its Subject Authority database. Because LC cataloging records are available through the LC Catalog, Cataloging in Publication (CIP), OCLC WorldCat, and other sources, all libraries in the United States and many around the globe can benefit from the work of LC catalogers, its authorities, and its MARC21 standards.

Searching Subject Authority

Searching the LC Subject Authority is very similar to searching the name or title authorities.[20] From the options in the box, select "Subject Authority Headings."[21]

Table 9.2. Searching the LC Subject Authorities

Steps	Action
1	Select "Subject Authority Headings" from the box of the LC Authority Headings.
2	Click "Search Authorities."
3	Type the word or phrase you anticipate is a main heading.
4	If what you typed is an LC subject heading, you will see it listed alphabetically and a number greater than zero will be in the second column, titled "Bib Records."
5	If what you typed is not an LC subject heading, you may see a red "References" button on the same line in the first column. In the "Bib Records" column there will be the number zero.
6	If this is the case, click on the red "References" button to see the LC subject heading.
7	For example, type "surf boards." The red "References" button appears with zero bib records. Click on the button and learn that the LC subject heading is "surfboards." "Surfboarding" is not an LC subject heading. It refers the searcher to "surfing." The LC uses a controlled vocabulary for its subject headings. While all of these words have to do with using surfboards, only certain ones have LC subject authority.

Remember, the LC Subject Authorities do not contain the majority of permissible subdivisions for subtopics, chronology, geography, language, or form. It is up to the cataloger to create appropriate subdivisions that follow and adhere to the LC rules.

6XX SUBJECT ACCESS FIELDS

We now return to the MARC21 (MARC) standards and template. The 6XX are the variable fields in the MARC record where LC authority subject headings are entered. The subject headings entered into the 6XX fields are read by patrons using the on-line catalog to obtain an immediate idea about what a library resource is about. For the book *Other Worlds, Other Universes, Playing with the Reality Game*, edited by Brad Steiger and John White, there are three subjects: (1) Life on other planets, (2) Unidentified flying objects, and (3) Astral projection. All three subjects are key ideas contained in this book, and patrons can look under any of them to find the bibliographic and item records.

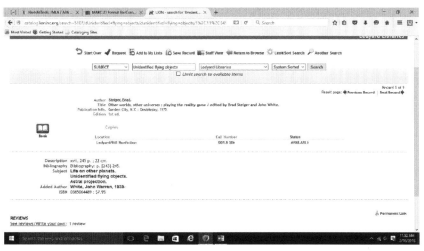

Figure 9.5.   Online Catalog Display with Subjects. Libraries PublicOnline, Middletown, CT.

There are twenty-one subject access fields in the 6XX series. Each one of these fields is designated for a specific type of subject heading. With library systems with integrated modules, inexpensive and almost limitless cloud storage, and the impressive reliability and processing speed of computers, catalogers are no longer restricted to just two or three subject headings per item. In fact, today with RDA (Resource Description and Access) cataloging rules, the Library of Congress encourages catalogers to use as many subject headings as they need to provide full access and searching exposure to the item.

Catalogers must match the kind or type of subject to the 6XX field. Table 9.3 contains the names and a short explanation of each of the twenty-one 6XX options:[22]

Table 9.3. Common 6XX Variable Subject Added Entry Fields

Tag	Type of Subject	Example
600	Personal Name	Hemingway, Ernest, 1899–1961 (used when the book is *about* Hemingway rather than being a book he authored)
610	Corporate Name	Ben & Jerry's (Firm)
611	Meeting Name	American Society of Newspaper Editors. Convention
630	Uniform Title	New York Times
648	Subject Added Entry—Chronological Term	Middle Ages
650	Subject Added Entry—Topical Term	Vampires
651	Subject Added Entry—Geographic Term	Grand Canyon (Ariz)
653	Index Term—Uncontrolled Index	Man ‡a Eyes ‡a Diseases (terms that are not derived from a controlled thesaurus or subject heading system)
654	Subject Added Entry—Faceted Topical Terms	Business letters—housing—United States (parts or aspects that make up a subject)
655	Index Term—Genre/Form	Detective and Mystery Fiction = Detective and Mystery Stories
656	Index Term—Occupation	Architects
657	Index Term—Function	Education, Humanistic
658	Index Term—Curriculum Objective	Library Technology Certificate
662	Subject Added Entry—Hierarchical Place Names	United States—Missouri—Mississippi River
690	Local Subject Added Entry—Topical Term	New York Yankees (Baseball team)—Statistics
691	Local Subject Added Entry—Geographic Name	Florida Everglades—Lake Okeechobee
695	Added Class Number	Place here an item or other number that is considered a subject.
696	Local Subject Added Entry—Personal Name	Connecticut—Norwich—Benedict Arnold
697	Local Subject Added Entry—Corporate Name	Empire State Building (New York, N.Y.)
698	Local Subject Added Entry—Meeting Name	Denver, CO—ISTE Conference 2016
699	Local Subject Added Entry—Uniform Title	Paris—Treaty of Versailles

After the cataloger determines the subjects of the item, the next step is to determine, among all of the choices of the 6XX divisions, what kind of subject each is, making the best match between the type of subject and the field description. All 6XX fields will appear on the public online catalog display as subjects. For research and bibliographic purposes, it is important to classify the subjects into the proper 6XX fields.

The most-used 6XX fields for public and school libraries are 600 (personal name), 650 (topical term), 651 (geographic term), 655 (genre), 656 (occupation), and the local information found in the 691 through 699 fields. Academic and special libraries may have greater use for 610, 611, 653, 654, 657, and 658 as these fields provide greater specificity of subjects.

Indicators

In the construction of any of the 6XX fields, as with the other MARC fields, there are indicators and subdivisions. Catalogers use the MARC tools to code indicators properly. For example, for the most commonly used 6XX field, 650, Subject Added Entry—Topical Term, the indicators are shown in table 9.4.

Table 9.4.   Indicators for 650 Field, Subject Added Entry—Topical Term

First Indicator	0	No level specified
	1	Primary
	2	Secondary
Second Indicator	0	Library of Congress Subject Heading
	1	LC Subject Heading for Children's Literature
	2	Medical Subject Heading
	3	National Agricultural Library Subject Authority File
	4	Source Not Specified
	5	Canadian Subject Heading (and so forth through 8, which indicates a Sears Subject Heading)

Most topical subject headings would be of primary importance and would be from LCSH, thus "1" should be used as the first indicator and "0" should be used as the second indicator:

10 Smartphones—Social Aspects—Japan

Subfields

There are four categories of subdivisions generally recognized in Library of Congress Subject Headings. These subdivisions convert into **subfields** in MARC records. Subfields require the MARC codes in table 9.5.[23]

Table 9.5.   Subfield Codes for 6XX Fields

Code	Subdivision
v	Form
x	Topical
y	Chronological
z	Geographic

Subfields v, x, and z in the 600 field are repeatable. Subfields v, x, y, and z do not have to be in alphabetical order. They will be in the order prescribed by the instructions given by the subject heading system. The form of the item (v) follows its (x) topical, (z) geographic, and (y) chronological subdivisions. Such subfields can be seen in the LC subject: Baseball—Museums—United States—Guidebooks (see table 9.6).

Table 9.6..   Explanation of Codes

650 0 Baseball|xMuseums|zUnited States|vGuidebooks	
650	MARC field for topical term subject
0	second indictor—this is a LC subject heading
Baseball	main subject heading
x Museum	"x" codes that "Museum" is a subtopic of Baseball
z United States	"z" codes that "United States" is the geographic location of the baseball museum
v Guidebooks	"v" codes that "Guidebooks" is the form of the book on baseball museums in the United States

ASSIGNING SUBJECT HEADINGS

Assigning materials to collections and creating subject headings are further examples of the ways that cataloging is indeed both a science and an art. As we learned in this chapter, there are rules established by the Library of Congress, such as its controlled vocabulary, that must be strictly adhered to so that there is uniformity for searching catalogs. Catalogers must check main headings through the LC subject authority before using topics, names, places, and concepts in the variable data fields of the 6XX tags.

Table 9.7.   Workflow for Assigning Collections and Subject Headings for Original Cataloging

1	If the item has CIP information on the back of the title page, use the subject headings the LC gave the item. Add local subject headings if needed.
2	If there is no CIP information, examine the item and search for any clues about its content. Clues might be found on the cover or in the front and backmatter descriptions, introduction, accompanying material, reviews, and so forth. Look at the table of contents and the index for key topics.
3	Determine if the item is fiction, nonfiction, or reference. Classify it into the appropriate library collection based on content or form.
4	Create list of three to five possible subjects. Search these subjects in the LC Subject Authority for accurate main headings.
5	Continue to examine item for form, geography, and chronology. Find subdivisions that are appropriate and would be helpful to future searchers.
6	With the list of 6XX variable fields in front of you (see table 9.3), select the best 6XX tab for each of the subject headings.
7	Construct each subject heading using appropriate MARC subfields x, v, y, and z.

However, the LC also has provided catalogers much leeway to create terms that are not in the LC Subject Authorities. They can add local places, events, names, and terms in natural language. As long as the cataloger follows the LC rules, there is much flexibility for the "art" of creating subject fields that reflect the essence of an item and will provide the most thorough description and access to patrons who may search for it in the future.

Every cataloger will establish their own workflow pattern for classifying materials into collections and to assigning subject headings. Table 9.7 provides a workflow approach to consider.

SUMMARY

This chapter provides beginning catalogers the basics of classification and organization schemes for collections. Through their application of the rules and authorities of Library of Congress Subject Headings, catalogers help users find the resources they seek through a well-maintained and fully functional online library catalog. When applied or created following the standards set by the Library of Congress, subject headings are a powerful access point to the resources of libraries found in both their individual and shared catalogs.

DISCUSSION QUESTIONS AND ACTIVITIES

Discussion Questions

1. What are collection codes and what purpose do they serve? Why are they part of the item record?
2. What is a status code and how does it benefit the patrons who are looking for a book?
3. Describe three alternative systems for classifying and cataloging library materials.
4. Explain the differences between main headings and subdivisions in LCSH. How do subdivisions complement main headings?
5. What are the most commonly used 6XX variable fields for subjects in public and school libraries? Why?
6. How would you go about determining a collection and subject headings for a local item that neither has been cataloged by the Library of Congress nor appears in any online catalog?

Activity 1: Using the Library of Congress Subject Authority

Find the LC controlled vocabulary for the following words by accessing the Library of Congress Subject Authority at authorities.loc.gov (see table 9.8).

Table 9.8. Find LC Controlled Vocabulary

Word or Phrase	LC Controlled Vocabulary
Rollerblading	
Sailboats—Masts and rigging	
Vineyard laborers—Wages	
Bobbleheads	
Valentine Day	

Activity 2: Selecting the Proper 6XX Variable Field

Select the appropriate 6XX variable field for the LCSH in table 9.9. Tell why you made this choice.

Table 9.9.   Select the 6XX Variable Field

LCSH	6XX Tag	Reason
Guitars Friend (Firm)	610	Corporate name
Maine—1930–1960		
Mystery and Detective Stories		
Sunscreens (Cosmetics)		
Biochemistry Engineers		
Texas Boys' Choir of Fort Worth		

NOTES

1. "Banned Books Week: Celebrating the Freedom to Read," American Library Association, at www.ala.org/bbooks/bannedbooksweek (accessed February 13, 2016).

2. Libraries Online, "Appendix I—LION cataloging codes," Bibliographic Manual, at www.lioninc.org/committees/bibliographic-2/bibliographic-manual/appendix-i-lion-cataloging-codes/ (accessed February 13, 2016).

3. McGill University Library, "Alpha Sub-library and Collection Codes," at www.mcgill.ca/library-csstaff/acq/sublibrary (accessed February 13, 2016).

4. Search results for *Go Set a Watchman: To Kill a Mockingbird Series, Book 2*, LION Catalog, at catalog.lioninc.org/search~S29?/tgo+set+a+watchman/tgo+set+a+watchman/1%2C4%2C8%2CB/exact&FF=tgo+set+a+watchman+to+kill+a+mockingbird+series+book+++++++++2&1%2C2%2C/indexsort=-. (accessed February 13, 2016)

5. "Fact Sheet NLM Classification," U.S. National Library of Medicine, last modified June 23, 2015, at www.nlm.nih.gov/pubs/factsheets/nlmclassif.html (accessed February 13, 2016).

6. Maricopa County Library District, "Quick Search Library Catalog," at mcldaz.org/default.aspx?ctx=1.1033.0.0.1 (accessed February 13, 2016).

7. Maricopa County Library District, "Introducing ShelfLogic," at mcldaz.org/custom/shelflogic.aspx (accessed February 15, 2016).

8. Rangeview Library District, "Anythink: A Revolution in Rangeview Libraries," at www.anythinklibraries.org/ (accessed February 15, 2016).

9. Cassidy Charles, "Is Dewey Dead?," *Public Libraries Online*, December 18, 2012, available at publiclibrariesonline.org/2012/12/is-dewey-dead/.

10. Kate Baker, "Folksonomies and Social-Tagging," *Idaho Librarian*, November 13, 2012, available at theidaholibrarian.wordpress.com/2012/11/13/social-tagging-2012/.

11. LibraryThing, home page, at www.librarything.com/ (accessed February 18, 2016).

12. "Library of Congress Subject Headings," Library of Congress, at id.loc.gov/authorities/subjects.html (accessed February 16, 2016).

13. "Library of Congress Children's Subject Headings," Library of Congress, at id.loc.gov/authorities/childrensSubjects.html (accessed February 18, 2016).

14. "1870—The Copyright Act of 1870," U.S. Capitol Visitors Center, at www.capitol.gov/html/EVT_2010061548065.html (accessed February 16, 2016).

15. "Library of Congress Subject Headings."

16. "Assigning and Constructing Subject Headings," Library of Congress Subject Headings—PowerPoint, last modified 2011, at www.library.illinois.edu/ (accessed February 16, 2016).

17. Ibid.

18. Ibid.

19. "Principles of Heading Construction," Cataloger's Reference Shelf, LCSH—Principles of Structure and Policies for Application Principles of Heading Construction, Library Corporation, at www.itsmarc.com/crs/mergedprojects/subjhead/subjhead/principles_of_heading_construction.htm (accessed February 16, 2016).

20. "Search Authorities," Library of Congress Authorities, at authorities.loc.gov/ (accessed February 17, 2016).

21. "Searching Subject Authority Headings," Library of Congress Authorities, at authorities.loc.gov/help/subj-auth.htm (accessed February 17, 2016).

22. "6xx Introduction," OCLC, at www.oclc.org/bibformats/en/6xx.html (accessed February 17, 2016).

23. "Assigning and Constructing Subject Headings."

REFERENCES, SUGGESTED READINGS, AND WEBSITES

American Library Association. "Banned Books Week: Celebrating the Freedom to Read." Accessed February 13, 2016, at www.ala.org/bbooks/bannedbooksweek.

Baker, Kate. "Folksonomies and Social-Tagging." *Idaho Librarian*, November 13, 2012. Accessed February 18, 2016, at theidaholibrarian.wordpress.com/2012/11/13/social-tagging-2012/.

Book Industry Study Group (BISG). "Complete BISAC Subject Headings, 2015 Edition." Accessed February 15, 2016, at www.bisg.org/bisac/complete-bisac-subject-headings -2015-edition.

Charles, Cassidy. "Is Dewey Dead?" *Public Libraries Online*. December 18, 2012. Accessed February 13, 2016, at publiclibrariesonline.org/2012/12/is-dewey-dead/.

Libraries Online. "Appendix I—LION cataloging codes." Bibliographic Manual. Accessed February 13, 2016, at www.lioninc.org/committees/bibliographic-2/bibliographic-manual/appendix-i-lion-cataloging-codes/.

———. LION Catalog search results for *Go Set a Watchman: To Kill a Mockingbird Series, Book 2*. Accessed February 13, 2016, at http://catalog.lioninc.org/search~S29?/tgo+set+a+watchman/tgo+set+a+watchman/1%2C4%2C8%2CB/exact&FF=tgo+set+a+watchman+to+kill+a +mockingbird+series+book+++++++++2&1%2C2%2C/indexsort=-.

The Library Corporation. "Principles of Heading Construction." Cataloger's Reference Shelf, LCSH—Principles of Structure and Policies for Application Principles of Heading Construction. Accessed February 16, 2016, at www.itsmarc.com/crs/mergedprojects/subjhead/subjhead/principles_of_heading_construction.htm.

Library of Congress. "6XX—Subject Access Fields—General Information." Last modified February 29, 2008. Accessed February 15, 2016, at www.loc.gov/marc/bibliographic/bd6xx.html.

———. "Library of Congress Children's Subject Headings." Accessed February 18, 2016, at id.loc.gov/authorities/childrensSubjects.html.

———. "Library of Congress Subject Headings." Accessed February 16, 2016, at id.loc.gov/authorities/subjects.html.

———. "Search Authorities." Library of Congress Authorities. Accessed February 17, 2016, at authorities.loc.gov/.

———. "Searching Subject Authority Headings." Library of Congress Authorities. Accessed February 17, 2016, at authorities.loc.gov/help/subj-auth.htm.

LibraryThing. Home Page. Accessed February 18, 2016, at www.librarything.com/.

Maricopa County Library District. "Introducing ShelfLogic." Accessed February 15, 2016, at mcldaz.org/custom/shelflogic.aspx.

———. "Quick Search Library Catalog." Accessed February 13, 2016, at mcldaz.org/default .aspx?ctx=1.1033.0.0.1.

McGill University Library. "Alpha Sub-library and Collection Codes." Sub-library codes. Accessed February 13, 2016, at www.mcgill.ca/library-csstaff/acq/sublibrary.

Online Computer Library Center (OCLC). "6xx Introduction." 6XX Fields. Accessed February 17, 2016, at www.oclc.org/bibformats/en/6xx.html.

Rangeview District Libraries. "Anythink: A Revolution in Rangeview Libraries." Accessed February 15, 2016, at www.anythinklibraries.org/.

University of Illinois at Urbana-Champaign. "Assigning and Constructing Subject Headings." Library of Congress Subject Headings—PowerPoint. Accessed February 16, 2016, at www .library.illinois.edu/.

U.S. Capitol Visitor Center. "1870—The Copyright Act of 1870." Architect of the Capitol. Accessed February 16, 2016, at www.capitol.gov/html/EVT_2010061548065.html.

U.S. National Library of Medicine. "Fact Sheet NLM Classification." Last modified June 23, 2015. Accessed February 13, 2016, at www.nlm.nih.gov/pubs/factsheets/nlmclassif.html.

PART 3

Cataloging Library Materials

CHAPTER 10

RDA, FRBA, and FRAD

LSS apply and manage the appropriate processes, computer technology, and equipment for cataloging and classification. (ALA-LSSC Cataloging and Classification Competency 1)

Key Terms

Analog. A term used to describe continuous data such as an audiocassette or videotape. Libraries circulated analog media prior to its being replaced by digital media.

Bibliographic. Data that identifies or describes a library item or resource such as its title, author, copyright date, ISBN, publisher, size, media format, and so forth.

Carrier. Format of device used to view, listen to, or read content such as a computer disk, sheet, audiocassette, or filmstrip.

Controlled access. A way of locating a library item through a unique term or element such as the International Standard Book Number (ISBN) or an LC authority for name of author.

Digital. Of or relating to information that is stored in the form of the numbers 0 and 1 such as computer programs, e-books, DVDs, CDs, high-definition television programming, audio files. Nearly all of the media formats and technology libraries use today are digital.

FRAD. The initialism for Functional Requirements for Authority Data, a conceptual model for organizing authority and controlled-access information based on the needs of users.

FRBR. The initialism for Functional Requirements for Bibliographic Records, a conceptual model of the relationships between works, expressions of the work, the manifestation or production of the work, and the final item to be cataloged.

Keyword searching. A search using natural language that does not weigh or control the context of the word, as would be the case for a LC subject heading.

RDA. The initialism for Resource Description and Access, the new cataloging standard that replaces the *Anglo-American Cataloguing Rules* (AACR2).

INTRODUCTION

It may be presumptuous to think that RDA, FRBR, and FRAD can be explained in just one chapter when it has taken a decade of books, journal articles, training sessions, and web resources for seasoned catalogers to become comfortably familiar with these rules. In fact, it may be easier for new catalogers to learn them as part of their initial instruction than to superimpose a new way of thinking about cataloging on top of the old. This chapter explains RDA and shares practical ways to apply its rules in cataloging.

Key Components of Cataloging

Four key components guide cataloging practices: rules, standards, authorities, and call numbers. The act of cataloging a library resource takes into consideration all of these elements, as each provides important guidelines for creating records. Because these elements are strictly adhered to, libraries of all types and sizes are able to share their records economically and efficiently in highly successful local and union catalogs. In this chapter we focus on the rules that govern cataloging.

ANGLO-AMERICAN CATALOGING RULES

Before we know where we are going, it is helpful to understand where we have been. As indicated in chapter 2, the second edition of the *Anglo-American Cataloguing Rules* (AACR2) has been the comprehensive and definitive "gold standard" for cataloging library materials for the United States, Canada, the United Kingdom, Australia, and other English-speaking countries for many years. Each action performed by catalogers in the process of creating a bibliographic record is done under the direction of a clearly defined and specific rule found in AACR2. Since 1978 AACR2 has been published and updated by the Joint Steering Committee (JSC), whose members are the American Library Association, the Library of Congress, the British Library, the Canadian Committee on Cataloging, the Australian Committee on Cataloging, and the United Kingdom Chartered Institute of Library and Information Professionals (CLIP). Table 10.1 has a chronology of events and publications that bring us to RDA today.

Cataloging rules were fairly stable without great need of revision through the mid-1970s. Then something happened that revolutionized the way libraries did business. Electronic equipment for media became smaller, more affordable, and easier to use. As a result, more electronics worked their way into family budgets and homes. The library became a natural place for people to borrow audiocassettes and videotapes for their new equipment. The demand was great, and collections of nonprint materials grew. Added to this was the onset of personal computers in the mid-1990s and the change from an **analog** to a **digital** world. The AACR2 rules that worked for books and serials did not neatly apply to multimedia and new digital resources like CDs, DVDs, and e-books. Thus, the many revisions in AACR2 between 1978 and 2002 were designed to keep cataloging practices current with the digital age.

Table 10.1. Chronology of the Development of Cataloging Rules in United States

1876	Charles Ammi Cutter's *Rules for a Dictionary Catalog* is published.
1883 (revised in 1900)	The American Library Association (ALA) publishes cataloguing rules, *Condensed Rules for an Author and Title Catalog.*
1902	An edition of the revised ALA rules is produced by the Library of Congress.
1904	Uniformity is created between the ALA rules and the fourth edition of Cutter's rules
1908	The first international cataloguing code is published in an American edition (titled *Catalog Rules, Author and Title Entries*) and a British edition (titled *Cataloguing Rules, Author and Title Entries*).
1941	A preliminary second edition of the American edition of the 1908 rules is published by the American Library Association.
1949	*ALA Cataloging Rules for Author and Title Entries* is published.
1967	Two versions of the *Anglo-American Cataloguing Rules* (AACR) are published, a North American text and a British text.
1978	The second edition of the *Anglo-American Cataloguing Rules* (AACR2) is published as one version.
1981	AACR2 is adopted by the Library of Congress, the National Library of Canada, the British Library, and the Australian National Library.
1988	The 1988 revision of AACR2 incorporates the 1982, 1983, and 1985 revisions plus subsequent unpublished revisions.
1998	The 1998 revision of AACR2 incorporates the 1993 amendments and revisions approved between 1992 and 1996.
2002	The 2002 revision of AACR2 incorporates the 1999 and 2001 amendments and changes approved in 2001.
2004	In December 2004, a draft of the first part of AACR3 is made available to the constituencies for review.
2005	A new approach is agreed on, and the decision is made to adopt the title *RDA: Resource Description and Access.*
2010	RDA is published, and certain libraries begin using it for their cataloging workflow.
2013	The Library of Congress announces full implementation of RDA for March 31, 2013.

Source: "A Brief History of AACR," Joint Steering Committee for Development of RDA, last modified July 1, 2009, at www.rda-jsc.org/archivedsite/history.html (accessed February 21, 2016).

Metadata

Even as AACR2 was revised in 2002, the potential to search library materials with their metadata was lurking on the horizon. As we learned in chapter 6, metadata are the many points of description about an item that give us access to it. For example, as I look at my coffee mug before me, I see its shape, dimensions (height and diameter), capacity, material, and color. I also know it is used as a container to drink from that holds liquid at a high temperature longer than other drinking utensils. In addition, I know the mug was made locally for a fund-raising project. All of this descriptive information is metadata, and each piece of information may help in locating (or obtaining access) to this resource—the coffee mug.

In 2002 neither the MARC record template nor AACR2 rules had provisions for including such robust descriptive information in a catalog record. At the time when digital formats were rapidly changing, the JSC decided a complete overhaul of AACR2 was necessary. The JSC could not keep putting patches on a tire that was constantly in motion! Libraries were acquiring subscriptions to e-books, databases, and other new digital resources that needed to be included in the public online catalog but which contained potentially more and yet different kinds of descriptive metadata for which there were no AACR2 rules and for which the MARC template did not allow.

At the same time, the Internet and databases were rapidly offering **keyword searching,** which neither AACR2 nor MARC were constructed to support. AACR2 rules were specific about what information a cataloger could include in a record, and MARC set up a limited number of computer fields for searching. Gradually, ILSs coded for keywords within a title, author, subject, and sometimes content note. But there was a real need for catalogers to be prompted to include in a record much more metadata in order to give patrons access through any of the numerous ways they might search.

AACR3? Now RDA!

It was evident to the JSC and others that more search fields were needed for digital and new resources libraries were rapidly using or acquiring. A commitment was made by the JSC to completely overhaul AACR2. It would be called AACR3. In December 2004 a draft of the first part of AACR3 was made available for constituencies to review.

But as the work on AACR3 progressed, it was apparent a new way of thinking about cataloging was emerging that no longer had definitive rules about how to use select bibliographic information; rather, it focused on how to use the many descriptions of a library resource. Even the definition of a library resource was under debate. Library resources of the same title may be available from different publishers, but could also now be available in different formats—print, CD, e-book, databases, and so forth. With some of the new formats, patrons accessed resources in ways other than traditional checkout at the circulation desk.

In 2004 Tom Delsey, a consultant for information modeling, was appointed editor of AACR3.[1] The edition was given the subtitle "Resource Description and Access." Delsey consulted on the "Functional Requirements for Bibliographic Records" (FRBR) and the "Functional Requirements and Numbering of Authority Records" (FRANAR) projects for the International Federation of Library Associations and Institutions (IFLA), a member of the JSC. FRBR was adopted as an important model or framework for AACR3 as it delineates users' needs, groups or entities, and relationships. In this chapter we look at each of these frameworks, which are the basis for all cataloging rules today.

TEXTBOX 10.1. RDA CATALOGING

RDA cataloguing involves each of the following:

1. Resources to be cataloged
2. Descriptions of the resources
3. Access to the resources

In 2005 the JSC agreed on a new approach and made the decision to adopt the title "RDA: Resource Description and Access" and drop AACR3. This was a radical departure, as AACR2 had been in use since 1967—almost two generations. But the decision was made within the JSC to educate catalogers about new methods of cataloging and, more importantly, about the new rules that could keep current with library resources and how patrons searched for them, no matter how they would change in the future.

RDA: RESOURCE DESCRIPTION AND ACCESS

RDA is the name for the rules of cataloging for Anglo-American libraries in the world. RDA originally was to be called AACR3. If that had been the case, RDA may have been less confusing and more widely accepted by catalogers. Today, some still struggle to understand or explain it.

RDA is made up of three distinct parts. The three parts are the rules, the set of functional requirements for bibliographic resources (FRBR), and the functional requirements for authoritative descriptions (FRAD). Many of the AACR2 cataloging principles have been imported into RDA. It may be easier if we think of RDA as rules (mostly old) and requirements (mostly new). Underlying RDA are conceptual models and terminology. Before we explore the rules, FRBR, and FRAD, we need a working vocabulary of RDA.

TEXTBOX 10.2. THREE COMPONENTS OF RDA

1. Rules (mostly adapted from AACR2, others newly added)
2. Requirements for Bibliographic Resources
3. Requirements for Authoritative Resources

Together, the rules, bibliographic requirements, and authoritative requirements compose the RDA standards and guidelines for today's cataloger.

RDA Cataloging Rules

While we talk of RDA as a complete revision of AACR2, much of AACR2 is still in place. One of the main reasons for this high level of compatibility between RDA and AACR2 was the JSC's intention to retain and not scrap the millions of catalog records already in existence, so the model is designed to have both AACR2 records and RDA records function together in the same catalog. Both use MARC21 standards, but RDA's MARC21 template has more tags and fields than the MARC21 template before RDA. While catalogers may certainly upgrade records made under AACR2 rules to RDA, RDA and AACR2 can function together in the same database. In 2013 the Library of Congress made RDA its standard for cataloging with the hope that libraries across the country would also understand the need to shift to RDA and make the local commitment to do so. The rules for cataloging are available from the American Library Association in an online subscription called the RDA Toolkit.

Some of the changes from AACR2 rules to RDA rules are significant. Major changes have to do with separation of content and presentation, core elements, classes of materials, transcription of data, less use of abbreviations, relationship designators, the rule of three, content, and carrier.[2] For example, in AACR2 catalogers prolifically used abbreviations but in RDA catalogers are to spell words out.

TEXTBOX 10.3. LESS USE OF ABBREVIATIONS

```
AACR2   256p. : ill (some col.) ; 28 cm
RDA     256 pages : illustrations (some color) ; 28 cm
```

Another significant difference between RDA and AACR2 is that under AACR2 catalogers were told to follow the rule of three—if there were more than three authors, an item would have a title main entry and no authors would be included in the record—but in RDA, all authors are important and there is no limit to author added entries.

RDA Toolkit[3]

The RDA Toolkit is on online database of the updated resource description and access instructions for catalogers. The toolkit also contains the cataloging rules from AACR2 that were carried over into RDA. A subscription to the toolkit provides workflows, maps, and other templates that teach catalogers how to create searchable Internet bibliographic records. RDA supports technology that today can provide new exposure to the items in library collections. The RDA Toolkit is a subscription with annual renewals. Libraries can purchase it according to the number of users, gaining a small discount per user for libraries that have multiple catalogers.

Figure 10.1.   RDA Toolkit Logo. American Library Association, Chicago, IL.

The rules of cataloging comprise the first part of the RDA Toolkit. Because the toolkit is a subscription, changes can be readily made. Each year libraries renew their subscription to the toolkit, and by doing so they will always have the most up-to-date rules and training supports.

Vocabulary

One can easily become confused and overwhelmed with the vocabulary that accompanies RDA. Table 10.2 lists and defines some of RDA's key terms and how they are applied. In order for this vocabulary to make sense, it has to be applied in FRBR and FRAD. Before we move into those explanations, let's look at an important and fundamental difference between AACR2 and RDA with attributes and elements.

Table 10.2. RDA Vocabulary

Attributes	An identifying characteristic or feature of a work in AACR2. RDA calls these characteristics "elements." Attributes of an item are part of its metadata. An example of an attribute in AACR2 is the measurement of a book.
Element	An identifying characteristic or feature of a work in RDA. These characteristics were called "attributes" in AACR2. Elements of an item are part of its metadata. In RDA there are element sets for Groups, FRBR, and FRAD.
Entities	In FRBR and FRAD, entities are the different levels of a group that relate to the item or resource in a special way. For example, the entities in Group 2 are those people or corporate bodies responsible for all steps in the production of the item.
Groups	A number of people or things who are connected or related in some way. In FRBR there are three groups of entities about the item, who contributed to it, or its concept or location that would normally be independent of each other in AACR2 but are now grouped in RDA because they have a common relationship to the item being cataloged.
Relationships	Common bonds between entities (people or things) that work toward the same end.
Authorities	In both AACR2 and RDA, forms of names, titles, and subjects are established for standardization and uniformity. Attributes or identifying characteristics of a name may be recorded in an RDA authority record, thereby enabling that authority record to serve current and future bibliographic needs in a much more dynamic way.

At the most basic level every item has attributes and elements. Both words as used here refer to the metadata or descriptors of an item. From the beginning of time, all items have had metadata. The word may be new to catalogers, but the idea has been around forever. The metadata in AACR2 were called attributes. What were the attributes of a book? To catalogers they were its size, number of pages, illustrations, language, index, Festschrift (if the work honored a scholar), genre, country of publication, and so forth. There were many pieces of metadata, but in AACR2 they were all treated equally.

Attributes or Metadata in AACR2 with Equal Treatment

pages	index	lang	illus	festchr	genre	carrier	place	date	size

Figure 10.2. Attributes or Metadata in AACR2 with Equal Treatment.

AACR2 and RDA group metadata differently. First, attributes are now known as elements. While this is a subtle change in terminology, the idea is to standardize a vocabulary. "Element" is another name for metadata. Elements in RDA are grouped by entities, not unlike the elements of the periodic table in chemistry.

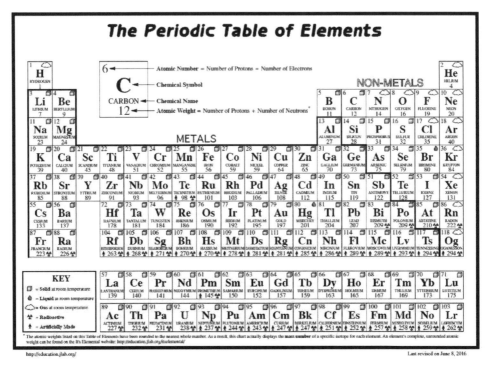

Figure 10.3.   Periodic Table of Elements.

In the periodic table, groups are formed around common characteristics of the chemical elements. In RDA, elements about a work to be cataloged with characteristics in common are also grouped. Figure 10.4 provides examples from the three groups found in the FRBR of RDA.

When catalogers accept that metadata—whether they are called attributes or elements—are grouped by entities with common characteristics or purpose, the ideas of FRBR and FRAD make more sense. Now that we undersand that like elements are grouped together, it is time to make the jump to FRBR and FRAD, two new cataloging practices that were adopted with RDA.

Example of Elements in the FRBR Group Entities of RDA

title	date	carrier

Group 1 Entities—Physical Characteristics of Works

author	creator	artist

Group 2 Entities—Responsible of Works

Group 3 Entities—Subjects of Works

Figure 10.4.   Example of Elements in the FRBR Group Entities of RDA.

FRBR

Functional Requirements for Bibliographic Records, or FRBR, is a model that helps catalogers think about and organize **bibliographic** metadata based on the needs of the patrons who will one day search for the item. FRBR applies the new vocabulary in the context of an item's bibliographic information. All bibliographic data or elements of an item are separated into one of three groups. Each group has entities or levels that cluster common metadata that could be both within and outside of the item (see table 10.3).

Table 10.3. FRBR Groups, Entities, and Examples of Bibliographic Elements

Group	Entities or Levels	Example of Bibliographic Elements
1. Products	Works	Title (of the intellectual content)
	Expressions	Language, sound recording, and so forth (how the work is expressed)
	Manifestations	Physical embodiment of the expression—that is, edition, various publishers, format (CD, DVD, text, audio)
	Items	The single manifestation or the item in hand to catalog
2. People	Person	Author, creator of an item
	Corporate Body	Sponsor, producer of an item
	Family	Two or more persons with legal status
3. Subjects	Concepts	Ideas, abstract models
	Objects	Physical things that can be touched or handled
	Events	Occurrences in the past, present, or future
	Place	Geographic locations within the universe
	Group 1	
	Group 2	

Groups

Each entity of bibliographic information has relationships to other entities within the group. An entity is also referred to as a level. Entities or levels in Group 1 of FRBR are sequential for the cataloger, who must (1) determine the title, (2) establish how it is expressed by either its language, type of text, media type, or other, (3) confirm the format or carrier of the work, and, finally, (4) catalog the item in hand, being confident about all of the previous entities.

This examination of the item in hand is no different than what catalogers have done since the nineteenth century when cataloging rules were first established. However, RDA with its FRBR model provides the cataloger with a process of thinking that makes sure all bibliographic options have been considered before creating or accepting a record. Once the bibliographic data of the item have been established, the next set of entities the cataloger must consider about the item are about responsibility.

If Group 1 is about the product, Group 2 is about the people. Group 2 entities are the people who created, produced, and disseminated the item in Group 1. Group 2 bibliographic metadata are about authorship, artistry, producers, publishers, and related people who inform the item, such as family members or musical or creative groups. Corporations that produce or sponsor an item are also in Group 2. Just as in AACR2 catalogers established the author, creator, or sponsor of an item, so in RDA catalogers do the same.

The third entities of bibliographic metadata are subjects, found in Group 3. Group 3 subjects have to do with concepts, objects, events, and places. Author names can also be subjects, as can special editions of works; therefore, Group 1 and Group 2 metadata could also appear in Group 3.

Let's go back and examine the coffee mug using FRBR:

Group 1—Products: Teachers are the Heart of Education (title), red, 10 cm. porcelain made in China

Group 2—People: Connecticut Education Association (organization), Academic Connection TM (manufacturer)

Group 3—Subjects: CEA Conference (event), coffee mug (object), teacher recognition (concept)

Practice classifying metadata into the FRBR groups. The more catalogers adopt FRBR into their conceptual thinking, the more skillful and confident with RDA they will become.

In the third part of this book we will practice placing the metadata of the FRBR bibliographic entities into MARC21 fields and subfields. Remember, the goal of the JSC was not to create a separate and incompatible set of catalog rules. Rather, RDA creatively works with AACR2, and thus MARC21 mostly remains the same today as it did prior to RDA. However, some new fields and subfields were required to accommodate the deep level of metadata, such as the descriptive tags for format and **carrier** metadata of Group 1, now extracted from items to be cataloged.

Table 10.4.   RDA and New MARC21 Fields

RDA Type	Description	MARC21 Field
RDA Content types	Sounds, text, computer program, cartographic moving image (MARC 336 field)	336
RDA Media types	Media form such as audio, microform, video, computer	337
RDA Carrier types	Format of device used to view, listen, or read the content such as computer disk, sheet, audiocassette, filmstrip (MARC 338 field)	338

We have now been introduced to both RDA rules and FRBR. The RDA authorities that govern the item are the third important part. These authorities are found in Functional Requirements for Authority Data, or FRAD.

FRAD

RDA is the acronym for Resources Description and Access. *R* represents *resources* and, in this chapter, we also link it to the revised cataloging *rules*. *D* reminds us of the increased number of bibliographic *descriptions* of product, people, and subject metadata using the model of FRBR. We will now look at the letter *A* for *access* points, but, before we do so, we need first to understand the importance of another *A*—*authorities*.

Photo 10.1. Metadata of a coffee mug.

Table 10.5.   Controlled Access Points in FRAD

Title	Name of the work. Check LC Authorities for uniform or preferred title if any doubt.
Names	Creators, authors, corporate bodies, editors, illustrators, performers, and others who contribute or have an important relationship to the work or its expression. Names of series also give controlled access.
Identifiers	Bibliographic metadata that is unique to the item such as ISBN, ISSN, edition, volume, issue, version, or searchable product codes.

Authorities

There is no difference in authority control between AACR2 and RDA. The rules and standards for name, uniform title, and subject authority control, determined and compiled by the Library of Congress, remain the same (see chapter 3). In fact, catalogers may use the LC Authorities even more in RDA because the bibliographic metadata for names and subjects have the potential to increase.[4] For example, the old rule of three whereby catalogers stopped adding authors after the third, even if there were more than three authors, no longer applies. Cataloger may check the LC Name Authorities four, five, or more times to give all authors credit for their work. Likewise, catalogers using RDA are now encouraged not to stop at just a few subjects. Each subject should be vetted through the LC Subject Authorities and its rules. There may also be more variant titles or versions that differ slightly from the uniform title. Again, the cataloger will rely on the LC Authorities to suggest different forms of the title if appropriate.

There are other authoritative data that comes under FRAD, such as ISBN, or International Standard Book Number. The ISBN is authoritative metadata because it is a single identifier of a source. Other identifiers may be ISSN for serials, software or media codes, logos, or other numbers or symbols by which an item can be found. While barcodes identify items in item records, they are assigned by libraries and are not part of the bibliographic record. In other words, the circulation barcode given to a copy of *The Hunger Games* in one library will not be the same barcode given to *The Hunger Games* in another library. However, the ISBN remains the same no matter where the version of the book is located. This permanent ISBN is an authoritative identifier.

Access

FRAD is also about **controlled access** points. Controlled access is the bibliographic authoritative elements a patron could use to reliably find an item. The controlled access points are from the LC Authorities and unique product identifiers.

Establishing the idea that authorities provide controlled access points is important in FRAD. Without authority, there would be no reliable control on access points. Just like in AACR2, catalogers must use the LC authority form of an author's name and not variations of it so that patrons can search the name and find all of the author's works. The relationships within the entities of FRBR and between the elements of FRBR and FRAD are the final part of RDA. Like all we have seen so far with RDA, there are very few changes to the bibliographic elements of an item from AACR2, but the way catalogers approach and think about their work has been modernized from plugging in data to approaching the catalog record as a way to enrich the searching process.

RELATIONSHIPS IN FRBR AND FRAD

We will first explore the relationships within Group 1 entities of FRBR. Group 1 entities have to do with the product. The FRBR entities of Group 1 are shown in figure 10.5.

FRBR Group 1 Entities

The Work →	The Expression →	The Manifestation →	The Item

Three actions take place in order to create the item in hand. These actions are related to each other in an orderly and sequential flow chart of steps.

Step 1	Step 2	Step 3	Step 4
The content, idea, or concept is →	Expressed in a language, sound, film, etc. →	And produced or manifested into a set of copies →	Whereby one copy is ordered by the library and is ready to be cataloged.

Figure 10.5. FRBR Group 1 Entities.

In the relationships, each step requires an action or verb. The verbs found in table 10.6 are used in RDA to describe the relationships that take place between the entities in FRBR Group 1.

Table 10.6. Verbs Used to Describe Relationships within FRBR

RDA Verbs	Definition	Relationships of Action Steps
Realized	to bring into concrete existence	The content of a *work* becomes fixed or concrete in the *expression* of how it is told whether by language, text, sound, film, etc.
Embodied	to make concrete and perceptible	The expression of the work is *manifested* or produced into a specific edition, publication, or product line.
Exemplified	to be an instance of	The item in hand to be cataloged is one example of other exact copies that were manifested or produced of the expression of the work.

There are other Group 1 relationships within FRBR. One that catalogers commonly confront is manifestation to manifestation. E-books are an example of this special relationship when an exact digital copy is made from a print work. The second manifestation (the e-book) is directly related to the first manifestation (the print book) when the e-book is, for example, an exact scanned PDF copy. The RDA Toolkit and other texts on RDA provide other examples of Group 1 relationships within FRBR.[5]

FRAD Relationships

FRBR Group 1 entities relate to each other and go sequentially from the *work* to the *expression* to the *manifestation*, ending with the *item* level and the entities of authority and access points of FRAD. FRBR Group 2 entities of *people, corporate bodies*, and *families* relate to FRAD entities of *authorities* and *access points*. Let's look at how FRBR Group 2 and FRAD work together.

To understand FRAD, we have to first look at its four categories of relationships. These four levels are listed in textbox 10.4.

TEXTBOX 10.4. FOUR LEVELS OF FRAD RELATIONSHIPS

Level 1: between main groups of entities
Level 2: between persons, families, corporate bodies, and FRBR works
Level 3: between names and persons, families, corporate bodies, and FRBR works
Level 4: between controlled access points

At the highest level of FRAD relationships are the RDA rules that require LC or other authority control such as adding, editing, or maintaining uniform titles, form of persons' names, and headings and assigning identifiers of ISBN and other codes and headings used for controlled access points. At level 1 FRAD specifies that the cataloging process must relate to and follow all rules for RDA authority and access to ensure the high quality of the record so it can be shared and used universally in library catalogs.

Level 2 relationships are between FRBR bibliographic entities of works and the FRAD entities of persons, families, and corporate bodies. These relationships may not be as obvious and often are explained in content or source notes in the MARC record. For example, years ago the poet and songwriter Patti Smith had a deep friendship with the photographer Robert Mapplethorpe that informed her early writing. This idea would be a level 2 FRAD relationship. Another example is the relationship between works. Playwright Author Miller said his writing of *Death of a Salesman* and other plays was influenced by his reading of Dostoevsky's novel *The Brothers Karamazov*.[6] RDA encourages level 2 FRAD and FRBR relationships be included in the catalog record to extend access to other sources.

Level 3 relationships are more familiar and direct between the FRAD entities of names and persons, families, corporate bodies, and the FRBR entity of works. In this relationship the term "known by" is used as a guide. The standard catalog process of "see" and "see also" to find other resources related to the item searched is a level 3 FRAD relationship. An example of a FRAD relationship between names could be "Mark Twain see Samuel Clemens." These two names are related because they refer ultimately to the same person. The LC Authorities dictate that books by Mark Twain should have controlled access with the birth name of Samuel Clemens. Mark Twain is *known by* Samuel Clemens and vice versa.

At level 4 we find the FRAD relationships between controlled access points when the element is in a different language, alphabet, or language script (such as a work in Mandarin also expressed in English); when the access point was created under another set of cataloging rules that are not RDA (from another country); or between a LC subject and a call number. For the beginning cataloger, FRAD relationships will usually be made by the cataloging supervisor as they often require more depth of knowledge or study about the item. However, if the support staff is the only cataloger in the library, he or she should receive training in FRAD to be able to competently apply it to the creation of records.

SUMMARY

RDA is in its infancy, and there will undoubtedly be bumps along the road and refinements to make the rules more understandable. Catalogers who learn the rules and authorities of RDA, FRBR, and FRAD will be able to apply and manage the appropriate current processes for cataloging and classification. Participating in RDA workshops, webinars, and other trainings is even more important today as catalogers become conceptual thinkers who can apply new rules and entities relationships in the process of creating quality records.

DISCUSSION QUESTIONS AND ACTIVITIES

Discussion Questions

1. What are the four key elements of the cataloging process? Why is each one important?
2. What is the definitive source for cataloging rules today? Where does the library obtain these rules? Do they own them or subscribe to them? Explain.
3. What do the terms "elements," "entities," "groups," "authorities," and "relationships" mean in RDA cataloging? How is each term used in the cataloging process?
4. What does FRBR mean and what it is its main purpose in cataloging?
5. What does FRAD mean and what is its main purpose in cataloging?
6. What are the three groups in FRBR and what are the entities in each group?
7. What are the four levels of FRAD relationships and how does the cataloger use them to create a bibliographic record for an item?

Activity 1

Each item that is cataloged originates as a creation or *work*, is *expressed* in a specific way such as in a particular language, song, or even film. It is *manifested* or produced in a format such as a print book, DVD, or perhaps a digital file. Those formats are sold as multiple *items*, one of which the cataloger holds in his or her hand to copy or create a record for the online catalog before it goes on the shelf.

In your library online catalog, search the famous title *The Adventures of Tom Sawyer*. Select two different editions of this novel, such as a paperback, a DVD, a hardback book, or an e-book. Make a chart using the categories shown in table 6.4, describing how each of these two items goes through the FRBR Group 1 Entities process from a *work* to an *item*. Describe what happens in each step using proper terminology. (See table 10.7.)

Table 10.7.   Four Steps of FRBR Group 1 Entities
(*The Adventures of Tom Sawyer*)

Step 1	Step 2	Step 3	Step 4
(WORK)	(EXPRESSION)	(MANIFESTATION)	(ITEM)

Activity 2: Level 3 FRAD Relationships

Level 3 FRAD are known relationships between persons, families, corporate bodies, and FRBR works. The standard catalog process of "see" and "see also" is a level 3 FRAD relationship.

For this activity you will use the LC Name Authorities found at authorities.loc.gov/.

Using this authority, find five famous families, groups, or corporate bodies and enter them in column 1. Click on the button "Authorized & Relationships" to the right of the name. Select one of the entities, such as a person, that has a relationship with this group and copy it into column 2. In column 3, explain what the relationship is (see table 10.8).

Table 10.8.   Level 3 FRAD Relationships

Group LC Name Authority	Enter a person who has a relationship with the group	Describe what the relationship is
Monkees (Musical group)	See Also: Jones, Davy, 1945–2012	Davy Jones was a musician and member of the band The Monkees

NOTES

1. "Tom Delsey Appointed as AACR3 Editor," Joint Steering Committee for the Development of RDA, Historic Documents, press release, September 17, 2004, at www.rda-jsc.org/archivedsite/aacr3editor.html (accessed February 24, 2016).

2. Amy Hart, *The RDA Primer: A Guide for the Occasional Cataloger* (Santa Barbara, CA: Linworth, 2010), 37.

3. "RDA Toolkit," American Library Association, at www.rdatoolkit.org/ (accessed February 25, 2016).

4. "Search Authorities," Library of Congress Authorities, at authorities.loc.gov/ (accessed February 26, 2016).

5. "RDA Toolkit."

6. Mark Lamos, "An Interview with Arthur Miller," *Michigan Quarterly Review* 46, no. 1 (2007), at hdl.handle.net/2027/spo.act2080.0046.113 (accessed February 27, 2016).

REFERENCES, SUGGESTED READINGS, AND WEBSITES

American Library Association. "RDA Toolkit." Accessed February 25, 2016, at www.rdatoolkit.org/.

Hart, Amy. "Getting Ready for RDA: What You Need to Know." *Library Media Connection* 29, no. 2 (October/November 2010): 30–32.

———. *The RDA Primer: A Guide for the Occasional Cataloger*. Santa Barbara, CA: Linworth, 2010.

IFLA Working Group on Functional Requirements and Numbering of Authority Records (FRANAR). *Functional Requirements for Authority Data: A Conceptual Model*. The Hague, Netherlands: IFLA, 2013. Available at www.ifla.org/files/assets/cataloguing/frad/frad_2013.pdf.

Joint Steering Committee for the Development of RDA. "A Brief History of AACR." Last modified July 1, 2009. Accessed February 21, 2016, at www.rda-jsc.org/archivedsite/history.html.

———. "The FRBR-RDA Puzzle: Putting the Pieces Together, Answers to Exercises." Accessed February 27, 2016, at www.rda-jsc.org/archivedsite/docs/2a-OLA-2011-FRBR-RDA-puzzle-answers-Brenndorfer.pdf.

———. "Historic Documents." Last modified July 15, 2009. Accessed February 21, 2016, at http://www.rda-jsc.org/archivedsite/docs.html.

———. "Tom Delsey appointed as AACR3 Editor." Last modified September 17, 2004. Accessed February 24, 2016, at www.rda-jsc.org/archivedsite/aacr3editor.html.

Lamos, Mark. "An Interview with Arthur Miller." *Michigan Quarterly Review* 46, no. 1 (2007). Available at hdl.handle.net/2027/spo.act2080.0046.113.

Library of Congress. *FRBR: FRBR, RDA, and MARC*. Cooperative and Instructional Programs Division, September 2012. Accessed February 27, 2016, at www.loc.gov/catworkshop/RDA%20training%20materials/LC%20RDA%20Training/FRBR_Module%203_FRBR%20&%20RDA%20&%20MARC/FRBR%20%20RDA%20%20MARC_studentversion_20120818.pdf.

———. *FRBR: Fundamental Concepts*. Cooperative and Instructional Programs Division, September 2012. Accessed February 27, 2016, at www.loc.gov/catworkshop/RDA%20training%20materials/LC%20RDA%20Training/FRBR_Module%201_Overview/FRBRFundamentals_20120809_student.pdf.

———. "MARC21, FRBR, RDA." Powerpoint Presentation. Accessed February 27, 2016, at www.google.com/url?sa=t&rct=j&q=&esrc=s&source=web&cd=2&ved=0ahUKEwiY1_nB8JLLAhXF_R4KHeCoAdcQFgghMAE&url=http%3A%2F%2Fwww.loc.gov%2Fcatworkshop%2FRDA%2520training%2520materials%2FLC%2520RDA%2520Training%2FFRBR_Module%25203_FRBR%2520%26%2520RDA%2520%26%2520MARC%2FFRBR%2520%2520RDA%2520%2520MARC_teacherversion_20120618.pptm&usg=AFQjCNH-bijOseVb_KIdWOYdzD3AUa5WEw&sig2=_gDPtTHsbJ2Nimap51eaeA&bvm=bv.115339255,bs.2,d.cWw.

———. "Search Authorities." Library of Congress Authorities. Accessed February 26, 2016, at authorities.loc.gov/.

Oliver, Chris. *Introducing RDA: A Guide to the Basics*. Chicago: American Library Association, 2010.

Open Metadata Registry. "The RDA (Resource Description and Access) Vocabularies." Accessed February 24, 2016, at rdvocab.info/.

Resource Description and Access (RDA). "RDA Registry." Last modified February 15, 2016. Accessed February 24, 2016, at www.rdaregistry.info/.

Shrout, Bill. *FRBR and RDA: RDA Training for Kentucky Public Libraries, Part 1*. Kentucky Department for Libraries and Archives, Summer 2013. Accessed February 27, 2016, at kdla.ky.gov/librarians/staffdevelopment/Documents/Part1FRBRRDAv5.pdf.

Tillett, Barbara. "The FRBR Model (Functional Requirements for Bibliographic Records)." Paper presented at the ALCTS Institute on Metadata and AACR2, San Jose, CA. April 4–5, 2003. Available at www.loc.gov/catdir/cpso/frbreng.pdf.

———. "FRBR: Things You Should Know, But Were Afraid To Ask." Library of Congress Webcast. March 4, 2009. Available at https://www.loc.gov/today/cyberlc/feature_wdesc.php?rec=4554.

———. "RDA Workshop." Lecture presented at the Georgia Cataloging Summit. August 10, 2011.

Welsh, Anne, and Sue Batley. *Practical Cataloging: AACR2, RDA, and MARC21*. Chicago: Neal Schuman, 2012.

CHAPTER 11

BIBFRAME—Preparing Catalogers for the Future

LSS apply and manage the appropriate processes, computer technology, and equipment for cataloging and classification. (ALA-LSSC Cataloging and Classification Competency 1)

LSS know and can explain the value and purpose of cataloging and classification to help users find the resources that they seek. (ALA-LSSC Cataloging and Classification Competency 7)

Key Terms

BIBFRAME. An acronym for the term "Bibliographic Framework," this Library of Congress initiative will replace MARC record cataloging in the future. Cataloging standards are changing to include more description and metadata that will be accessed universally through search engines rather than proprietary MARC record systems. MARC records will transfer to BIBFRAME. The Library of Congress will determine when to abandon the MARC standard.

BIBFRAME Annotation. One of the four high-level classes, an Annotation may share opinions about a resource such as a review, provide institution specific information, or enhance a description, such as cover art or a summary.

BIBFRAME Authority. One of the four high-level classes, an Authority is used to identify agents such as authors, editors, or distributors of a Work; places such as towns, countries, or continents; and subjects that the work is about, such as topical concepts, places, agents, and the like.

BIBFRAME Instance. One of the four high-level classes, an Instance reflects an individual, material embodiment of a BIBFRAME Work that can be physical or digital. A BIBFRAME Instance includes properties specific to the publication, production, manufacture, and distribution of the material.

BIBFRAME Work. One of the four high-level classes, a Work reflects a conceptual entity such as an unpublished story written by an author or the song of a musician that is

---

not yet produced. A BIBFRAME Work is an abstract entity, as there is no single material object one can point to.

Class. In BIBFRAME this is one of fifty-three groups of common data, similar to a tag or field in a MARC record. The first letter of a class name in BIBFRAME is capitalized to distinguish it from a property. There are four high-level classes: Work, Instance, Authority, and Annotation.

HTML. An initialism for hypertext markup language, the accepted tagging and coding of text files for Internet web pages that create variations in font, color, graphic layout, design, and hyperlink effects.

Monograph. A written account of a single topic, most commonly published as a book (print or digital), or a one-volume scholarly work such as a thesis or manuscript.

Natural language. Not computer code or artificial programming commands, this is the ordinary day-to-day speaking and writing used by humans to communicate with each other in their native tongues such as in English, Spanish, or Mandarin Chinese.

Properties. Terms in BIBFRAME that identify, describe, or relate specific data (in lower case) found in a broader group or class; they are called "elements" in RDA and "subfields" in MARC records.

RDF/XML Code. The computer code or language that will mostly replace HTML as the computer language for Web 3.0. This code will have customized tagging schemes and common formats that will enhance the interchange of data on the semantic web.

Semantic web. This is a name for the upcoming Web 3.0 that will replace the current Web 2.0. On the semantic web it will be easier to find, share, reuse, and combine information through customized tagging schemes and common formats for the interchange of data that Web 2.0 does not offer.

INTRODUCTION

The rules and practices of Anglo-American cataloging have a long history of change. In previous chapters we discussed how cataloging rules, call numbers, formats, standards, and authorities have evolved. The need for significant revisions to cataloging practices often resulted from external events, such as the passing of the U.S. Copyright Act of 1870, the development of government mainframe computers in the 1950s, and the evolution of high-speed networks and other technologies that enabled libraries to share their catalogs in the twenty-first century.

In this chapter we examine a major revision to cataloging practices that is currently ongoing. This revision is called **BIBFRAME**. A main purpose of BIBFRAME is to link library items to websites and related information found on the Internet. In the future BIBFRAME will replace the MARC21 standard.

BIBFRAME BACKGROUND

MARC has been around since the 1960s. MARC, or machine readable cataloging, was created by the Library of Congress (LC) as the standard format for entering bibliographic data. Library catalogers first used MARC to standardize the way information was typed on catalog cards. When cards were replaced by integrated library systems (ILSs), MARC created the computer record or file for each item with links to cataloging, circulation, and the online public catalog. As cataloging rules changed, even recently with RDA, the MARC format adjusted to accommodate new fields or subfields.

Table 11.1 compares a simple main title entry (245 tag) in MARC to the same entry in BIBFRAME. You may be very surprised to see the comparison! In this chapter we explore the reasons cataloging is undergoing such significant changes.

Table 11.1. Title Entry in MARC vs BIBFRAME for the work *Environmental Science & Technology*

MARC	BIBFRAME
245 00 Environmental science & technology	http://id.loc.gov/resources/bibs/11160818, a
	bf:Work ;
	bf:hasInstance [a bf:Instance ;
	bf:keyTitle [a bf:Title ;
	bf:label "Environmental science & technology" ;
	bf:titleValue "Environmental science & technology"]]

BIBFRAME is the acronym for Bibliographic Framework and will be a new way of representing and exchanging bibliographic data.[1] BIBFRAME will use the future potential of Web 3.0 and will replace the MARC format.

Evolution of the Web

Why are the LC and others undertaking such a radical change to replace their MARC cataloging format? One reason is the evolution of the web. The LC has continually demonstrated leadership in exploring government use of computers and revising cataloging practices to use new technologies. The LC established authorities for names and subjects and created standard fields and subfields for data entry. Because of its foresight in standardizing entries, library catalogs and services can be shared and networked locally, regionally, and globally, unlike the databases used in other professions. With BIBFRAME the LC is continuing its practice of aligning cataloging practices with future technology, and library catalogs will be fully ready to use the new resources with the upcoming Web 3.0.

To understand Web 3.0, we should look back at where we have been. Each generation of the web can be identified by clusters of new applications or services that open up new ways of using the Internet. Some would say that Web 1.0 was the Internet from 1990 through 2000 and Web 2.0 evolved from 2000 through 2015. Currently, the world is transitioning to Web 3.0 and may be using its resources fully by 2020. Regardless of the exact dates, the Internet today is evolving significantly from where it has been for the past decade.

What is the connection between the web and cataloging? How does the relationship affect the cataloger? In short, the web has been our delivery system for MARC records and authorities. Not unlike UPS or FedEx, catalogers use the web for receiving and sending MARC records to and from other library catalogs or systems. But this is about to change. The cataloger who understands how the web is evolving may be more receptive to learning how it will provide new opportunities for moving MARC cataloging to BIBFRAME. A cataloger who understands the relationship between the new web and the new cataloging model of BIBFRAME will be an invaluable member of the cataloging department as it grapples with radical changes in its work.

Before Web 1.0, personal computers were primarily used to create, store, and retrieve information from files and databases, but they could not link users to outside information sources. Email was not web-based at this time. When **HTML** was developed and became the code for the Internet, information could be shared between computers because they "spoke" the same language. Exact words or phrases could retrieve information from other computers' databases and websites. Web 1.0 was "one-way": information was downloaded in one direction from an outside source to the user. Catalogers immediately were ready for and used Web 1.0 at its onset because we had already adopted the MARC format standard at our local libraries and could download MARC records from OCLC or the LC to use with our cataloging systems. In other words, because of the standardization of MARC, local cataloging computers were compatible with outside library sources.

Web 2.0 defined partnerships and sharing with others. Think of Web 2.0 as "two-way" exchanges of files, communications, and services. Examples of Web 2.0 applications are Wikis, social media, portals, software as a service (SaaS), online shopping and banking, the cloud, streaming, texts, email, and other interactions via the Internet that go back and forth. Keyword searching and overwriting catalog records are just two of the many Web 2.0 services and applications libraries rely on today.

Web 3.0

What is Web 3.0? It contains all of the Web 2.0 resources and more! Web 3.0 will connect data, concepts, applications, and ultimately people.[2] Also called the **semantic web**, it will provide an easier way to find, share, reuse, and combine information through customized tagging schemes and common formats for the interchange of data. There will be a common language for recording how data relate to real-world objects, allowing a person or a machine to start off in one database and then move through an unending set of databases connected not by wires but by *being* about the same thing. Web 3.0 will have deeper and more extensive links to and among related ideas, concepts, and data. Thus, searching will no longer depend on a user coming up with keywords; rather, he or she will be able to find information through semantics with search engines applying the meanings, words, or associations to concepts.

Web 3.0 can be understood as made up of three distinct components: the semantic web, the mobile web, and the immersive Internet.[3] All three types inform the BIBFRAME model of cataloging. With the semantic web, software has been developed that can understand the meaning of data and use natural-language searches. Searches will be automatically tailored to users' needs, location, and identity. In a way that is similar to how we use the cloud today, the mobile web will allow us to effortlessly move from one device or location to another. In the immersive Internet, virtual worlds, augmented reality, and 3-D environments are the norm. All three types of Internet will be integrated and work together for the user in Web 3.0.

TEXTBOX 11.1. THREE COMPONENTS OF WEB 3.0

Semantic web. Search engines use natural language and interpret the conceptual meaning of data.
Mobile web. Users can search from any device in any location.
Immersive web. Users actively participate in virtual worlds, augmented reality, and 3-D environments.

Web 3.0 and BIBFRAME

RDA was developed to work with both MARC and BIBFRAME. In the previous chapter on RDA cataloging rules, we saw that catalogers now consider the relationships between and among bibliographic and authority elements and entities of an item. The MARC format has been adapted to create searchable access points for RDA descriptive data. In the near future with Web 3.0 and the replacement of MARC by BIBFRAME, the potential for searching library items will greatly expand.

Rather than filling out a MARC form, where the data can only be accessed through its own unique tags and fields, the BIBFRAME cataloger will be coding bibliographic information into **RDF/XML** computer language that will be commonly used across the Internet. Because BIBFRAME uses RDF/XML, people using sematic searches of topics, names, or concepts in Web 3.0 will find in their results concepts and relationships that may link to the bibliographic and authoritative data of library items. No longer will the patron need to know the bibliographic data of an item to locate it.

Table 11.2. Comparison with Examples of the Three Stages of the Web

Web 1.0	Progression	Web 2.0	Today	Web 3.0
1990–2000		2000–2015		2020–2030
One-way movement of data: download		Two-way movement of data: download and upload		An interconnection of relationships
websites		portals		semantic searching
Boolean searches		keyword searches		mashups
databases		collaboration		semantic databases
groups		social media		widgets
e-mail		SaaS		distributed searching
HTML		wikis		intelligent personal
Java		the cloud		agents
		Flash		
		RSS		

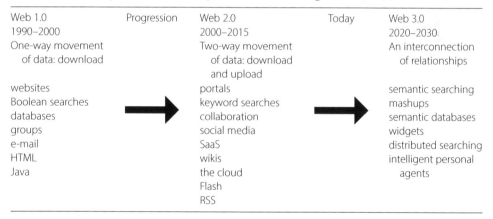

Web 3.0 is also known as "Linked Data" and the "semantic web." Web 3.0 is connecting and linking information in order to provide context that can be discerned by a nonhuman entity or search engine.[4] As we saw in RDA, in Web 3.0 objects are categorized based on their relationship to other data objects, giving a context to the object and allowing library data to be integrated with external, nonlibrary data. The LC Authorities, AACR2, and RDA have resulted in trustworthy data, making libraries a reliable point of linking. With RDA rules and the BIBFRAME code of RDF/XML, library catalogs will be an important link to authoritative information across the 3.0 Internet.

BIBFRAME INITIATIVE

The LC has declared the BIBFRAME Initiative as the future of cataloging; the initiative will take place on the web and be networked around the world.[5] BIBFRAME integrates library catalogs with the global information community of the web as it also serves the local information needs of libraries. Accepting RDA rules is a first step in the implementation of BIBFRAME and is slated to occur around 2020. There are three main goals of the BIBFRAME Initiative:

TEXTBOX 11.2. GOALS OF THE BIBFRAME INITIATIVE

1. Differentiate between conceptual content and its physical or digital manifestation(s)
2. Clearly identify information entities, such as authorities
3. Leverage and expose relationships between and among entities[6]

Unlike MARC, where an item's bibliographic data was recorded as it appeared onto the appropriate field or subfield, the BIBFRAME model differentiates the item's bibliographic data into types following the entities of RDA.

Table 11.3. Examples of RDA Bibliographic Data in BIBFRAME

RDA Entities	Description	Example
Work	FRBR Conceptual Creation	Title and author
Manifestation	FRBR Physical Details	Page numbers, edition, illustrations
Authorities	FRAD Relationship	Author and publisher authority and relationship
Subjects	FRAD Concepts	Subjects associated with a resource

Table 11.3 shows how catalogers will approach their work much differently. In MARC, bibliographic information focuses on the work and its manifestation. RDA and BIBFRAME equally value the relationships associated with the item as important points of access. With Web 3.0 poised to support semantic and **natural language**, patrons will expect to find library items through associations as they do with their other searches. The cataloger will populate the BIBFRAME records with both bibliographic and conceptual information that will support this new way of searching across the web—not just in ILS catalogs—for library resources.

BIBFRAME CLASSES AND PROPERTIES

MARC tags and fields are used to group common or like data. Subfields are used to identify specific data of the field. A BIBFRAME **class** is also a group of common data (with initial capitals), and **properties** identify and relate specific data (rendered in lower case) in the class. In the BIBFRAME model there are currently fifty-three classes (see table 11.7). Of the fifty-three classes, there are four primary or high-level classes:[7]

Table 11.4. High-Level Classes in BIBFRAME with Parallel Concepts in RDA and MARC

Class in BIBFRAME	Entities in RDA	Elements in RDA	Fields or Subfields in MARC
Work	Works and Expressions	Elements of works and expressions	Uniform title authority information
Instance	Manifestation	Elements of manifestations	Approximately corresponds to MARC bibliographic descriptions
Authority			MARC names and subjects (but not titles— these are in BIBFRAME Works)
			Other types of authority such as classification, publisher, and the like.
Annotations	Items		

Each class group has unique properties that help sort or explain the item's data and its relationship to other sources on the web. The numerous properties (currently there are 289 properties) are specific metadata or elements that have a relationship to one or more of the fifty-three classes.

A **BIBFRAME Work** is an abstract conceptual entity that has not yet been made into a physical item.[8] Like the RDA Work, it could be an author's novel, a director's film, or a songwriter's lyrics and music that have been created but not manifested into a specific format or publication. Common properties of Works include contextual relationships to BIBFRAME Authorities related to the topic, subject, person, and so on of the work as well as the entities of person, organization, jurisdiction, and so forth associated with its creation. Works can relate to other Works, reflecting specific relationships.

A **BIBFRAME Instance** reflects an individual, material embodiment of a work that can be physical or digital in nature.[9] In RDA, this is called the manifestation. A BIBFRAME Instance could be a book, film, a streamed video, or any other library resource. Common properties are specific to the publication, production, manufacture, and distribution of the material.

The **BIBFRAME Authority** defines relationships reflected in the Work and Instance. Examples include people, places, topics, organizations, and the like. One important concept in Authority is domain, which is the entity taking responsibility for the recognition, organization, and maintenance to ensure authoritative resources. The editor agent is an example of a domain. Common properties are the authorities responsible for the integrity of the Work or Instance, including the agents, place, time period, and topic. We use the LC Authorities for subject and author BIBFRAME Authority.

A **BIBFRAME Annotation** provides information about a BIBFRAME Work, Instance, Authority, or another Annotation.[10] Annotations express opinions about a resource—for example, a review could be an Annotation. They can also provide institution-specific information, such as holdings. Annotations can provide description about cover art or item summaries. Common properties are annotations, tables of contents, indexes, reviews, notes, or summaries.

Cataloging prior to RDA and BIBFRAME was mostly "data neutral," which means that, other than title, author, and subjects, there was no greater significance placed on one subfield than on another. Catalogers did not think about how the data of an item interacted; rather, they looked for information from the item to slot into the correct field or subfield of a MARC record.

With RDA and even more fully with BIBFRAME, catalogers will look to see how properties (metadata) relate and "fit" with other metadata in broad categories of classes and specific data of other properties. Catalogers will research the items in hand and draw conclusions about how the metadata fit into a bigger picture—the world wide web of information—and how it can be retrieved with multiple points of access.

Table 11.5 shows just four of the fifty-three classes and only a handful of the 289 properties that go with each class. Remember, there are so many properties because libraries have numerous types of resources. Many of the properties for print books will differ from the properties for online films. Many of the properties are also used with multiple classes. Full listings of classes and properties can be found on Bibframe.org.

Table 11.5. Examples of Classes and Properties

BIBFRAME Class	Examples of Properties for the BIBFRAME High-Level Classes
Work	agent, arrangement, audience, barcode, carrier, cartography, classification, classification number, contains, contributor, copy, cover art, dimensions, distribution, expression of, format, frequency, genre, identifier, illustration, index, ISBN, ISSN, key title, language, material, music, part of, performer, place, precedes, production, provider, publication, publisher, relationship, reproduction, responsibility statement, review, series, subject, summary, supersedes, system number, table of contents, title, translation, union, video
Instance	abbreviated title, accompanied by, arrangement, award note, carrier, category, change date, CODEN, color content, contents note, credits note, derivative of, dimensions, duration, graphic scale note, handle, illustration note, instance of, ISBN, ISMN (international standard music number), manufacture, music medium, notation, note, place, preceded by, provider, related instance, related resource, stock number, title, UPC, URN
Authority	agent/entity having a role in a resource (person, organization, and so on); place/ geographic location; temporal concept/chronological period; topic/concept or area of knowledge
Annotation	authorized access point, identifier, label, related to, annotates, annotation asserted by, annotation body, annotation source, assertion date, cover art, held material, review, summary, table of contents

Source: "Key title—Property," Bibliographic Framework Initiative, Library of Congress, at bibframe.org/vocab/ keyTitle.html (accessed March 7, 2016).

BIBFRAME MODEL

The cataloging process of every item in BIBFRAME can be divided into two parts: the Work and the Instance (see figure 11.1). The process of gathering and identifying the data of the Work leads the cataloger to the LC Subject and Name Authorities and to the relationships found with each. The steps in gathering and identifying the data of the Instance are more concrete and physical where the item in hand is examined closely for its elements.

The model can twist and turn, looking slightly different for each item. For example, cataloging an item that is the manifestation of the third edition of a hardcover book would have relationship links to other past versions that a first-edition paperback would not have. In each case the Work and Instance are examined and the other two classes—Authority and Annotations—are considered. For each class appropriate properties are selected. This is very different from MARC, where the cataloger basically began with the 008 field and worked downward to the 800 fields. The pattern of work in MARC was rote, and the cataloger was not challenged to think about how concepts or relationships to outside sources could be found.

With the BIBFRAME model there are classes and properties, but there is also an extensive list of vocabularies for catalogers to consider and use.

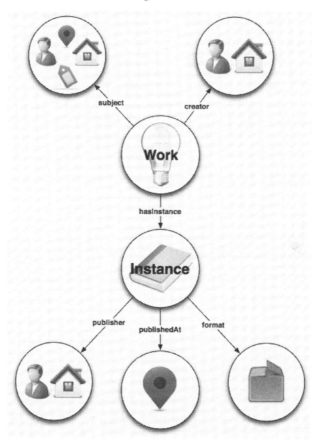

Figure 11.1. BIBFRAME Model. Library of Congress.

BIBFRAME VOCABULARIES

To understand where the vocabulary of BIBFRAME comes from, we return to RDF/XML. Earlier in this chapter we learned that BIBFRAME is coded in RDF/XML. RDF stands for Resource Description Framework, which is written in XML computer language and is used for describing resources on the web.[11] RDF is used for describing properties of items and especially for finding website content by search engines and digital library resources. It was designed to be a common way to describe information so that it can be understood by many different kinds of computer applications. It is ideal for the semantic web whereby computers integrate information from various web sources and then use URLs to identify the resources. RDF can describe resources in great detail and can describe their property values; for catalogers, those values are the elements and entities found in RDA, FRBR, and FRAD.

Table 11.6. RDF Classes Used in BIBFRAME

Agent	Description Admin Info	Manuscript	Provider
Annotation	Electronic	Meeting	Related
Archival	Event	Mixed Material	Relator
Arrangement	Family	Monograph	Resource
Audio	Held Item	Moving Image	Review
Authority	Held Material	Multimedia	Serial
Cartography	Identifier	Multipart Monograph	Summary
Category	Instance	Notated Music	Table of Contents
Classification	Integrating	Organization	Text
Collection	Intended Audience	Person	Title
Cover Art	Jurisdiction	Place	Topic
Dataset	Language	Print	Work

Source: "Bibliographic Framework Initiative," BIBFRAME, Library of Congress, at www.loc.gov/bibframe/ (accessed March 2, 2016).

Similar to MARC, the BIBFRAME Vocabulary has a defined set of elements and attributes called classes and properties.[12] A class in a BIBFRAME resource is much like a MARC field, such as the author field. Properties in a BIBFRAME resource are like subfields in MARC that more specifically identify aspects of the concept.

Table 11.7. MARC and BIBFRAME Similarities

MARC	BIBFRAME
Field *is similar to*	Class
Subfields *are similar to*	Properties

The BIBFRAME Vocabulary is comprised of the RDF properties, classes, and relationships within and connected to the data of the item to be cataloged. Refer back to table 11.5 for the RDF classes BIBFRAME currently uses.

Each RDF BIBFRAME class has multiple properties. The list of properties is too long to include here, but an example in figure 11.2 shows how the class called "cover art" can be subdivided or refined by multiple properties (similar to subfields in MARC).

Catalogers will become familiar with BIBFRAME classes and their properties. There are many resources to help with identifying properties; for example, the model view of BIBFRAME vocabularies has links to suggested properties for each class.[13]

Figure 11.2. Example of a Cover Art and Its BIBFRAME Properties.

RDF/XML CODING FOR BIBFRAME

BIBFRAME is still a work in progress in both the discussion and development phase. The LC says on its website that when it is more mature, vendors and suppliers will need time to adjust services to accommodate it. And then we can expect a mixed environment for some time.[14] Catalogers are urged to learn all they can about BIBFRAME so that they will be comfortable and ready for the transition from MARC.

There are many resources, including editing and conversion tools, being developed for BIBFRAME. It would be unrealistic for catalogers to become sophisticated RDF/XML coders. As web designers use software to create websites, so catalogers will use software to "code" in RDF/XML. However, catalogers will need to understand the rules of RDA, FRBR, and FRAD and how they apply to the BIBFRAME model of Works, Instances, Authority, and Annotations. These conceptual models are complex and require much study and practice. The LC continues to build new resources and share information on its BIBFRAME sites, and these are available for all to review. Much information is also available about Web 3.0 and RDF/XML. Curious catalogers who explore these initiatives will be invaluable employees in their libraries when the BIBFRAME transition takes place.

BIBFRAME TOOLS

While BIBFRAME is still in the future, tools are being developed that will support catalogers. While catalogers will not have to obtain degrees in RDF/XML coding, their work with MARC is already a level of programming, one that will continue with BIBFRAME. In addition to programming bibliographic data, catalogers using BIBFRAME will also engage in a high level of research to fully understand the relationships that can and should be created around the Work, Instance, Authority, and Annotation of every library resource being cataloged so that many points of access will be had in Web 3.0. A few of the tools that are being developed and beta-tested today for future catalogers are described below.[15]

BIBFRAME Editor (BFE)

The BIBFRAME Editor is a simple stand-alone tool that enables input of any BIBFRAME vocabulary element.[16] It can be used as an editor for RDF data. A demo version for experimentation is available from the Library of Congress.

The BIBFRAME Editor provides much guidance to catalogers for examining and finding the metadata of an item. For example, the editor prompts for the classes and properties of the instance or manifestation, such as the title proper, the statement of responsibility, and the publication information. Next to each of these prompts is the RDA cataloging rule that governs why the metadata is needed. The editor template is very helpful to the work of the cataloger and also very instructive as catalogers learn to match RDA rules with BIBFRAME requirements. Libraries will have to subscribe to the RDA Toolkit to obtain the rule information. When you click on the "RDA Work" elements in the toolkit, a textbox appears for data entry. All of the classes or properties required are supplied in the editor template.

BIBFRAME Profile Editor

A BIBFRAME profile is primarily a means for an application, such as a cataloging tool, to guide a cataloger in the creation or modification of a BIBFRAME record.[17] It may also be used to create templates in BIBFRAME editors. The BIBFRAME Profile Editor was written under contract to the Library of Congress by Smart Software Solutions. This software is open source and may be freely downloaded and used. The profile is a document or set of local cataloging practices that is edited to work with FRBR, FRAD, and possibly other models. A set of "resource templates" is used to describe possible metadata structures and applied to the properties of BIBFRAME. Academic, special, and large public libraries with unique collections and classification needs may need to use the profile editor in order to continue alternate but important cataloging practices of their institutions. Demonstration sites that are under development are available from the Library of Congress. Two tools under design to help evaluate and transform MARC bibliographic records to BIBFRAME are the Comparison Service and the Transformation Service.

MARC to BIBFRAME Transformation Tools: Comparison Service

This service is currently being beta-tested. The Comparison Service produces a comparison between a MARC/XML record and its BIBFRAME representation.[18] Currently, the only comparisons that can take place are LC MARC/XML records. The Bib ID found in the 001 tag of the record is entered into the box. At the time of this writing, very few records can be compared.

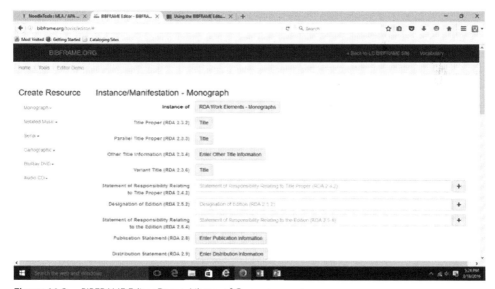

Figure 11.3. BIBFRAME Editor Demo. Library of Congress.

MARC to BIBFRAME Transformation Tools: Transformation Service

A demonstration site is also available for the Transformation Service. As with the Comparison Service, only MARC/XML records that have URLs can be transformed and viewed as BIBFRAME resources.

These demonstration sites let catalogers become familiar with the BIBFRAME standard and allow the Library of Congress to test many of the "what ifs" in the enormous project of conversion of MARC to BIBFRAME.

THE FUTURE IS NOW

Throughout this book the reader finds examples of how cataloging in the United States and other English-speaking countries is in a state of transition. For many years the Library of Congress MARC record has been the "standard" for cataloging bibliographic data for library resources that are converted into patron-friendly displays in an online catalog.

The first step of the new age of cataloging occurred when the RDA Toolkit replaced AACR2 to govern the practice of cataloging. With the Toolkit, catalogers no longer just record or "slot" data into tags and fields but rather delve deeper into descriptions, authorities, and relationships within groups of entities. When BIBFRAME is fully functional and ready for all catalogers to use, we will be able to share our records across the Internet so anyone can search any library's materials. The day is coming with Web 3.0 and BIBFRAME.

LSS CATALOGERS CAN BE PREPARED

Our objective is to be prepared for BIBFRAME and all that goes with it by understanding why cataloging is changing, gaining knowledge incrementally, and practicing new methods for your library's transition to BIBFRAME. Here are steps we can take:

1. Read, study, and practice. By reading this chapter, you have already decided to be a proactive learner. Look at the References, Suggested Readings, and Websites list at the end of this chapter.
2. Follow the Library of Congress and Bibframe.org websites for updates, demonstrations, and opportunities for practice.
3. Attend workshops, webinars, and any professional learning offered by your library or library consortium. Any new pieces of information will be invaluable to the transformation.
4. Continue to use the RDA Toolkit, the LC Authorities, and the Dewey or LC classification systems. These are not going away with BIBFRAME. Become good at and knowledgeable about these components of cataloging.
5. Learn from each other. RDA and BIBFRAME are major shifts in thinking for seasoned catalogers. For new catalogers they could be overwhelming. The language from the LC is dense and sophisticated—and even confusing! The LC's primary audience is their own catalogers.
6. Accept cataloging as a challenge that requires lifelong learning. Because every library resource is different, there are many research subtleties that make the work exciting!

SUMMARY

RDA rules and the current MARC21 and emerging BIBFRAME standards challenge catalogers to apply and manage appropriate processes, computer technology, and equipment for cataloging and classification. More than ever before, catalogers must continually learn new ways to extract and input bibliographic data so library resources can be searched and located on the semantic web. Library staff who know and can explain the value and purpose of cataloging and classification can apply their knowledge to help users find the resources they seek. Cataloging remains both a science and an art that is rapidly changing to make library resources as accessible as all other information found on the Internet.

The last chapters in this book are designed to give the reader practice in cataloging a variety of library resources using the current RDA rules and the MARC21 template that is still in use at the time of this publication.

DISCUSSION QUESTIONS AND ACTIVITIES

Discussion Questions

1. Why is the evolution of the Internet from Web 2.0 to Web 3.0 important to the development of new cataloging rules and standards?
2. What do the terms "semantic web" and "natural language" mean? Why are these two concepts changing cataloging?
3. What is the difference between a BIBFRAME class and a BIBFRAME property?
4. What are the four high-level BIBFRAME classes? Describe what is important or distinctive about each.
5. What are two BIBFRAME tools currently under development and how will catalogers use them in the future?

Activity 1: Finding BIBFRAME Properties

This activity provides practice in identifying the BIBFRAME properties of a book, a DVD, and a music CD.

- For each of these different items (or others that you chose for yourself), identify ten of its BIBFRAME properties from the vocabulary properties box—the second box found at bibframe.org/vocab-list/.
- For each property that seems appropriate for the item, click its link and read its description. For example, for Adele's album *25*, some of the properties would be agent, cover art, music medium, music number, and so forth.
- Repeat this process for each of the resources.

Activity 2: Gain Practice Using the Demo of the BIBFRAME Editor (BFE)

1. By practicing with the BIBFRAME Editor, you will begin to learn its different classes and properties and make associations with the MARC record format.

2. Find the BFE at bibframe.org/tools/editor/#.
3. You will see several different types of library materials such as monograph, noted music, serial, and so on.
4. With a book of your choice in hand, click on "Monograph" and select "Work."
5. Using the bibliographic data of the book as well as relationship data you can glean from the book jacket, reviews, and other sources, fill out as much information as you can on the editor template.
6. When finished with the "Work," go back and select "Instance" under Monograph and continue to input data and properties from the item at hand.

NOTES

1. "Bibliographic Framework Initiative," BIBFRAME, Library of Congress, at www.loc.gov/bibframe/ (accessed March 2, 2016); "BIBFRAME Frequently Asked Questions," BIBFRAME, Library of Congress, at www.loc.gov/bibframe/faqs/ (accessed March 6, 2016).

2. "Semantic Web," Webopedia, at www.webopedia.com/TERM/S/Semantic_Web.html (accessed March 6, 2016).

3. Michael Green, "Better, Smarter, Faster: Web 3.0 and the Future of Learning," *TD* 11, no. 4 (April 2011): 70.

4. Leif Pedersen, "Linked Data for Libraries," *Information Today* 32, no. 4 (May 2015).

5. "BIBFRAME Frequently Asked Questions."

6. Ibid.

7. Sally McCallum, *MARC Tags to BIBFRAME Vocabulary: A New View of Metadata* (Washington D.C.: Library of Congress, 2014), available at connect.ala.org/node/221077 (accessed March 6, 2016).

8. "BIBFRAME 1.0 Vocabulary: Terminology and Conventions," BIBFRAME, Library of Congress, at www.loc.gov/bibframe/docs/vocab-conventions.html (accessed March 7, 2016).

9. Ibid.

10. Ibid.

11. "W3Schools," Powerful XML Editor, at www.w3schools.com/xml/xml_rdf.asp (accessed March 7, 2016).

12. "BIBFRAME Frequently Asked Questions."

13. "The BIBFRAME Model," Bibframe.org, at bibframe.org/vocab-model/ (accessed March 7, 2016).

14. "BIBFRAME Frequently Asked Questions."

15. "Tools," Bibframe.org, at bibframe.org/tools/ (accessed March 18, 2016).

16. "Using the BIBFRAME Editor," BIBFRAME, Library of Congress, at www.loc.gov/bibframe/implementation/bfe-howtouse.html (accessed March 18, 2016).

17. "BIBFRAME Profiles: Introduction and Specification," BIBFRAME, Library of Congress, at www.loc.gov/bibframe/docs/bibframe-profiles.html (accessed March 18, 2016).

18. "MARC to BIBFRAME Comparison Service," Bibframe.org, at bibframe.org/tools/compare/ (accessed March 18, 2016).

REFERENCES, SUGGESTED READINGS, AND WEBSITES

Green, Michael. "Better, Smarter, Faster: Web 3.0 and the Future of Learning." *TD* 11, no. 4 (April 2011): 70–72.

Library of Congress. "BIBFRAME Frequently Asked Questions." Accessed March 6, 2016, at www.loc.gov/bibframe/faqs/.

———. "The BIBFRAME Model." Accessed March 7, 2016, at bibframe.org/vocab-model/.

———. "BIBFRAME Model and Vocabulary." Accessed March 6, 2016, at www.loc.gov/bibframe/docs/.

———. "BIBFRAME Profiles: Introduction and Specification." Accessed March 18, 2016, at www.loc.gov/bibframe/docs/bibframe-profiles.html.

———. "BIBFRAME Vocabulary: Terminology and Conventions." Accessed March 7, 2016, at www.loc.gov/bibframe/docs/vocab-conventions.html.

———. "Bibliographic Framework Initiative." Accessed March 2, 2016, at www.loc.gov/bibframe/.

———. "Complete List of Classes." Bibframe.org. Accessed March 16, 2016, at bibframe.org/vocab-list/#link_classList.

———. "Instance/Manifestation—Monograph." BIBFRAME Editor Demo, Bibframe.org. Accessed March 16, 2016, at bibframe.org/tools/editor/#.

———. "Key title—Property." Bibframe.org. Accessed March 7, 2016, at bibframe.org/vocab/keyTitle.html.

———. "MARC to BIBFRAME Comparison Service." Bibframe.org. Accessed March 18, 2016, at bibframe.org/tools/compare/.

———. "Tools." Bibframe.org. Accessed March 18, 2016, at bibframe.org/tools/.

———. "Using the BIBFRAME Editor." Accessed March 18, 2016, at www.loc.gov/bibframe/implementation/bfe-howtouse.html.

McCallum, Sally. *MARC Tags to BIBFRAME Vocabulary: A New View of Metadata*. Washington, DC: Library of Congress, 2014. Available at connect.ala.org/node/221077

Miller, Eric. "BIBFRAME and the World Wide Web." BIBFRAME Webcasts & Presentations. LC Bibliographic Framework Initiative Update Forum, 27, 2013. Accessed March 6, 2016, at www.loc.gov/bibframe/pdf/ALAmw2013-bibframe-lcupdate-20130127_Miller.pdf.

Pedersen, Leif. "Linked Data for Libraries." *Information Today* 32, no. 4 (May 2015): 18.

QuinStreet. "Semantic Web." Webopedia. Accessed March 6, 2016, at www.webopedia.com/TERM/S/Semantic_Web.html.

Refsnes Data. "W3Schools." Powerful XML Editor. Accessed March 7, 2016, at www.w3schools.com/xml/xml_rdf.asp.

CHAPTER 12

RDA and MARC21 Cataloging Exercises and Answers

LSS know the role of technology in creating, identifying, retrieving, and accessing information resources and demonstrate facility with appropriate metadata storage and retrieval tools. (ALA-LSSC Cataloging and Classification Competency 8)

These exercises are developed to give the reader guided practice cataloging books, e-books, audio, video, software, and serials based on the current MARC21 template and RDA rules. Use information from the previous chapters and references found in this book. Do not look at the answers provided from the LC Catalog until after you have practiced on your own.

Photo 12.1.   Image: Nonfiction book.

Table 12.1.   Practice Item 1: Nonfiction Book

Link	Bibliographic Descriptive Data
www.abc-clio.com/LibrariesUnlimited/ product.aspx?pc=F1152C	**Author:** Marie Keen Shaw **Title:** Block Scheduling and Its Impact on School Library Media Centers **Series:** Greenwood Professional Guides in School Librarianship **Hardcover:** 256 pages **Publisher:** Greenwood Press, Westport, CT **LCCN:** 98-22900 **Language:** English **ISBN-10:** 0313304947 **ISBN-13:** 978-0313304941 **Product Dimensions:** 25 cm

Catalog the nonfiction book using a MARC21 template and RDA rules. Begin cataloging with the 010 tag.

Leader/06	Type of record	a
Leader/07	Bibliographic level	m
Leader/18	Descriptive catalog form	i
Leader/19	Multipart resource record level	#
007/008	Physical description	t
008/35–37	Fixed data elements—language	eng
010	LCCN	$a
020	ISBN	$a
040	Cataloging source	rda (*answer supplied here*)
050	LC Classification	$a
082	Dewey Classification	$a
100	Main entry—Personal name	$a, $d, $e
245	Title statement	$a / $c
250	Edition statement	$a
264	Clarification of these subfields	$a, $b, $c
300	Physical description	$a, $c
336	Content type	$a, $b
337	Media type	$a, $b
338	Carrier type	$a, $b
490	Series statement	$a
504	Bibliography	$a
505	Content note	$a
650	Subject added entry—Topical	$a
650	Subject added entry—Topical	$a
963	Publisher contact information	

Photo 12.2.   Image: Fiction Book.

Table 12.2.   Practice Item 2: Fiction Book

Link	Bibliographic Descriptive Data
www.kensingtonbooks.com/book.aspx/31225	**Author:** Susan Kietzman **Title:** The Summer Cottage **Paperback:** 352 pages **Publisher:** Kensington Books **Language:** English **Copyright:** 2015 **ISBN-10:** 1617735493 **ISBN-13:** 978-1617735493 **Product Dimensions:** 21 cm

Catalog the fiction book using the MARC21 template and RDA rules. Begin cataloging with the 010 tag.

Leader/06	Type of record	a
Leader/07	Bibliographic level	m
Leader/18	Descriptive catalog form	i
Leader/19	Multipart resource record level	#
007/008	Physical description	t
008/35–37	Fixed data elements—language	eng
010	LCCN	$a
020	ISBN	$a
040	Cataloging source	rda (*answer supplied here*)
050	LC Classification	$a
082	Dewey Classification	$a
100	Main entry—Personal name	$a, $d, $e
245	Title statement	$a / $c
250	Edition statement	$a
264	Clarification of these subfields	$a, $b, $c
300	Physical description	$a, $c
336	Content type	$a, $b
337	Media type	$a, $b
338	Carrier type	$a, $b
490	Series statement	$a
504	Bibliography	$a
505	Content note	$a
650	Subject added entry—Topical	$a
650	Subject added entry—Topical	$a
963	Publisher contact information	

Photo 12.3.   Image: Magazine (Serial).

Table 12.3.   Practice Item 3: Magazine (Serial)

Link	Bibliographic Descriptive Data
www.sikids.com/about-us	**Title:** Sports Illustrated for Kids **Format:** Magazine **Publisher:** Time Magazine, New York **ISSN:** 1042-394X **Published** monthly, begin in January 1989 with volume 1, no. 1 **Size:** 30 cm.

Catalog the magazine or serial using the MARC21 template and RDA rules. Begin cataloging with the 022 tag.

Leader/06	Type of record	a
Leader/07	Bibliographic level	s
Leader/18	Descriptive catalog form	i
Leader/19	Multipart resource record level	#
007/00	Physical description	t
008/35–37	Fixed data elements—language	eng
022	ISSN—International Serial Number	$a
040	Cataloging source	rda (*answer supplied here*)
050	LC Classification	$a
082	Dewey Classification	$a
245	Title statement	$a / $c
250	Edition statement	$a
264	Clarification of these subfields	$a, $b, $c
300	Physical description	$a, $b $c
310	Current publication frequency	$a
336	Content type	$a, $b
337	Media type	$a, $b
338	Carrier type	$a, $b
362	Dates of publication and/or sequential designation	$a
500	General note	$a
530	Additional physical form	$a
650	Subject added entry—Topical	$a
650	Subject added entry—Topical	$a
710	Corporate name	$a

Photo 12.4.   Image: Ebook.

Table 12.4.   Practice Item 4: E-book

Link	Bibliographic Descriptive Data
catalog.lioninc.org/search~S29?/tclockwork+orange/ tclockwork+orange/1%2C4%2C16%2CB/ frameset&FF=tclockwork+orange&11%2C%2C13	**Title**: A Clockwork Orange **Author**: Anthony Burgess **Publisher:** not identified **Description:** online resource **ISBN:** 9780393343045 (electronic book) **Original ISBN:** 9780393312836 **Electronic reproduction**: W. W. Norton & Company, New York **Date:** 2015 **E-book Reader Requirements:** Adobe Digital Editions (file size: 237 KB) or Amazon Kindle (file size: N/A KB). **Downloaded:** from Overdrive

Catalog the e-book using the MARC21 template and RDA rules. Begin cataloging with the 020 tag.

Leader/06	Type of record	a
Leader/07	Bibliographic level	m
Leader/18	Descriptive catalog form	i
Leader/19	Multipart resource record level	#
007/008	Physical description	t
008/35–37	Fixed data elements—language	eng
020	ISBN	$a
040	Cataloging source	rda (*answer supplied here*)
050	LC Classification	$a
082	Dewey Classification	$a
100	Main entry—Personal name	$a, $d, $e
245	Title statement	$a / $c
250	Edition statement	$a
264	Clarification of these subfields	$a, $b, $c
300	Physical description	$a, $c
336	Content type	$a, $b
337	Media type	$a, $b
338	Carrier type	$a, $b
520	General note	$a
533	Electronic reproduction	$a, $b
650	Subject added entry—Topical	$a
650	Subject added entry—Topical	$a
776	Original ISBN (print copy)	$a
856	Electronic location and access	$u

Photo 12.5.   Image: Audio Disc.

Table 12.5.   Practice Item 5: Audio Disc

Link	Bibliographic Descriptive Data
www.blackstonelibrary.com/zom-b-gladiator	**Author:** Shan, Darren **Read by:** Galvin, Emma **Title**: Zom-B gladiator [sound recording] **Series:** The Zom-B Series, book 6 **Publication:** Blackstone Audio, Ashland, OR **Date:** 2014 **Edition:** Unabridged **Genre:** Fiction **Audience**: Children (8–12) **Physical:** 3.1 hrs., 3 CDs **Sound characteristics:** digital **File characteristics:** audio file, CD audio

Catalog the audio disc using the MARC21 template and RDA rules. Begin cataloging with the 020 tag.

Leader/06	Type of record	a
Leader/07	Bibliographic level	m
Leader/18	Descriptive catalog form	i
Leader/19	Multipart resource record level	a
007/00	Physical description—material category	s
007/01	Physical description—material designation	d
007/06	Physical description—material dimensions	g
007/12	Physical description—playback characteristics	e
008/35–37	Fixed data elements—language	eng
020	ISBN	$a
037	Source of acquisitions	$b
040	Cataloging source	rda *(answer supplied here)*
050	LC Classification	$a
082	Dewey Classification	$a
100	Main entry—Personal name	$a, $d, $e
245	Title statement	$a / $c
250	Edition statement	$a
264	Clarification of these subfields	$a, $b, $c
300	Physical description	$a, $c
336	Content type	$a, $b
337	Media type	$a, $b
338	Carrier type	$a, $b
344	Sound characteristics	$a $2rda
347	Digital file characteristics	$a, $b $2rda
490	Series statement	$a
500	General note	$a
520	Summary	$a
650	Subject added entry—Topical	$a
650	Subject added entry—Topical	$a
700	Added entry—Personal name	$a, $e narrator
710	Added entry—Corporate name	$a
963	Publisher contact information	

Photo 12.6.   Image: Video Disc.

Table 12.6.   Practice Item 6: Video Disc

Link	Bibliographic Descriptive Data
www.dove.org/review/10050 -chuggington-chief-wilson/	**Title:** Chuggington, Chief Wilson **Director**: Sarah Ball **Producer:** Jacqueline White **Publication:** Ludorum (place of publication not identified) **Date:** 2013 **Produced:** Anchor Bay Entertainment, Beverly Hills, CA **ISBN:** 0013132601557 **Description:** 1 videodisc (64 min.) : sound, color ; 4¾ in. + activity book with stickers. Two-dimensional moving image **Not rated** **Closed captioned** **Television program** **Publisher number:** DV60155

Catalog the video disc using the MARC21 template and RDA rules. Begin cataloging with the 028 tag.

Leader/06	Type of record	g
Leader/07	Bibliographic level	m
Leader/18	Descriptive catalog form	i
Leader/19	Multipart resource record level	#
007/00	Physical description—material category	v
007/01	Physical description—material designation	d
007/03	Physical description—color	c
007/04	Physical description—video format	v
007/05	Physical description—sound on medium	a
007/06	Physical description—medium for sound	i
007/08	Physical description—configuration of playback	q
008/35–37	Fixed data elements—language	eng
028	Publisher number	$a
040	Cataloging source	rda *(answer supplied here)*
050	LC Classification	$a
082	Dewey Classification	$a
100	Main entry—Personal name	$a, $d, $e
245	Title statement	$a / $c
264	Clarification of these subfields	$a, $b, $c
300	Physical description	$a, $b, $c
336	Content type	$a, $b
337	Media type	$a, $b
338	Carrier type	$a, $b
344	Sound characteristics	$a, $b, $g, $h
346	Video characteristics	$a, $b
347	Digital file characteristics	$a, $b
490	Series statement	$a
511	Performer note	$a
500	General note	$a
520	Summary	$a
521	Target audience, rating	$a
538	System details note	$a
546	Closed captioned note	$a
650	Subject added entry—Topical	$a
650	Subject added entry—Topical	$a
700	Added entry—Personal name	$a, $e narrator
710	Added entry—Corporate name	$a
730	Added entry—Uniform title	$a
963	Publisher contact information	

Photo 12.7.   Image: Computer File.

Table 12.7.   Practice Item 7: Computer File

Link	Bibliographic Descriptive Data
www.atozmapsonline.com/a-z_maps_online_login.asp	**Title:** AtoZ maps online [electronic resource] **Publication:** World Trade Press, Petaluma, CA **Date:** 2006 **Description:** Updated monthly. **Mode of access:** World Wide Web. Access restricted to viewers. **Varying form of title:** A to Z maps online **Additional Information see Product Sheet:** http://www.atozmapsonline.com/Preview/MapsOnline_PS.pdf

Catalog the online data file using the MARC21 template and RDA rules. Begin cataloging with the 050 tag.

Leader/06	Type of record	a
Leader/07	Bibliographic level	i
Leader/18	Descriptive catalog form	i
Leader/19	Multipart resource record level	#
007/00	Physical description—material category	c
007/01	Physical description—material designation	r
007/03	Physical description—color	c
008/35–37	Fixed data elements—language	eng
040	Cataloging source	$e rda *(answer supplied here)*
050	LC Classification	$a
082	Dewey Classification	$a
100	Main entry—Personal name	$a, $d, $e
245	Title statement	$a / $c
246	Varying form of title	$a
264	Clarification of these subfields	$a, $b, $c
300	Physical description	$a, $b, $c
310	Frequency of updates	$a
336	Content type	$a, $b
337	Media type	$a, $b
338	Carrier type	$a, $b
344	Sound characteristics	$a, $b, $g, $h
346	Video characteristics	$a, $b
347	Digital file characteristics	$a, $b
500	General note	$a
520	Summary	$a
650	Subject added entry—Topical	$a
650	Subject added entry—Topical	$a
710	Added entry—Corporate name	$a
856	Electronic location and access	$u
963	Publisher contact information	

Answers to Exercises
This section contains the Library of Congress cataloging for the exercise items above.

1. NONFICTION BOOK

```
008 980421t19991999ctua b 001 0 eng
010 98022900
020 0313304947 (alk. paper)
050 00 Z675.S3|bS538 1999
082 00 027.8/0973|221
100 1 Shaw, Marie Keen.
245 10 Block scheduling and its impact on the school library
media center /|cMarie Keen Shaw.
264 1 Westport, Conn. :|bGreenwood Press,|c[1999]
264 4 |c(c)1999
300 xi, 236 pages :|billustrations ;|c25 cm
336 text|btxt|2rdacontent
337 unmediated|bn|2rdamedia
338 volume|bnc|2rdacarrier
504 Includes bibliographical references and index.
650 0 School libraries|zUnited States.
650 0 Instructional materials centers|zUnited States.
650 0 Block scheduling (Education)|zUnited States.
Greenwood professional guides in school librarianship.
```

2. FICTION BOOK

```
008 150819s2015 nyu 000 1 eng d
010 2015297335
020 9781617735493|q(paperback)
020 1617735493|q(paperback)
035 (OCoLC)886505436
050 00 PS3611.I3994|bS86 2015
082 04 [Fic]
099 9 PR JE
100 1 Kietzman, Susan,|eauthor.
245 14 The summer cottage :|ba novel /|cSusan Kietzman.
264 1 New York, NY :|bKensington Books,|c[2015]
300 326 pages ;|c22 cm
336 text|btxt|2rdacontent
337 unmediated|bn|2rdamedia
338 volume|bnc|2rdacarrier
500 Includes discussion guides.
520 "Helen Street spent every summer of her childhood at her
family's cedar-shake cottage on Long Island Sound. The
```

youngest of four, she shared her mother Claire's athletic genes and relished the orchestrated games and competitions that filled those warm, endless days. Unlike her older siblings—fiery Charlotte, ambitious Thomas, middle-child Pammy—Helen rarely felt the pressure of her mother's high expectations. Thirty years later, with her brother and sisters scattered, Helen is the sole caregiver for Claire, now terminally ill. Knowing her death is imminent, Claire has put Helen in the awkward position of telling the others that she plans on leaving everything, including the cottage, to Helen when she dies—unless everyone comes to the shore for a long weekend over the Fourth of July. During this time together, Helen, Charlotte, Pammy, and Thomas will revisit their long-ago decisions and assumptions. And they will face new choices that could shatter their fragile kinship—or reveal a family's extraordinary power to remember, to forgive, and to grow" —|cProvided by publisher.

650 0 Terminally ill|xFamily relationships|vFiction.
650 0 Families|vFiction.
0 Domestic fiction.

3. MAGAZINE (SERIAL)

008 890113c19899999nyumr p uu 0 0eng
022 0 1042—394X
032 003554|bUSPS
037 |bSports Illustrated for Kids, P.O. Box 830609, Birming-ham,
AL 35283—0609
082 10 796|211
210 0 Sports illus. kids
222 0 Sports illustrated kids
245 00 Sports illustrated kids.
246 3 Sports illustrated for kids.
264 1 [New York] :|b[Time, Inc.],|c[1989—]
264 4 |c[(c)1989—]
300 volumes :|billustrations ;|c30 cm
310 Monthly|b1989—
336 text|btxt|2rdacontent
337 unmediated|bn|2rdamedia
338 volume|bnc|2rdacarrier
362 0 Vol. 1, no. 1 (Jan. 1989—)
362 0 May 2006 changed title to Sports Illustrated kids.
500 Title changed to Sports illustrated kids 2006.
500 Title from cover.

515 Vol. 1, no. 1 also called premiere issue.
650 0 Sports|vPeriodicals.
856 |zClick here for recent issues.|uhttp://catalog.oslri.
net/
search/X?SEARCH=t:
(%22sports%20illustrated%20for%20kids%22%202014)%20or%20t:
(%22sports%20illustrated%20for%20kids%22%202015)%20or%20t:
(%22sports%20illustrated%20for%20kids%22%202016)&SORT=D

4. E-BOOK

008 150731s2015 nyu s 000 1 eng d
020 9780393343045|q(electronic bk)
037 700C381C-2E73—44F4-BE4E-EC7B9E46C405|bOverDrive, Inc.
|nhttp://www.overdrive.com
100 1 Burgess, Anthony.
245 12 A clockwork orange|h[electronic resource].|cAnthony
Burgess.
264 1 [Place of publication not identified] :|b[publisher not
identified],|c2015.
300 1 online resource
336 text|btxt|2rdacontent
337 computer|bc|2rdamedia
338 online resource|bcr|2rdacarrier
520 Great Music, it said, and Great Poetry would like quieten
Modern Youth down and make Modern Youth more Civilized.
Civilized my syphilised yarbles. A vicious fifteen-year-old
droog is the central character of this 1963 classic. In
Anthony Burgess's nightmare vision of the future, where
the criminals take over after dark, the story is told by
the central character, Alex, who talks in a brutal
invented slang that brilliantly renders his and his
friends' social pathology. A Clockwork Orange is a
frightening fable about good and evil, and the meaning of
human freedom. When the state undertakes to reform Alex to
"redeem" him, the novel asks, "At what cost?" This edition
includes the controversial last chapter not published in
the first edition and Burgess's introduction "A Clockwork
Orange Resucked."
533 Electronic reproduction.|bNew York :|cW. W. Norton &
Company,|d2015.|nRequires Adobe Digital Editions (file
size: 237 KB) or Amazon Kindle (file size: N/A KB).
650 7 Classic Literature.|2OverDrive
650 17 Fiction.|2OverDrive
655 7 Electronic books.|2local

776 1 |cOriginal|z9780393312836
856 4 |3Excerpt|uhttp://samples.overdrive.com/?crid=700c381c-
2e73-44f4-be4e-ec7b9e46c405&.epub-sample.overdrive.com
|zSample
856 40 |uhttp://lion.lib.overdrive.com/
ContentDetails.htm?ID=700C381C-2E73-44F4-BE4E-EC7B9E46C405
|zClick to access digital title.

5. AUDIO DISC

008 131015t20142014orunnnnd f n eng d
020 9781478981862|qLibrary ed.
020 1478981865|qLibrary ed.
020 9781478981893
020 147898189X
028 02 Z8921|bBlackstone Audio, Inc./Hachette Audio
035 (OCoLC)860805950
040 BLACP|beng|cBLACP|dOCLCO|dTEF|dCWJ|dOJ4|dLEO
043 e-uk-en
049 LEOA
050 14 PZ7.S52823|bZs 2014ab
082 04 [Fic]|223
100 1 Shan, Darren.
245 10 Zom-B gladiator|h[sound recording] /|cDarren Shan.
246 3 Zombie gladiator
250 Unabridged.
264 1 [Ashland, Or.] :|bBlackstone Audio, Inc. ; Hachette
Audio,
|c[2014]
264 4 |c©2014
300 3 audio discs (3 hour) :|bdigital ;|c4 3/4 in. .
336 spoken word|bspw|2rdacontent
337 audio|bs|2rdamedia
338 audio disc|bsd|2rdacarrier
490 1 Zom-B ;|v[6]
500 Title from web page.
500 Compact discs.
500 Duration: 3:00:00.
500 "Tracks every 3 minutes for easy bookmarking"—Container.
511 0 Read by Emma Galvin.
520 B Smith has decided to live and to fight for good as long
as possible, but London is swarming with human mercenaries
whose sense of right or wrong dissolved when society did
and when they capture B, escape will not be easy.
650 0 Zombies|vFiction|vJuvenile sound recordings.

650 1 Zombies|vFiction.
651 0 London (England)|vFiction|vJuvenile sound recordings.
651 1 London (England)|vFiction.
651 1 England|vFiction.
655 0 Young adult fiction.
655 7 Horror fiction.|2gsafd
655 7 Audiobooks.|2lcgft
700 1 Galvin, Emma.
710 2 Blackstone Audio, Inc.
710 2 Hachette Audio (Firm)

6. VIDEO DISC

008 130923s2013 xx 064 j vaeng d
028 42 DV60155|bAnchor Bay Entertainment
040 TEFMT|beng|erda|cTEFMT|dTEF|dOJ4|dGK5|dJP3|dLEO|dnwc
050 4 PN1992.77|b.C48 2013
082 04 791.45/75|223
245 00 Chuggington. |h[videorecording]|pChief Wilson|cDirec-
tor:
Sarah Ball ; producer: Jacqueline White.
246 30 Chief Wilson
264 1 [Place of publication not identified] :|bLudorum,|c2013.
264 2 Beverly Hills, CA :|bAnchor Bay Entertainment,|c[2013]
300 1 videodisc (64 min.) :|bsound, color ;|c4 3/4 in. +
|eactivity book with stickers.
336 two-dimensional moving image|btdi|2rdacontent
337 video|bv|2rdamedia
338 videodisc|bvd|2rdacarrier
344 digital|boptical|2rda
347 video file|bDVD video|2rda
500 Bonus features: Bonus badge quest episode: Chug patrol;
Chugger spotlight: Hodge; Chugger spotlight: Zephie;
Coloring & activity sheets.
520 Chief Wilson finds himself on one exciting adventure after
another, including a magnetized wild ride, a wet and wild
trek through the forest, and a run for the mayoral Chugger
of the Year award! Also, Chief Wilson performs a series of
rescue tests on the Chugasonic Speedway and his best
friend Koko learns to make high-speed stops!
538 DVD, region 1, NTSC, anamorphic widescreen presentation
1.78:1, Dolby surround 2.0.
546 Closed captioned.
650 0 Railroad trains|vJuvenile films.
650 1 Railroads|xTrains|vDrama.
655 7 Animated television programs.|2lcgft
655 7 Children's television programs.|2lcgft

710 2 Anchor Bay Entertainment, Inc.,|efilm distributor.
730 0 Chuggington (Television program)

7. COMPUTER FILE

008 090513c20069999cau e s 0 eng d
034 0 a
035 (OCoLC)320896214
040 VWM|cVWM|dVWM
049 LEOA
090 G1021|b.A86
245 00 AtoZ maps online|h[electronic resource] /|cby World
Trade
Press.
246 3 A to Z maps online
246 3 AtoZmaps online
264 Petaluma, Calif. :|bWorld Trade Press,|c2006—
300 1 online resource
310 Updated monthly.
336 maps|btxt|2rdacontent
337 computer|bc|2rdamedia
338 online resource|bcr|2rdacarrier
500 Title from home page (viewed May 13, 2009).
505 0 Animal & plant distribution maps—Antique map collection
—Bible maps—Canada maps—Climate change maps—
Current event maps—Earthquake maps—Education-
teaching tools—Environmental maps—Flags of the world
—Geography databases—Geology maps—GIS data—
Glossaries—Google Earth—Hurricane maps—Map games
& puzzles—Modern map collection—NASA maps—
Software—USA maps—Volcano maps—Weather maps.
506 Access restricted to subscribers.
520 "AtoZMapsOnline.com is the worlds largest subscription-
based database of proprietary, royalty-free world,
continent, country, and state maps. Included in the 4,000+
maps are: political maps, physical maps, outline maps,
population maps, precipitation maps, climate maps, and
other thematic maps. New maps are added to the collection
every month."—Database home page.
538 Mode of access: World Wide Web.
650 0 Atlases|vDatabases.
650 0 World maps|vDatabases.
650 0 Maps|vDatabases.
710 2 World Trade Press.
856 40 |uhttp://www.atozmapsonline.com|zAccess restricted to
patrons from subscribing libraries. Check with your local
library with questions.

BIBLIOGRAPHY

Libraries Online. "LION Catalog." Accessed March 25, 2016, at catalog.lioninc.org/.

Library of Congress. "Library of Congress Online Catalog." Accessed March 25, 2016, at catalog.loc.gov/.

———. "MARC21 Format for Bibliographic Data." Accessed March 25, 2016, at www.loc.gov/marc/bibliographic/.

Ocean State Libraries. Online Catalog. Accessed March 25, 2016, at catalog.oslri.net/.

RDA Toolkit. "Complete Examples—Bibliographic Records." RDA Complete Examples, October 2015. Accessed March 25, 2016, at www.rdatoolkit.org/sites/default/files/6jsc_rda_complete_examples_bibliographic_revisedoct2015.pdf.

Glossary

AACR2. The abbreviation for the *Anglo-American Cataloguing Rules*, second edition. These rules govern the work of those who catalog in English-speaking countries including the United States, Canada, the United Kingdom, and Australia.

Abridged Dewey. A shortened version of the Dewey Decimal classification system used by small libraries.

Access points. Words or terms, such as author, title, series, subject, or keyword, that can be used to locate a bibliographic record in a library catalog.

Accession book. A ledger used by librarians to record bibliographic and item information about each item acquired by the library in the order that it was received.

Acquisitions. The processes of reviewing, ordering, purchasing, and receiving library resources.

Analog. A term used to describe continuous data such as an audiocassette or videotape. Libraries circulated analog media prior to its being replaced by digital media.

Area. Called a "field" in MARC21, it is the term for a line of bibliographic information in AACR2.

Authority control. The establishment of one standard form of a name, word, or term for an access point that occurs in multiple MARC records.

BIBFRAME. An acronym for the term "Bibliographic Framework," this Library of Congress initiative will replace MARC record cataloging in the future. Cataloging standards are changing to include more description and metadata that will be accessed universally through search engines rather than proprietary MARC record systems. MARC records will transfer to BIBFRAME. The Library of Congress will determine when to abandon the MARC standard.

BIBFRAME Annotation. One of the four high-level classes, an Annotation may share opinions about a resource, such as a review, provide institution-specific information, or enhance a description, such as cover art or a summary.

BIBFRAME Authority. One of the four high-level classes, an Authority is used to identify agents such as authors, editors, or distributors of a Work; places such as towns, countries, or continents; and subjects that the Work is about, such as concepts, places, agents, and the like.

BIBFRAME Instance. One of the four high-level classes, an Instance reflects an individual, material embodiment of a BIBFRAME Work that can be physical or digital. A BIBFRAME Instance includes properties specific to the publication, production, manufacture, and distribution of the material.

BIBFRAME Work. One of the four high-level classes, a Work reflects a conceptual entity such as an unpublished story written by an author or the song of a musician that is not yet produced. A BIBFRAME Work is an abstract entity, as there is no single material object one can point to.

Bibliographic. Data that identifies or describes a library item or resource such as its title, author, copyright date, ISBN, publisher, size, media format, and so forth. In cataloging the term refers to the descriptive information and data of a library resource that is entered into the fields of a MARC record.

Bibliographic record. Information such as the title, author, publisher, ISBN, size, or edition that describes a unique book or other library item.

Bibliographic utility. A source of MARC bibliographic records that a library purchases or to which it subscribes that can be imported to the local catalog. The cataloger searches the utility to find matches of records to the item in hand that needs cataloging.

Call number. The Dewey Decimal or Library of Congress classification number used to organize library collections by topic or subject.

Carrier. Format of device used to view, listen, or read content such as computer disk, sheet, audiocassette, or filmstrip.

Catalog display. This is the patron view of a MARC record that does not include the computer coding language.

Cataloging. The process of analyzing and selecting key identifying information about an object and organizing this information in ways that can be easily retrieved by those who wish to locate and use the object.

Cataloging in Publication. Also known as CIP, this is both the print display form found on the reverse side of the title page and the MARC record that is created by the Library of Congress during the prepublication stage of a new book or manuscript.

Cataloging module. The software application in an integrated library system (ILS) dedicated to creating, editing, and importing bibliographic records with attached item records into the online catalog.

Circulation parameters. These are the rules for check-in and checkout established by the library for each type of resource.

Class. In BIBFRAME this is one of fifty-three groups of common data, similar to a tag or field in a MARC record. The first letter of a class name in BIBFRAME is capitalized to distinguish it from a property. There are four high-level classes: Work, Instance, Authority, and Annotation.

Classification. The process of assigning subjects and location codes to library materials. Library of Congress (LC) and Dewey Decimal are the common codes used in the United States. LC subjects are assigned so that materials can be searched by topic.

Cloud computing. A library leases storage space for their catalog data on computer servers located off-site and managed by a company that guarantees technical support, backup, and security.

Collections. These are groupings of library materials, often assembled by genre, material format, age, reading level, historic value, or some other useful demarcation.

Consortium. Libraries that form a partnership to share an ILS.

Controlled access. A way of locating a library item through a unique term or element such as the ISBN or an LC authority for name of author.

Controlled vocabulary. The words and phrases chosen by the Library of Congress to be included in or excluded from its subject authority database.

Copy cataloging. The process of making a local record based on an acquired bibliographic record created from another source.

DDC23. The abbreviation for the twenty-third edition of the Dewey Decimal Classification System.

Delimiters. The letters or numbers used as part of the computer code that separates subfields of information in a line of a MARC record.

Depository. A library or government facility where copies of works are kept and preserved. A depository does not necessarily circulate items.

Digital. Of or relating to information stored in the form of the numbers 0 and 1, such as computer programs, e-books, DVDs, CDs, high-definition television programming, and audio files. Nearly all of the media formats and technology libraries use today are digital.

Element. A word, phrase, or groups of characters forming a field or subfield.

Enumeration. A complete order or listing, usually by number, such as the assignment of numbers to represent specific topics in the Library of Congress Classification System.

Expansion. A system of classifying books and other materials whereby main classes of subjects are further subdivided for specificity.

Field. A unique piece of bibliographic information about an item such as its author, title, ISBN, or media type that corresponds to an area in AACR2. The term also refers to the place where specific information related to the topic of the tag is inputted on a line of a MARC record.

Fixed field. Data in a MARC record that is limited to an exact number of characters.

Fixed location. Prior to Dewey, a new book was assigned a designation, such as an accession number, that set its permanent location at a specific place on a shelf.

Folksonomies. An alternative classification system generated through social media to share suggestions of library resources without having to know library cataloging terminology.

FRAD. The initialism for Functional Requirements for Authority Data, a conceptual model for organizing authority and controlled-access information based on the needs of users.

FRBR. The initialism for Functional Requirements for Bibliographic Records, a conceptual model of the relationships between works, expressions of the work, the manifestation or production of the work, and the final item to be cataloged. FRBR supports RDA, which expands access points in bibliographic MARC records.

Genre. Categories of literature, music, or art that further define a broader category such as fiction, nonfiction, poetry, drama, and so forth.

Holding library. The library in a consortium that owns or "holds" a particular item.

Holding record. Attached to the bibliographic record, this record contains the location information for an item in an individual library.

HTML. An initialism for hypertext markup language, the accepted tagging and coding of text files for Internet web pages that create variations in font, color, graphic layout, design, and hyperlink effects. Hypertext markup language is the computer code most commonly used to create websites. It permits text and images to be linked to internal and external web pages. Many digital library resources, such as websites, articles, e-books, and documents, can contain hyperlinks because they are written in HTML.

Indicator. Used in variable fields, these two numeric characters are part of the programming of a MARC field that helps to set up the patron display screen properly. Each indicator's meaning varies according to the tag.

Initial articles. The articles "a," "an," or "the" when used as the first word of a book title.

Integrated library system (ILS). The hardware and software used by a library or libraries to provide a common online catalog and circulation, cataloging, acquisitions, interlibrary loans, reserves, and other library services.

Inversion. Some Library of Congress subject headings transpose or reverse the order of the noun and verb because it is more logical to search by the noun.

ISBN. The initialism for International Standard Book Number, a unique thirteen-digit number that identifies a specific edition of a book.

ISSN. The initialism for International Standard Serial Number, a unique eight-digit number that identifies a specific title (not volume) of a magazine, newspaper, or journal.

Item record. Attached to the bibliographic record, this second record contains local information, unique to a specific library, about the resource being cataloged such as its circulation rules, call number, barcode, replacement cost, and collection type.

Itype. A code that identifies the location or ownership of a specific type of library resource, such as DVDs, in a shared online catalog.

Keyword searching. A search using natural language that does not weigh or control the context of the word, as would be the case for a LC subject heading.

Library of Congress. An agency of the legislative branch of the federal government. Among its many services is its leadership in establishing cataloging standards and the rules and practices for librarians to follow in the United States.

Library of Congress Authorities. Free and online searchable MARC authority records of the preferred forms of names, titles, places, subject phrases, and topical terms to be used for author, title, subject, tracings, and added entry access points.

Library support staff (LSS). The term used by the American Library Association for people who work in libraries who do not have professional (graduate) library degrees. These staff constitute approximately 85 percent of library workers today and perform a wide variety of duties and services.

Main class. This is the broadest, most general division of topics.

Main heading. The key topic, term, name, place, or other concept that is the subject of a library resource.

MARC authority. Records available in the Library of Congress Authorities of standardized headings for names, titles, places, subject phrases, or topical terms to be used by catalogers in the United States.

MARC record. An acronym for machine readable cataloging, the computer coding system developed by the Library of Congress in the 1970s that established a standard way to enter and format bibliographic data about library material.

MARC21 record. The standard for creating a bibliographic catalog record based on the rules of AACR2.

Metatag. A top line of computer code on a web page for inputting searchable subjects that will enhance the page's ranking. Such lines of code influence search engine results by matching the user's search terms with the subjects found in the code. Library programmers can influence the ranking of their websites by using metatags.

Modules. The different functions or services of the ILS, such as circulation, cataloging, online catalog, and so on.

Monograph. A written account of a single topic, most commonly published as a book (print or digital), or a one-volume scholarly work such as a thesis or manuscript.

Natural language. Not computer code or artificial programming commands, this is the ordinary day-to-day speaking and writing used by humans to communicate with each other in their native tongues, such as in English, Spanish, or Mandarin Chinese.

Nonfiling. A word, such as an initial article, that is ignored or not used for filing purposes.

Notation. Numerals, letters, and symbols are used to represent the main and subordinate divisions of a library classification scheme. In the Dewey Decimal classification system, Arabic numbers are used to represent all topics or subjects. In the Library of Congress system, letters represent the main classes and divisions, and numbers and punctuation are used for greater specificity.

Online Public Access Catalog. Also known as the OPAC, this is how patrons view, place holds, and manage their accounts both within and outside the library using the Internet.

Open source. Software available to the public at either minimal or no cost.

Properties. Terms in BIBFRAME that identify, describe, or relate specific data (in lower case) found in a broader group or class; they are called "elements" in RDA and "subfields" in MARC records.

RDA. Resource Description and Access, the new cataloging standard that replaces the *Anglo-American Cataloguing Rules* (AACR2). Created in 2010, RDA is a content standard that works with AACR2 to expand description access points in bibliographic MARC records. Most libraries have adopted it as their standard for cataloging.

RDF/XML Code. The computer code or language that will mostly replace HTML as the computer language for Web 3.0. This code will have customized tagging schemes and common formats that will enhance the interchange of data on the semantic web.

Relative index. An alphabetical listing of the topics of knowledge found in DDC23, with associated call numbers.

Relative location. Location of an item with or near other books on the same topic or subject using the Dewey classification system, but not located in a permanent or fixed place on a shelf. Item locations will shift or change shelves according to how a collection grows.

Repository. A building, usually in a central location, such as a library, where things may be stored.

Reserves. Temporary collections of books or other library resources set aside at the circulation desk or other accessible location for students in a specific class to use for a set amount of time inside the library.

Schema. A representation or plan, such as the Library of Congress classifications, that represents all topics of knowledge or the placement of books in the LC.

Semantic web. This is a name for the upcoming Web 3.0 that will replace the current Web 2.0. On the semantic web it will be easier to find, share, reuse, and combine information through customized tagging schemes and common formats for the interchange of data that Web 2.0 does not offer.

Status code. The term or abbreviation used in the ILS cataloging program to describe the current state or location of a library item, such as available on the shelf, checked out to a patron, on display, or in use in other ways. A code is also used if the item is missing, in storage, or lost.

Subclass. A second or more specific division of general knowledge in a subject area.

Subfield. A part or subdivision of a variable field that relates to the main theme of the tag. Subfields are separated in the tag line by alphabetical or numerical delimiters.

Tag. The three-character code that begins a line of bibliographic information in a MARC record.

Tagging. The actual process of creating one or more keyword labels (tags) and associating them with a library catalog record. A folksonomy is the classification system that arises from these tags.

Template. The format for coding bibliographic information and data of an item in MARC so that it can be read and interpreted by software applications.

Topics of knowledge. Another name for all possible subjects known to humankind and able to be classified by Melvil Dewey's system.

Tracings. The 400-level tags of a MARC record where alternate forms of an author's name are entered so that any searches using these forms will retrieve the records with LC name authority headings.

Unabridged Dewey. The full version of the Dewey Decimal classifications recommended for libraries with more than twenty thousand items in their collections.

Uniform access. The ability to search and obtain access to all items by the same author or with the same title or subject in one search.

Uniform title. The preferred title chosen by the Library of Congress for a work that is published or known by multiple titles.

Union catalog. A library catalog that contains the bibliographic records of more than one library interfiled in the dictionary format.

URI. The initialism for Uniform Resource Identifier. In the future, cataloging records will be created in BIBFRAME and each line of code will be a URI or web address pointing to linking descriptive or authority information stored on the servers of the Library of Congress and other libraries.

Variable field. This field in a MARC record allows a flexible number of characters.

XML. An initialism for Extensible Markup Language, a type of code recommended for posting data or information on the Internet and used to code and edit new websites. XML works with HTML so that relationships between lines of code can be made. It has become a common language for programming websites to enhance searching and is the coding language of BIBFRAME.

Z39.50. An international information retrieval standard that enables one computer to speak to another in order to find and obtain information.

Index

About the Author

Marie Keen Shaw is the program coordinator for the library technology assistant certificate program at Three Rivers Community College in Norwich, Connecticut, where she has also been an adjunct professor since 1999. She teaches courses in cataloging and classification, digital resources, reference services, and management strategies. She serves on the advisory board of the Connecticut Digital Library and is current chair of the boards of the Connecticut Library Consortium and the Groton Public Library. Marie received a doctorate of education in educational leadership and adult learning from the University of Connecticut, a sixth-year degree in educational leadership from Southern Connecticut State University, and an MS in library and information science and educational media from Purdue University. A retired certified high school library media specialist and curriculum instructional leader, she has been a speaker at state library and educational media conferences in Rhode Island, Illinois, and Connecticut. Marie is the author of the books *Library Technology and Digital Resources: An Introduction for Support Staff* (Rowman & Littlefield, 2015) and *Block Scheduling and Its Impact on the School Library Media Center* (1999). Her doctoral dissertation, "Teacher's Learning of Technology: Key Factors and Process," was accepted by the University of Connecticut in 2010.